take a hint from the heavens...

1986 is packed with promise. Make the most of it with the predictions, insights, clues and suggestions America's most popular astrologer, Sydney Omarr, has prepared for you!

Learn about the "geometry" of relationships—who you get along with, and why . . . pore over celebrity sun signs and personality profiles . . . discover how and why the movements of the zodiac affect men and women so differently . . . and much, much more. Whatever your desire, whatever your dilemma, let Sydney Omarr's time-tested wisdom guide you through 1986, and watch your dreams become exciting realities!

For Expanding Your Personal Knowledge of
Astrology, SIGNET Brings to You

SYDNEY OMARR'S
ASTROLOGICAL GUIDES
FOR YOU IN 1986

- [ ] **ARIES** .... (136764—$2.75)*
- [ ] **TAURUS** .... (136772—$2.75)*
- [ ] **GEMINI** .... (136780—$2.75)*
- [ ] **CANCER** .... (136799—$2.75)*
- [ ] **LEO** .... (136802—$2.75)*
- [ ] **VIRGO** .... (136810—$2.75)*
- [ ] **LIBRA** .... (136829—$2.75)*
- [ ] **SCORPIO** .... (136837—$2.75)*
- [ ] **SAGITTARIUS** .... (136845—$2.75)*
- [ ] **CAPRICORN** .... (136853—$2.75)*
- [ ] **AQUARIUS** .... (136861—$2.75)*
- [ ] **PISCES** .... (136888—$2.75)*

*Price is $3.25 in Canada

Buy them at your local bookstore or use this convenient coupon for ordering.

NEW AMERICAN LIBRARY
P.O. Box 999, Bergenfield, New Jersey 07621

Please send me the books I have checked above. I am enclosing $_____
(please add $1.00 to this order to cover postage and handling). Send check or money order—no cash or C.O.D.'s. Prices and numbers are subject to change without notice.

Name_____

Address_____

City _____ State _____ Zip Code _____
Allow 4-6 weeks for delivery.
This offer is subject to withdrawal without notice.

SYDNEY OMARR'S
DAY-BY-DAY ASTROLOGICAL GUIDE FOR
Libra
(SEPTEMBER 23–OCTOBER 22)
1986

A SIGNET BOOK

NEW AMERICAN LIBRARY

NAL BOOKS ARE AVAILABLE AT QUANTITY DISCOUNTS
WHEN USED TO PROMOTE PRODUCTS OR SERVICES.
FOR INFORMATION PLEASE WRITE TO PREMIUM MARKETING DIVISION,
NEW AMERICAN LIBRARY, 1633 BROADWAY,
NEW YORK, NEW YORK 10019.

Copyright © 1985 by Sydney Omarr

All rights reserved

Sydney Omarr is syndicated worldwide by Los Angeles Times Syndicate.

SIGNET TRADEMARK REG. U.S. PAT. OFF. AND FOREIGN COUNTRIES
REGISTERED TRADEMARK—MARCA REGISTRADA
HECHO EN CHICAGO, U.S.A.

SIGNET, SIGNET CLASSIC, MENTOR, PLUME, MERIDIAN and NAL BOOKS
are published by New American Library,
1633 Broadway, New York, New York 10019

First Printing, July 1985

1 2 3 4 5 6 7 8 9

PRINTED IN THE UNITED STATES OF AMERICA

CONTENTS

1 **Defining Terms** — 7
   - *Astrology* — 7
   - *The Zodiac* — 8
   - *Sun Sign* — 9
   - *Element* — 9
   - *Quality* — 11
   - *Element and Quality Together* — 12
   - *Planet* — 13
   - *House* — 15
   - *Rising Sign* — 16
   - *Horoscope* — 17
   - *Aspect* — 18
   - *Transiting Planet* — 19

2 **Your House of the Sun** — 21
   Your "Piece of the Pie"

3 **The Geometry of Relationships** — 32
   What Signs You Get Along with—and Why

4 **Twelve Places at the Table** — 35
   Personality Profiles of the Signs

5 **Moods of the Moon** — 44
   Day-by-Day Changes

6 **Venus and Mars** — 55
   Love and Sex . . . Peace and War . . .
   Cooperating and Competing

7	**Venus Sign Position Chart 1910–1975**	*70*
8	**Mars Sign Position Chart 1910–1975**	*76*
9	**The Planets As "Stars"** Astrological Cast of Characters	*80*
10	**Astrotrivia—Rating Yourself in the Best Game in Town**	
	I Sun Signs of the Rich and Famous	*95*
	II More Celebrity Sun Sign Lore	*97*
	III Fascinating Facts About the Signs	*99*
	IV Where Do You Belong?	*100*
	V Which Animal Best Suits You?	*102*
11	**Sun Sign Changes 1920–1975**	*105*
12	**LIBRA: The Big Picture**	*113*
13	**LIBRA: Objectives and Obstacles** A Game Plan for Being the Most Successful LIBRA Under the Sun	*117*
14	**Pairing Off with LIBRA** Your Compatability with Other Signs of the Zodiac	*122*
15	**The LIBRA Sex Role Dilemma**	*126*
16	**The LIBRA Female** Child ... Young Woman ... Mate ... Mother	*129*
17	**The LIBRA Male** Child ... Young Man ... Mate ... Father	*133*
18	**LIBRA Help Wanted** Selecting a Career/Your On-the-Job Style	*137*
19	**How "Pure" a LIBRA Are You?** Your Moon Sign ... Your Rising Sign	*140*
20	**Find Your Rising Sign**	*145*
21	**LIBRA Astro-Outlook for 1986**	*148*
22	**Fifteen Months of Day-by-Day Predictions**	*150*

1

Defining Terms

What Are Those Astrologers Talking About?

Everyone knows it is more fun to visit another country if you know a bit of the language, and it's a lot easier to find your way around, too. The same idea applies to astrology, which is still foreign territory to many people. Astrology has its very own language, but it really isn't difficult to get a handle on it as long as you understand a few important terms. What follows is a kind of "Astrological Phrase Book," a brief compendium of the most basic words and concepts in the astrological language. Once you've learned them, you'll find you know a lot more about the why of your sun sign as well as information that will help you understand other astrological factors that make you what you are. Best of all, your new language can help you enjoy and explore one of the most exciting, underdeveloped territories under the sun—modern astrology!

Astrology Is an Ancient and Practical "Science"
The first definition of astrology in the standard dictionary is "astronomy," and at one time in history the two studies were synonymous. The word astrology derives from Greek and literally means "the science (or study) of the stars." However, even in earliest times astrology has had much less to do with the "fixed" stars, which appear to remain in one place, than the planets, which move. (The word "planet" means wanderer.) Early man noticed that, as these heavenly bodies moved, their movements coincided with certain earthly events—mainly the changing of the seasons. Gradually, the movement

of the planets was observed to coincide with other important worldly events, such as wars, and the science of "divination" (prediction) by the planets was born. Astronomy and astrology lived happily together until the Christian church banned the latter in about 1550, condemning it as mere superstition. Astrology bounced back in the 1700s, when it came into use as an indicator of human personality, as well as a way to foretell future events. However, this so-called modern astrology is based on the same premise the ancients set down thousands of years ago: "As above, so below." Simply put, what it means is that the positions of the planets, which represent the cosmic order, are related in a significant and observable way to both human behavior and events in human life.

The Zodiac Is a "Circle of Signs"

The zodiac ("circle of animals") is an invisible band in the sky which corresponds to the apparent yearly path of the sun, moon, and the major planets around the earth. It is the "apparent" path in the sense that it is what we *observe* from here on earth. Obviously we know that the earth and other planets revolve around the sun, but the study of astrology (and astronomy) takes earth as the reference point.

The 360-degree circle of the zodiac around the earth is divided into twelve thirty-degree segments—the twelve astrological signs. Throughout the year, as the sun appears to move, it passes through each of these segments in about thirty days. Zero degrees Aries, the vernal equinox or beginning of spring, is the beginning of the zodiac and the start of the seasonal year. It is at that point, on or about March 22, that the sun crosses or intersects with the *ecliptic*—another imaginary band that is (in the mind's eye) the extension of the earth's equator. Another major intersection of the sun's path and the ecliptic takes place at the fall equinox about September 22, the beginning of the seventh sign of the zodiac, Libra. (Equinox means equal days and nights, which is what we experience briefly in the early spring and early fall.) The zodiac "finishes" with the end of the twelfth sign Pisces, about March 21, then begins again with Aries.

Though the segments of the zodiac (the astrological signs) are *named* for the constellations of stars in the sky, they do not correspond with them. The constellations served as convenient visual markers for the ancient astrologer/priests, but the zodiac—and astrology—has always been based on the seasonal year, which never changes. The position of the constellations have changed with reference to our point of view here on earth, however, due to the slipping of the earth's axis. The constellations return a couple of degrees every year and have been doing so for centuries. That's why when the modern *astronomer* says "Aries," he is referring to a group of stars that is in a different position in the sky than the segment of the zodiac the *astrologer* calls "Aries."

Your Sun Sign is Determined by the Month and Day You Were Born

The twelve segments of the zodiac are the twelve astrological signs, from Aries through Pisces, and it takes the sun exactly one year to pass through all twelve signs. A person born when the sun is passing through a particular segment of the zodiac is said to be born under that sign, and it is his/her sun sign. For example, a person born October 14 is said to be born under the sign of Libra. Your sun sign is the most important component of your astrological personality, it is the "real you." However, there are nine other planets besides the sun, and at the moment of a person's birth, those planets are passing through certain segments of the zodiac, or signs, as well. You will learn about some of these lesser influences on your personality in this book later on.

An Element Is Part of a Sign

Obviously your sun sign is a lot more than simply a piece of the sky, or it wouldn't have any meaning. The meaning it has is based on two ancient astrological concepts, the *four elements* and the *three modes*. When these two factors are combined they form the basis of all astrological descriptions of human personality. You can't *see* an element or a quality; they are only to be understood in terms of analogy, but they are fundamental to everything else in astrology, so it is important to understand them.

The four elements, defined by ancient philosophers as the basic components of everything and everybody, are *fire, earth, air,* and *water.* It is doubtful that even in earliest times this breakdown was to be taken as a physical reality: The elements are really four different ways we experience both things and people. For instance, if a thing or a person was experienced as hot rather than cold, sharp rather than dull, active rather than passive, it was said to partake of the *fire* element. And it's easy to see the connection.

Later on, during the Renaissance, the four elements were called "humors," starting a whole new way of typing people. *Fire was the humor choler*, and people who were said to have too much of it were those angry, impatient types who are subject to modern-day diseases like high blood pressure and heart attacks. *The earth element was called black bile* and could cause extreme melancholia (depression) in a person who had too much of it. *Air was the sanguine or rosy humor* and meant a lighter personality. *The water element was the humor phlegm,* and people with too much of it had rather "soggy" personalities and tended to be fat, as well. If the relationship between the elements (or humors) and the signs of the zodiac is beginning to ring a bell, it should. Here's the way the twelve signs break down into elements:

Fire signs: Aries, Leo, Sagittarius
Earth signs: Taurus, Virgo, Capricorn
Air signs: Gemini, Libra, Aquarius
Water signs: Cancer, Scorpio, Pisces

The four elements as four primal types of being exist today in the way many psychologists categorize people's thought processes. Once again, the relationship to the ways in which the twelve astrological signs really do perceive and react to the world is uncannily correct:

The fire signs are instant reactors who put it all together very quickly; things rarely have to be spelled out for a fire sign. These types of people also see the future possibilities inherent in the present and want to bring them about *now*. Obviously, fire signs tend to be impatient, but they have strong wills. Fire is the principle of *action*.

The earth signs are more pragmatic and slower to react. If they can't literally see something or touch it, they have difficulty visualizing it. They operate out of *sense perceptions* and are the realists of the zodiac—the builders who provide stability and continuity. Earth is the principle of *sustenance*.

The air signs see everything as connected to everything else. They are sequential thinkers for whom there must be a beginning, a middle, and an end to everything. For the most part these people operate on *logic* and act only when they can see the sense of their actions. The air signs are endlessly curious and represent the principle of *connecting and reasoning*.

The water signs tend to feel their way through life. What is most real to them is what their emotions tell them; they do what their emotions tell them to do as well. They are imaginative thinkers, the poets and artists of the zodiac. The water principle is that of *caring, nurturing, and protecting*.

A Quality Is Part of a Sign

There are only four elements, but there are twelve signs. In astrological arithmetic, the *three qualities* which divide the *four elements* make up the difference. It isn't easy to grasp the concept of the elements, but the qualities (or "modes" as they are sometimes called) help a lot, because they make the elements a lot more tangible. Called *cardinal*, *fixed*, and *mutable*, the three modes can best be understood as *kinds of motion*.

Cardinal motion is start-up movement. It is the principle of bringing into being. Cardinal goes forward, so, the cardinal signs are *initiators*.

The four cardinal signs are those that start the four seasons:
   Aries (*spring*)
   Cancer (*summer*)

Libra (*fall*)
Capricorn (*Winter*)

Fixed motion means staying in place. Fixed things have come into being, and now simply are. The fixed signs represent stability, and are difficult to move. The four fixed signs represent the middle of each season:
Tarus (*spring*)
Leo (*summer*)
Scorpio (*fall*)
Aquarius (*winter*)

Mutable motion means flexible motion. Things that are mutable are changing, able to turn into something else. The mutable signs represent the *ability to adjust, and to accept change*. The four mutable signs are those that end the seasons:
Gemini (*spring*)
Virgo (*summer*)
Sagittarius (*fall*)
Pisces (*winter*)

Elements and Qualities Together Add Up to Signs
When you put elements and qualities together you begin to get a picture of what they add up to—the twelve astrological signs. Here is how each quality modifies each element.

Fire element/Cardinal quality = **Aries**
This get-up-and-go sign has all the flash and dash of fire plus an added dose of a pioneering spirit by virtue of its cardinal quality.

Fire element/Fixed quality = **Leo**
Leo burns with the ardor and enthusiasms of fire, but gives off very steady heat due to its fixed quality.

Fire element/Mutable quality = **Sagittarius**
Sagittarius represents the kind of fire that spreads, igniting everything and everybody in its path—which is rather erratic because of Sagittarius's mutable quality.

Earth element /Cardinal quality = **Capricorn**
Capricorn is the most active builder of the earth signs because of its cardinal quality. Capricorn's brand

of reality demands that something be brought into being.

Earth element/Fixed quality = **Taurus**
This strong sign stands and waits, holding things and people together. Taurus is the warmest and most nurturing of the earth signs, and is always "there."

Earth element/Mutable quality = **Virgo**
Virgo's practical sense knows that all things must change. This mutable sign represents the principle of stability with flux; that is, permanence in the face of change.

Air element/Cardinal quality = **Libra**
Libra's air nature moves forward, actively connecting people and things into partnerships via its cardinal quality of initiation.

Air element/Fixed quality = **Aquarius**
Aquarius is the most immovable of the air signs, representing the permanance of ideas and their practical application.

Air element/Mutable quality = **Gemini**
This very movable sign represents changing thoughts and opinions, the breaking up of static ideas so that new ones can come about.

Water element/Cardinal quality = **Cancer**
Cancer is the most initiating of the water signs because of the cardinal quality. Though shy, Cancer generally moves quietly but effectively to the forefront.

Water element/Fixed quality = **Scorpio**
Scorpio's powerful self-control comes from the emotional water element that is contained and compressed because of this sign's fixed quality.

Water element/Mutable quality = **Pisces**
Pisces extreme emotionalism—as well as this sign's creativity—comes from feelings that constantly change and move into new areas, creating new outlets.

Planets Are the Most Important Factor in Astrology
"Planet" is probably an even more important word in the astrological language than "sign." How can that be?

Because it is the placement of the planets in various signs which indicates personality and it is the movement of the planets through the zodiac that indicates events. In other words, without the planets the signs would have no application to people and what happens to them.

As early man noticed that the planets moved in fairly regular patterns, he began to associate certain characteristics with each of the planets, and each planet gradually took on a "personality." In a number of different cultures, certain planets were hooked up with certain gods, because it was the gods who really controlled life on earth. The moon was virtually always a female god—like Diana or Artemis. Jupiter, always a "good guy" planet, was known as Vishnu, the preserver, to the Hindus. Before he got his Roman name of Jupiter, the Greeks knew him as Zeus, a lusty fellow who had a heart of gold. (You'll get a complete rundown on each of the planets in Chapter 9, "The Planets As Stars.")

From these planetary "personalities" came the idea that each planet caused a certain kind of behavior or event by virtue of its own nature. For instance, Mars, always the war god, is still regarded by modern astrologers as an indicator of strife and conflict. When predicting events, the astrologer looks at what sign and what house Mars will be passing through at a certain point in time to see what kind of influence it is most likely to bring into a person's life.

When looking at personality, the astrologer determines which sign a person's Mars is in at the time of the person's birth to see how that individual is most likely to assert him-/herself. The sun, the most important planet makes us what we are in totality according to which sign the sun is placed in at our birth; i.e., our sun sign's Venus is the planet of relationships, and its placement in a specific sign shows how a person is likely to relate to others.

In short, planets indicate *action*, and the signs in which the planets are placed indicate *the kind of action*.

Since ancient times, astrologers have recognized seven planets. The sun (which is really a star), the moon (which is really a satellite of our own planet, earth) Mercury, Venus, Mars, Jupiter, and Saturn.

With the development of the telescope, three more planets were discovered (although there is some evidence that early astrologer/priests divined their existence). Uranus was first spotted in 1781, Neptune in 1846, and Pluto as late as 1930. Some astrologers/astronomers anticipate that there are two more to be found, so that there would be twelve planets instead of the current ten.

A House Is an Area of Life—and a Planet's "Home"

Just as there is a great circle in the sky called the zodiac, and it is divided into twelve equal units of *space*, there is another circle which is based on units of *time*. As we all know, the earth makes one complete rotation on its own axis every twenty-four hours. Imagine yourself standing in one place during a twenty-four-hour period and making a mark on the sky every two hours while that sky appears to pass by you as the earth turns. At the end of twenty-four hours, you will have marked off twelve different units of sky. A "house" is simply one of those pieces of sky that has passed by during your day-long vigil. Toward the end of your day of skywatching, twelve houses will have gone by, and "house one" will be coming up again.

When an astrologer draws up a natal horoscope—which is simply a map of the sky when you were born—he/she does it by drawing a picture of the sky as it appeared from the exact place of birth, at the exact time of your birth. What happens is that the twelve houses are lined up in a very specific way—a very different way than if you had been born *in another place at the same time* or *at the same time in another place*.

What is most important about the particular lineup of the houses is that each house represents a different area of human life, and how those areas are positioned *for you* has a tremendous effect on your astrological makeup. For instance, the second house is the house of income and personal possessions and has a lot to do with attitude toward money and how easy or how difficult it will be to come by in your lifetime. The seventh house is the house of partnership and offers clues about who you are likely to marry. If you know the time of your birth within one hour or so, you can add a very important dimension to your astrological self-knowledge by reading the chapter "Your House of the Sun—Your 'Piece of the Pie,'" because the house of the horoscope into which the sun falls in your horoscope usually indicates what area of life will absorb you during your lifetime.

Your Rising Sign Is the One that Starts the First House

Your rising sign is sometimes called the ascendant, because it is the sign of the zodiac that was "ascending" on the eastern horizon at the time of your birth, no matter what time your birth occured. It is the "sunrise sign," corresponding to the nine o'clock position on the face of an ordinary clock. The astrologer's "clock" starts at this position and is read counter-clockwise around the circle of the face. If you were born around sundown, your rising sign will be the one 180 degrees *opposite* the sign you were born under. For instance, if you are an Aries born at sundown, your rising sign will be Libra. If you are an Aries born at sunrise, your rising sign is probably Aries as well.

Why is your rising sign so important? Because it starts the first house of personality, or your very individual way of presenting yourself to the world. No matter what your sun sign is, your rising sign will cover it to a greater or lesser degree (which is why it is so difficult to guess someone's Sun Sign when you first meet them). The rising sign has to do with appearances and can actually influence your physical looks.

If you don't know the time of day you were born, you can't determine your rising sign (although some astrologers can by doing what is called a "rectification," based on the events in your life so far). However, even those who do not know their rising sign can have their horoscopes read; what the astrologer does is put your sun sign on the first house, and do an analysis of what is called a solar horoscope. If you *do* know your birthtime within an hour or so, you can use the rising sign chart in this book to determine yours.

Planets in Signs in Houses Make Up a Horoscope

The whole basis of astrology is that anyone born in a particular moment in time partakes of the qualities of that moment in time. Actually, the same applies for things; for instance, a business that has its beginnings at a precise astrological moment also has a horoscope which can be read, and tells a lot about its potential for success or failure.

An astrologer looks at the particular moment in drawing up a horoscope—or "picture of the hour." A horoscope is basically a map of the sky, showing exactly where the planets were in relation to the signs and the houses, to each other, and from the particular reference point of your birthplace. It is also called a "natal chart" or "natal map."

Everyone's horoscope has ten planets and twelve houses. Those ten planets can be in a variety of signs, and in a variety of houses. Each planet means something different according to its own nature, how that nature operates in a particular sign, and what area of life the planet is most likely to affect by virtue of which house of the horoscope it falls into. Sound complicated? It is, and only a highly trained astrologer can interpret the many factors and put them together for you in a meaningful way. The most exciting part of astrology is the fact that *no two individuals are ever exactly alike*—not even twins, who are born a few minutes apart.

Although you can find out a lot about your astrological personality right in this book, many people like to take the next step and have a personalized horoscope drawn up for them and interpreted by a professional astrologer. There are a number of ways to find a good person to do this for you; in astrology, as in every other profession, there are variations in the level of competence. Two places you can start your search are:

National Astrological Society
62 West 39th St.
New York, NY 10018

American Federation of Astrologers
Tempe, AZ 85282

An Aspect Is the Distance Between Planets

Among the more sophisticated factors an astrologer looks for in your horoscope are the *aspects*. Within the 360-degree circle of the horoscope (and the zodiac), planets form certain aspects to each other by virtue of the distance between them. Some distances are considered harmonious, and some are inharmonious, in terms of how those two (or more) planets work together. It's all a matter of mathematics. The soft or harmonious aspects are the sextile (60 degrees apart) and the trine (120 degrees apart). The hard or inharmonious aspects are formed when planets are in square to each other (90 degrees apart) or in opposition, 180 degrees or exactly half a circle apart. These are only the major aspects, and there are lots and lots of minor ones between, but you can get a good picture of interplanetary relationships with only these few.

For example, if your sun sign is Aries, and at the time of your birth the planet Saturn was in the sign of Libra, or 180 degrees away from Aries, you are likely to have a more serious (Saturnine) disposition than the typical "happy" Aries. Depending on your point of view, this can be a positive note in your horoscope, because you will have greater powers of concentration than many an Aries—or a negative note, because you will be less happy-go-lucky. In another example, a person with a Capricorn sun sign may have a horoscope in which Jupiter, the planet of expansiveness, is 120 degrees away from the sun—either in the sign of Virgo or Taurus— and therefore in "trine" aspect to his/her sun. The result: a much more outgoing, giving Capricorn than the run-of-the-mill type. On the other hand, such an easy aspect could expand Capricorn's acquisitive nature too much, and make for a megalomanic (someone who craves worldly goods and power).

The ancients separated aspects into "favorable" and "unfavorable," but psychologically-thinking modern astrologers know that it is not that simple; it all depends on the total horoscope, plus the individual's reactions to the particular vibrations of the planets in that horoscope.

A Transiting Planet Affects Your Life Now

When someone goes to an astrologer for the first time, he/she usually has *two* readings—separate, but interrelated. The first will be an interpretation of your natal chart or birth horoscope. This tells you about your given personality—the traits, problems, abilities, and advantages you are most likely to have by virtue of the placement of the planets in the sky at the time of your birth. The second reading will have to do with what you can expect in your life at the present time and the near future. Your birth horoscope always remains the same, but the planets in the sky keep changing their relationships to your birth horoscope throughout your lifetime. The astrologer will acquaint you with the current "transit"—or movements—of the planets and how you, the individual, can expect them to affect you. For instance, if an astrologer notes that Uranus, the "earthquake planet," is approaching your fourth house (the house of emotional security, the place where we really live), the astrologer might alert you to the fact that big changes are in the offing: even a total shaking of the foundations, or a pulling up of roots. This is a major transit, and many people change their residence, partners, or jobs when it occurs. Similarly, but on a less critical note, the astrologer may notice that the planet Venus is going to make a transit over the place in the zodiac occupied by Mars in your birthchart. This could indicate a firey romantic interlude or the rekindling of an old flame.

There are two important things to keep in mind about astrological predictions. The first is that your natal horoscope—your "birth imprint"—really determines how you will react to life's events. To put it even more strongly, your innate personality will really *create* the events of your life, because "character is destiny." There is no doubt that the planets create conditions, but we must take responsibility for how we cooperate with those conditions. The second thing is that *there are very few hard and fast rules.* There are guidelines, to be sure, and most of them have ancient roots; a lot of astrological prediction is based on the case history technique. However, since no two sets of conditions—

the one in the sky and the one in an individual birthchart—are ever *exactly* the same, it is virtually impossible for any astrologer to tell you specifically what is going to happen.

2

Your House of the Sun

Your "Piece of the Pie"

The prime symbol in the very symbolic language of astrology is the perfect circle; it represents the sky around us, the cosmic atmosphere into which we are all born. All astro-math is based on division of the 360-degree figure, which since ancient times has been regarded as having mystical qualities. When thinking about the houses of the horoscope, however, it helps to use a very down-to-earth analogy. Look at that circle as a great "pie in the sky," which is divided into twelve cosmic slices—each slice representing one house and a different facet of human experience.

Just as there are ten planets in everyone's horoscope, there are twelve houses. However, not all those houses may be occupied by a planet; it all depends on where the planets were in the sky at the moment of your birth. The placement of any planet in a specific house is a *very* important factor in your individual horoscope, but the most important is the placement of the sun. No matter what your sun sign, your House of the Sun has a lot to tell you about the life you've been "given" to live on this earth. As your sun sign is the prime indicator of *character and personality,* your house of the sun points to the *area of human affairs* that you are most likely to find yourself concentrating on in your lifetime.

In the sense that it helps define the boundaries of your life, your house of the sun is your "piece of the pie"—that slice of life within which you will live. Does your house of the sun totally box you in? In a way it does, but it is more productive to think of the dimensions of your house of the sun as *guidelines* about where you can most profitably focus your energies.

Here's the way it works:

- The *sun* is the most important planet in your horoscope. It is the planets that do the "acting," and the sun plays the leading role.
- Your sun sign determines *how* your sun (the real you) acts, i.e., the characteristics of the character you play.
- Your house of the sun is the "stage" on which you will play out your role.

For instance, if your sun sign is Scorpio (the great investigator) and your house of the sun is the twelfth (hidden things), you find yourself drawn to some kind of career in which you must "dig" to do your investigating. Ergo, you might make a good psychoanalyst, archeologist, or genetic researcher. Or, your greatest pleasure in life might be reading mystery novels or spy thrillers—or writing or editing them.

In order to figure out which piece of the pie you've been served, you have to know your birth-time within an hour or so. If you were born during Daylight Savings Time or War Time, you have to subtract one hour from your birth time to determine the "real sun time."

Each house is described here from three different angles:

- The matters or principles connected with it
- The people/places/things related to it
- The problems and the possibilities of having your sun in that house.

Birth time, 4 to 6 a.m.: **Sun in First House**

- *First house matters:* Exploration ... use of the physical body ... being on the scene ... breaking new ground ... independent action ... emergencies ... conquest ... controversy ... strategy ... competition ... being in the vanguard.

- *First house people/places/things:* Entrepreneurs ... acrobats ... cutting instruments ... rock music ... metals ... satire ... hardware ... the head and face ... opticians ... adrenalin ... new products ... commodities ... salesmen ... fighters ... firemen.
- *Problems and possibilities:* With your sun in the first house, your sun sign personality is quite strong. Regardless of what your sun sign is, you should be able to make clear-cut decisions and have a good sense of your own identity. If you are to gain control over your life, you are going to have to banish fear from it and develop both the moral and the physical courage that is available to you. Though your will should be strong, you will have to keep yourself from a tendency to tyrannize others. When you feel most defeated is the time your first house sun will come to your rescue. The one thing that could keep you from living out the very vivid life this house placement gives you is inflexibility and intolerance. Be willing to listen.

Birth time, 2 to 4 a.m.: **Sun in Second House**

- *Second house matters:* Calmness ... conservation ... ability to make grow ... eroticism ... collecting ... comforting ... administrating ... luxury ... stabilizing ... building up ... perpetuating ... patience ... using ... making stronger ... indulging.
- *Second house people/places/things:* Possessions ... money ... the voice ... landscape gardeners ... brokers and bankers ... love/passion ... personal adornment ... life-sustaining skills ... buying and selling ... security needs ... nurses ... food and shelter ... good music ... creature comforts.
- *Problems and possibilities:* You should be able to establish yourself firmly and securely in whatever you choose to do; self-adjustment should come easily to you. Your economic life could be relatively worry-free but you must resist valuing money and

possessions for their own sake and becoming overly materialistic. You must develop the will that is given you and turn it into willpower, or you could lose self-respect. You are a good manager, but if you allow yourself to become too settled, you will fear to take the necessary risks to make your life less limited. Though things come to you fairly easily, do not let yourself over-indulge in any of them, including rich food.

Birth time midnight to 2 a.m.: **Sun in Third House**

- *Third house matters:* Connecting ... associating ... verbalizing ... dexterity ... inquisitiveness ... distribution ... novelty ... thinking and reasoning ... cause and effect ... exchanging ... bringing the news ... being responsive ... "here today, gone tomorrow."
- *Third house people/places/things:* Short journeys ... realatives (especially siblings) ... speech/languages ... high school teachers ... role-playing/entertaining ... computers ... graphic arts ... handwork ... transportation ... the nervous system ... handwriting .. repair men ... gossip ... comedy ... ventriloquists.
- *Problems and possibilities:* You should be an excellent communicator who reports things clearly and accurately. In your desire for information, however, you could become rather superficial and a bit of a talebearer. If you don't focus your mental energies carefully, you may waste the gift of curiosity your third house sun gives you. You must also learn to live with uncertainty, and to keep your opinions flexible. If life scares you, you are likely to become very defensive and locked in to your ideas. Develop your capacity for listening as well as your talent for talking.

Birth time 10 p.m. to 12 a.m.: **Sun in Fourth House**

- *Fourth house matters:* Adaptability ... change ... instinctiveness ... fluctuation ... protecting ...

imagination ... softness ... the subconscious ... survival ... enveloping ... integrating ... fertility ... mothering.

- *Fourth house people/places/things:* Dreams ... the past ... roots ... home and family ... physical sensation ... museums ... caterers ... water and other liquid ... introverts ... obstetrics ... boats ... domestics ... imagination.
- *Problems and possibilities:* Via your fourth house sun, you are given the possibility of understanding yourself and your motivations quite thoroughly. If you handle your life in a mature way, you will establish a warm and comfortable home for you and your family. However, you must strive for real self-knowledge if you are not to become simply self-absorbed and self-centered. Your imagination is considerable, and you could be highly creative; the down side is that you could develop irrational fears that verge on paranoia. Work to see the world clearly at all times and try to conquer your tendency to play the introvert. No mater what your sun sign, the placement of that sun in the fourth house will make you instinctively avoid the limelight. Get out there and shine!

Birth time 8 to 10 p.m.: **Sun in Fifth House**

- *Fifth house matters:* Being at the heart of things ... pleasures ... power ... ambition ... generosity/giving ... "gilding the lily" ... showmanship ... stability ... management ... territorial rights ... self-expression ... autocracy ... organization.
- *Fifth house people/places/things:* Philanthropy ... corporations ... impresarios ... holidays and vacations ... romantic love ... children ... gamblers ... gold ... circuses ... nursery teachers ... fashion and fashion designers ... public life.
- *Problems and possibilities:* Even if you have a "shy" sun sign, your fifth house placement of the sun will force you into some form of self-expression that is possibly very creative. You also have a capability

for approaching life with a joyful, expectant manner; however, your pursuit of pleasure and play could become extreme. Consciously avoid any pleasure that threatens to get out of control. Your affairs of the heart could be many, but it is important to keep alert for anything that smacks of an abusive partner; it's possible you could enjoy the drama of an unhappy situation. Develop your capacity for warmly accepting others.

Birth time 6 to 8 p.m.: **Sun in Sixth House**

- *Sixth house matters:* Competence/skill ... specialization ... refining ... categorizing ... analyzing ... obedience ... realism ... responsibility ... purifying ... invention ... making things work ... ministering ... discriminating.
- *Sixth house people/places/things:* Service ... critics ... crafts ... libraries ... closets ... public health ... the harvest ... small animals ... dependents ... dental hygienists ... research ... diagnosing ... numbers work ... chemists.
- *Problems and possibilities:* With your sun in the sixth house you have the potential of becoming a true master at something; however, if you allow yourself to get bogged down in life's details, you could possibly end up being a wage slave. No matter what your sun sign, your instincts tell you to be of service to others. While you are capable of great self-sacrifice, you must avoid the temptation to be overly humble and to assume the servant role. You are mentally very keen, and can break things and jobs down into smaller parts in order to accomplish them. Do not let the state of your own health become an obsession. With the sun is the sixth house, your basic constitution should be quite strong. Don't worry!

Birth time 4 to 6 p.m.: **Sun in Seventh House**

- *Seventh house matters:* Sharing ... comparing ... give-and-take ... peacemaking ... negotiation ...

making things beautiful ... creating balance ... fairness ... sociability ... gratification ... advocacy ... diplomacy ... aestheticism.

- *Seventh house people/places/things:* Divorce lawyers ... love poetry ... marriage brokers ... the kidneys and lower back ... illustration ... resort managers ... public relations ... fine arts ... receptionists ... boutiques ... jugglers ... tailors ... pianos.
- Possibilities and problems: You have a great need to identify with others, and can create a wonderful rapport with them easily. However, your need for a life partner could make you overly dependent. If you have an independent sun sign, this could create a serious life conflict. With this placement, you are able to adjust to new people and new situations easily, but you must avoid a tendency not to stick with a position when you really believe in it. You have the potential of forming very warm, balanced and intimate relationships; however, if you do not handle this gift in a mature manner, you could develop a fear of intimacy, and shy away from it or become an outrageous and insincere flirt.

Birth time 2 to 4 p.m.: **Sun in Eighth House**

- *Eighth house matters:* Release of blockages ... probing ... anonymity ... procreation ... rejuvenation ... willpower ... endurance ... controlling ... investigation ... aloneness ... demolishing and rebuilding ... crisis ... elimination.
- *Eighth house people/places/things:* Puzzles ... generals ... political parties ... labor lawyers ... the healing arts ... death and dying ... taxes ... spies ... superathletes ... crime detection ... statesmen ... sex symbols ... geologists ... explorers ... mating instinct ... sanitation engineers.
- *Problems and possibilities:* A light sun sign (like Gemini or Libra), the placement of the sun in this house will add depth to your character. You will feel compelled to investigate things that are hidden or

even dangerous. While it is good to probe, you must beware of a tendency to concentrate on what is morbid. All things being equal, you will be highly sexed; however, with insufficient self-knowledge, your healthy sexual instincts could turn into obsession with the subject—or a total advoidance of it. Learn to live with your dynamic physical body and you will live with others quite happily. Also, encourage your religious or mystical feelings, which are quite real. You have the potential of totally transforming your life at one point or another.

Birth time noon to 2 p.m.: **Sun in Ninth House**

- *Ninth house matters:* Anticipating ... aspiring ... moving around ... expanding things ... speculating ... idealism ... advising ... unpredictability ... search for truth ... search for opportunity ... taking aim ... magnanimity ... excess.
- *Ninth house people/places/things* Casinos ... ambassadors ... passport offices ... luck ... international transportation ... trading/high finance ... dancers ... aristocrats ... large animals ... higher studies ... lawmaking ... profiteers ... veterinarians.
- *Problems and possibilities:* Even if you have a routine-loving sun sign (like Virgo), this placement of the sun will give you the desire and the ability to constantly renew your life, and to adapt to new patterns of behavior. You will feel strongly about one religious or ethical system or another, or at least have a very strong personal philosophy. However, you could become rather dogmatic and rigid in your opinions. Your adaptability is admirable, but a desire for the new and novel could be the "downside" of your openness to new experience. Exercise control. With certain sun signs, there may be a tendency toward inner battles between opportunity-seeking and a firm set of principles. You are a spender—of both your money and your physical resources.

Birth time 10 a.m. to 12 a.m.: **Sun in Tenth House**

- *Tenth house matters:* Realism ... structure ... ambition ... rigidity ... integrating ... limitation ... disciplining ... reputation ... social position ... creating the useful ... contraction ... coolness ... convention.
- *Tenth house people/places/things:* Figures ... fame ... common sense ... property ... correctional systems and facilities ... ceramics ... money lenders ... efficiency experts ... the bones ... the elderly ... sculptors ... watches and clocks.
- *Problems and possibilities:* You have the capacity of becoming a respected member of whatever group you move in, because your public image is very important to you. If you play your cards right, you can arrive at a sense that you are fulfilling your destiny. However, if you become obsessed with power and appearances, you could end up living a shallow, meaningless life behind your strong facade. It is most important with this placement of the sun to find the right outlet for you to express yourself and get positive feedback from others. You won't be happy starving in a garret, because both money and recognition are too important to you. This position of the sun often brings fame.

Birth time 8 to 10 a.m.: **Sun in Eleventh House**

- *Eleventh house matters:* Helping ... experimentation ... humanitarianism ... association ... liberalism .. freedom ... suddenness ... awakenings ... combining ... freethinking ... rationality ... caring ... breaking through ... observing coolly ... predicting.
- *Eleventh house people/places/things:* Paradoxes ... stunt men ... electricity ... zealots ... divorce ... fireworks ... the social sciences ... reform ... geniuses ... aviation ... weathermen ... brotherly love ... magnetism ... groups ... friends ... causes.
- *Problems and possibilities:* If you are a very personal

sun sign (like Cancer), you will gain a lot of objectivity with the placement of the sun in this house. You should have very high aims and goals, and some of them will undoubtedly involve helping the less fortunate in some way or another. Though this is admirable, if you don't set yourself on a definite path in life and stick to a definite plan, you could simply drift along, with only vague ideas about where you can shine. It is important to be quite realistic with the sun in this house. Your own crowd is important to you, but you must avoid becoming such a part of the group that you lose a sense of your own individuality—which is potentially very great. Some people with the sun in the 11th house are downright wacky, but often very achieving people.

Birth Time 6 to 8 a.m.: **Sun in Twelfth House**

- *Twelfth house matters:* Dissolving ... ambiguity ... disguising ... retreating ... sensualism ... enchantment ... paying dues ... healing spiritually ... insubstantiality ... confinement ... persuading ... comprehending the incomprehensible ... merging ... pretending.
- *Twelfth house people/places/things:* Makeup ... escapism ... alcohol and drugs ... drama and dramatic actors ... films ... advertising ... pastoral work ... fishing ... astrophysics ... con men ... magicians ... hospitals ... alibis ... myths ... prisons.
- *Problems and possibilities:* Yours is not an easy house of the sun to have—especially if you are a very self-expressive sun sign type like Leo. You may feel that life is confining you in some way or another; what you are really sensing is your gift of the ability to transcend self to a much higher spiritual level. You should be an expert at coping with intangibles and sensing the nuances of any situation. In a sense, you have a kind of ESP which can be developed for life success. However, the real down side of the twelfth house sun is that it

can lead to a very confused, unfocussed attitude toward life. It is essential that you give yourself a definite structure to work within if you are to free yourself from the worries and cares of life. By all means avoid any form of escapism that is dangerous.

3

The Geometry of Relationships

What Signs You Get Along with—and Why

The first thing most people want to know about their sun sign is what other signs they are compatible with. It's a natural question, and a good one to ask an astrologer, because one aspect of astrology, called "synastry" (literally, "stars together") concentrates on the subject of relationships. When practising synastry, the astrologer compares the two birth charts of the two people involved to find what connections there are between them. It is a complicated process, but it provides excellent clues about how two people will relate to each other. What chart comparison does is *describe the nature of the relationship*. Actually, to an astrologer there are no "bad" or "good" relationships; there are just a lot of different kinds and each has a special character. Of course it is true that some relationships end up on the rocks, sometimes devastating one or both parties involved. But, even in such cases, the astrologer looks at it as a "karmic" relationship—one in which people *had* to come together in order to learn some life lessons.

While comparing two complete horoscopes is the ideal way to look at a relationship, there is a very simple method of looking at two sun signs, and coming up with an overall prediction of how two people will relate to each other. This method goes back to the great circle of the zodiac and to the division of the twelve signs into four elements: fire, earth, air, and water.

Here's the lineup of signs in each element:

Fire: Aries, Leo, Sagittarius

Earth: Taurus, Virgo, Capricorn
Air: Gemini, Libra, Aquarius
Water: Cancer, Scorpio, Pisces

The general rules of thumb for element-mixing are as follows:

Great	Good	Semi-tough or Difficult
Fire and air	Fire and fire	Fire and water
Water and earth	Earth and earth	Earth and air
	Air and air	Fire and earth
	Water and water	Air and water

Here's the way it looks mathmatically:
If you divide the 360-degree circle of the zodiac by the twelve signs, you find that each sign is 30 degrees away from the next.

- Signs that are 30 degrees apart—or next to each other—are semi-tough.
- Signs that are 60 degrees (two signs) or 180 degrees (six signs) away from each other are the best combinations. (The latter, 180 degrees away from each other, makes these signs polar opposites, and in astrology polar opposites attract.)
- Signs that are 120 degrees apart—four signs away from each other—are in the same element, and their relationship is good, but far from perfect.
- Signs that are 90 degrees or three signs away from each other have the most difficult relationships of all. They are said to be in "square aspect" to each other.

When you look at the four elements in terms of what they signify in the physical world, you get a good idea why some elements get along more easily.

Fire turns water into steam (hot air).
Water puts fire out.
Fire scorches earth.

Earth smothers fire.
Air fans fire and makes it brighter.
Fire warms up cool air.
Water softens up hard earth.
Earth makes water keep its shape.
Water and air do nothing (unless you add heat).
Air blows earth around.

What about combinations of the same element, such as fire with fire? In effect, they tend to neutralize or cancel each other out. Or, they can simply be too much of one element for comfort.

- Two fire signs together could experience "burn out" fairly quickly.
- Two air signs might analyze each other to the death of the relationship.
- Two earth signs could depress each other a lot.
- Two water signs could make for an overly "heavy" relationship.

4

Twelve Places at the Table

A Mini Astrodrama in Which the Twelve Signs Play Themselves

No matter how accurate or colorful any description of a zodiac sign may be, it is still a description—not the real thing. A sign is simply an abstract concept until it takes form in a living, breathing human being. There are obviously as many different types of people as there are individual horoscopes, and no two are exactly alike. However, the twelve signs of the zodiac are still the best guidelines we have for sorting out human behavior into broad but meaningful categories. There are even fiction writers who use the zodiac signs as prototypes for characters they create because it makes them more realistic, i.e., more like people you are likely to meet.

What follows is fiction, but it gets closer to the truth about each zodiacal sign than a general description ever can. The twelve characters in this docudrama are obviously caricatures, because their behavior is highly exaggerated. But it is exaggeration for emphasis, and for the purpose of bringing to life the twelve signs of the zodiac, which don't really exist except as real people. Like real people, these twelve characters have foibles; but they have fine points too. As you read this drama, you may find yourself drawn to some signs and put off by others. Make mental notes of which signs you find yourself most sympathetic with and check out your findings in the parts of this book about astrological compatibility. It could prove very interesting—

and very revealing. As each sign of the zodiac has a sex or gender, they are portrayed here as male or female accordingly. But the basic behavior pattern is applicable to both sexes.

The twelve signs of the zodiac are invited to dinner at that great dining room in the sky. When they arrive, they find that their host (who shall remain signless) has slipped up, and there are only eleven places set at the table. Since it is a fancy affair, each sign is trying to be on his/her best behavior. However, the situation is a bit unsettling, so in the course of trying to resolve it, they all relapse into their natural zodiacal characteristics.

Aries An energetic young man, he comes bounding into the room, almost tripping on an untied shoelace. He is dressed rather casually for the occasion, and looks as if he got dressed rather quickly. When he realizes what the situation is, there's no doubt in his mind how to handle it.

"Only eleven places? Don't worry; Pisces will probably never show anyway. But, I got here before anybody else (the doorman will prove it) so I should definitely get a seat. In fact, I should sit down *first*. No, I don't need to wash my hands or anything. I'm *starved*, so I hope you aren't having anything like the gooey mess with the French name you had before. A hamburger will do just fine. And don't serve it cold like you did the last time. Hey, there's a great-looking dish over there, ha ha! Seat me next to her, will you Cancer? Well, she looks like a nice warm type, so I think I'll go let her warm me up. By the way, I'm organizing a sky-diving club. Want to join? Seriously, if you can't afford the membership fee, I'll put it up for you, because I'd love to have you join. Oh, you're doing okay now? Glad to hear you're off the rack. Got any pretzels?"

Taurus An attractive young woman with faint dimples in her roundish cheeks and a slightly unruly but pretty mass of curly hair comes sauntering into the room. She is dressed in a soft and pretty outfit that looks expensive, and has her handbag clutched tightly under her arm. She looks around the room with moderate curiosity. As the host walks up to her, she gives him a warm smile; when she speaks, her voice is low and melodious—but firm.

"Only eleven places? You mean, only eleven *chairs*. All you have to do is set another place and give me a pillow to sit on. I don't mind, as long as I'm comfortable. And I smell something wonderful, so I know the food is going to be delicious. To be honest with you, that's really why I came. I don't like to go out much, you know. What I really like is curling up in my warm and comfy bed—with someone warm and comfy, of course. (Are you busy later on?) But, now that I'm *here*, there's no way I'm not going to eat. What's for dessert? Who's that nervous-looking lady over there? Virgo? I'll go try to make her feel comfortable."

Gemini It's hard to tell just how old this fellow is as he springs in the door; he could be any age, though he looks about eighteen. He is dressed in the very latest style, though nothing he has on is really extreme. His eyes dart all over the room, and he is carrying a notebook under his arm. When the host tells him about the eleven places, he is so busy listening to another conversation, he almost misses it. When he reacts, it is in a typically casual way.

"Don't worry about me; I don't need a place. I'll just float around the room, because what I really came here for is the conversation. I'm writing a book, you know—it's called *1001 Opening Conversational Gambits* and tonight I'm researching. I see you've got some really fascinating types here. How did you make up the guest list? Are they all married? Why did they come alone? What's the menu? Who's the chef? Can I see the wine list? Who's that blowsy-looking type over there? Taurus? I'll bet *she's* got a story. Where's the telephone? I've got to make a call."

Cancer A sexy, voluptuous woman of indeterminate age pauses at the door; she seems shy, but conscious of the impression she is making. Her clothes are a bit unusual, and some things are from the thrift shop. However, her antique jewelry is genuine, and the whole effect is glamorous. When she discovers there are only eleven places, she is visibly upset, and there is a touch of a whine in her voice as she speaks.

"I wish I'd known; I could have stayed home with the children. They have colds, you know. If you want, I'll simply leave; but I really don't want to go home by myself; I'll get scared and have bad dreams. Upset? Yes, I am upset, and when I get upset I can't eat. Unless it's really soothing and nourishing. Did you know that a touch of heavy cream in mashed potatoes is simply heavenly? Chicken soup? I make it by the gallon. Say, you look as if you could stand a little fattening up. Well, all right. I *guess* I'll stay—unless I change my mind, of course."

Leo This is a fine figure of a man—fairly tall, rather muscular, and with a thick crop of curly hair that is somewhere between blond and red. He is elegantly dressed and his gold cufflinks probably put a real drain on Fort Knox. His grand entrance is smooth and practised, and his handshake is hearty and warm. When his host tells him the news, he takes it very personally.

"Well, let me tell you, this is embarrassing! I mean, all these people here to see me, and I may have to stand? I've given bigger parties than this, and they've always gone off without a hitch. Let me handle things for you the next time. For now, just get that chair over there and squeeze someone in—Virgo won't mind. No, *here*; not *there!* While we're all waiting I guess I can entertain everyone with my tantrum act. What? No, I'm only kidding—though I am mad. I'll do my Hamlet number instead. Like my cufflinks? They match my Gold Card. I've ordered another pair with sapphires, too."

Virgo A rather prim woman stands quietly at the door looking as if she would like to blend into the woodwork. She is dressed very neatly, but conservatively, with flat-heeled sensible shoes. In her handbag she carries a surgical mask to wear in case any of the other guests has a cold. Her reaction to the news that there are only eleven places is swift and shrill.

"Well, it certainly isn't *my* fault. I answered the invitation the minute I got it. I *always* do! Why didn't you check on things more carefully? If you had, this wouldn't have happened, and you wouldn't have all these people standing around thinking terrible things about you. I don't mind for myself, you understand, I don't eat much anyway; you never know what you're going to get. I'll stay in the kitchen and help the cook clean up. You can't be too careful about these things, you know. You wouldn't believe the sanitary conditions I've found in *some* kitchens. Not mentioning any names, of course. Oh, *why* did you mess things up this way; you are simply impossible. . . ."

Intermission: Our host walks away as Virgo continues to complain. As he checks on the guests, he discovers that Libra has just arrived. Sagittarius and Pisces are nowhere to be found, but Scorpio, Capricorn, and Aquarius are waiting to greet him. Because he looks like he's a bit uncomfortable, the host talks to Libra first.

Libra A very attractive male, wearing all the right things, walks tentatively into the room, looking as if he is searching for someone. He is visibly uncomfortable alone. His gaze scans the room, quietly appraising everything and everybody in it. He seems to approve, but in his nervousness, he approaches the table, and starts rearranging one of the settings, then rearranging it again. All this is done very tactfully and gracefully. In fact, he looks as if he couldn't make an awkward gesture if he tried. His host approaches him and breaks the news. Libra's reaction is smooth and unruffled.

"Oh, how *clever* of you to arrange this little puzzle for us. It will make things so much more fun. Of course, we've got to make things absolutely fair; we wouldn't want to hurt anyone's feelings. I could leave if it would help, but . . . Oh, how nice of you to tell me I'll definitely have a place; it makes me feel a lot less awkward. I rarely go places alone, you know. Who would I like to sit next to? Well, the Capricorn lady looks like a sturdy and sensible type. But on the other hand, Scorpio is a *knockout*. Is she attached? Hmmm, Taurus looks like she'd like to chat, but oh, that Cancer! Decisions, decisions; I'll make up my mind later on. Where did you get that *great* painting?

Scorpio A slim and sexy woman dressed totally in black comes slinking into the room. Her style and movement are absolutely magnetic, and every eye turns to look at her. But she gives no visible response that she is aware of it. She doesn't seem to be feeling anything at all, but when her host approaches and tells her what is going on, she is seething with quiet rage.

"Do you really think you are going to get away with this? I suspected something when I got that weird invitation. Who in the world would ever come as they are and let everybody else know what they're really like? No matter how many times you tell me it was an innocent mistake to set only eleven places, I'll never believe it. Nothing in this world is innocent. And when it comes to drawing straws, just remember you owe me one from the last time. You know, the *last* time! Who's that wimpy looking guy over there? Gemini? Maybe I'll amuse myself with him for a while. I need a new conquest; I'm getting out of practice."

Sagittarius While Scorpio has been talking with the host, a tall rather rangy male has come loping into the room carrying a suitcase. He is a bit disheveled because his flight was late. He throws the suitcase in a corner and starts putting himself back together—a bit absentmindedly because he is looking around the room with a big smile and a lot of anticipation. He moves toward the host and gives a slap on his back that is almost *too* hearty.

"Only eleven places? Why worry? We'll work it out somehow. Life's too short to get uptight anyway. Had the greatest trip, and I'm turning right around tomorrow and going to the Orient so I can practice my Chinese. Say, are you serving Chinese food? I love Chinese food—and a good beer to go with it. At least I hope you're serving better wine than you did last time. You're looking a little pale . . . been partying too much lately? Ha ha, only kidding. Who's that guy over there with the flashy cufflinks? And the mouse with the sensible shoes? Think I'll see if I can loosen her up a bit. Did you hear I'm going to win the lottery again? What do you mean, how do I know? I just *know*. And I've got a great idea for an international fast food chain I'm going to bankroll with my winnings. I'm gonna call it 'The Great Gobler' and serve only turkey sandwiches. Hey, I'm thirsty. Where's the bar?"

Aquarius An intellectual-looking gentleman—sort of an absentminded professor type—has been standing in the doorway quietly puffing his pipe and scrutinizing the crowd. His jacket and pants don't match, but he isn't aware of it. An even stranger—but typical—sartorial note is his electric blue tie with orange stripes. He's got his earphones with him; if things get too dull, he'll listen to some hard rock or electronic music and be in seventh heaven. When he finds out about the missing place, he gives a thoughtful answer and makes an impractical suggestion.

"Oh, well, rather than make anyone feel left out, we could cancel the whole dinner and bring the food to the local shelter for the homeless. Ah, you don't care for that idea. Too bad; I'm becoming more and more concerned about poverty in our own backyard. Of course, I'm no bleeding heart like Pisces, but fair's fair. Want to hear about a new invention I'm working on? It's an electronic stamp sorter that will revolutionize the whole philatelic world. Huh? Oh, that's stamp collecting. Glad you asked me to come alone, since I'm free as a bird now. My last attachment got so *sticky!* I've sworn off. At least off those emotional types who want you to get so involved. No, I never get lonely—I've got too many friends for that. By the way, I can just sit on the floor in the lotus position, and get some meditating in at the same time."

Capricorn A rather handsome, perfectly put together woman has been quietly observing the crowd and the room, mentally putting a price tag on everything. What she has on is very expensive, but understated and in excellent taste. In her handbag she carries a petition with her name on it. She wants to run for local office, and is hoping to pick up some supporters tonight. If they are "her kind of people," that is. Her reaction to the host's situation is sober but logical.

"Well, it's obvious someone will have to go, but I

trust your judgment to decide who is most important—if you know what I mean. Your appointments are in excellent taste; I see you like Tiffany as much as I do. Who's that rather tacky looking type over there? Cancer? Where *does* she get her clothes? I have little sympathy for people who can't get their act together and run their lives successfully. She's probably a poet. Ah, well, different strokes for different folks; fantasy has no place in *my* life, you know. By the way, I have some excellent ideas about how to shape things up in the community; will you sign my petition? At dinner, are we going to discuss great books? I just bought a whole series . . . all leather-bound, of course. They look smashing in my living room."

Pisces   Meanwhile, a rather wispy but very pretty woman has been wandering in and out of the doorway, looking as if she isn't quite sure she is in the right place. She is dressed in a misty fabric of very pale colors; there doesn't seem to be a clear-cut edge anywhere. In fact, if you don't rub your eyes, you might think you are seeing an apparition. The host knows it's Pisces and catches her just as she's about to drift out the door again. He doesn't bother telling her about the missing place, because he knows she wouldn't understand why that was important.

"Late? Am I late? I lost my watch two weeks ago. Or was it three? Oh well, what's time anyway in the larger scheme of things? Hungry? Not really, though I can't remember the last time I ate. *Love*—it's *love* that's food for the soul, and that's what I care about nourishing. I wonder if any of these people have had any *real* soul food lately. No, don't worry, I won't try to convert anyone tonight. I'm too, too drained because of my current work. What kind? Well, it really isn't a job-job, I mean where you make money, and all. I've started a shelter for homeless animals in my apartment; I cry so much when I see a stray that I can't stand it. Who? Ho, he left some time ago. Something about there being 'other fish in the sea.' What in the world do you suppose he meant by that? By the way, I'm a little short of cash. Do you think you could lend me . . .?"

At this point, things are at a stalemate, but the situation will quickly resolve itself in one of twelve ways. Take your pick: This time *you* can choose the ending you like—and the one you think makes best astrological sense.

A. Aries gets in a fight with Leo and has to go to the emergency room.
B. Taurus gets really tired and hungry and decides to go home, cook a hamburger, and go to bed early.
C. Gemini runs out of note paper and gets laryngitis at the same time.
D. Cancer gets a call from the babysitter and is so worried she goes home to take care of her children.
E. Leo gets so irritated that no one is paying attention to the bruises Aries gave him that he leaves in a huff.
F. Virgo gets a stomach ache and decides to leave. Besides, it's time for her mineral bath.
G. Libra isn't able to make up his mind and gets a headache in the process.
H. Scorpio decides it's definitely a plot to humiliate her, and bows out less than graciously.
I. Sagittarius gets a little drunk and leaves early to get the plane.
J. Capricorn leaves as soon as she gets her petition filled up because there isn't anyone there *really* worth knowing.
K. Aquarius decides to go teach people at the shelter to use his stamp-sorting machine so they can get jobs.
L. Pisces remembers she has a date with her spiritual advisor and that she forgot to feed the animals.

5

Moods of the Moon

How to Successfully Navigate Its Day-by-Day Changes

Never underestimate the power of the moon. It is the closest planet to earth, and the only one whose effect on human life can actually be measured. Even the most skeptical antiastrology person has to admit that the moon rules the tides. If you stand on the beach for even a half hour or so, you can literally *see* how the moon works its magic as the water flows higher or lower, according to the time of day. There are places in the world where the tide rises as much as forty feet from its lowest to its highest point—that's *power*. If you think about the fact that humans are about 98 percent water in our chemical makeup, it's much easier to accept the fact that the moon has the same powerful effect on us as it does on the tides.

Like the "female" she symbolically is, the moon also changes her mind—or her sign—more quickly than any other planet. If you look at the day-by-day predictions in this book, which gives the position of the moon for every day, you will see that this changeable planet moves into a different sign about every two days.

As it moves from sign to sign, the moon brings a different kind of energy to the earth's atmosphere. Those who are particularly sensitive—like Cancers—feel it most strongly. But even the most stolid types are often moved by the effect of the particular sign the moon occupies on any given day, though they may not want to admit it.

Are we then slaves to the moods of the moon? Not if we understand its energies and cooperate with them. If you work *with* the moon and not against her, you can actually make life a lot easier for yourself. For instance, there are certain activities that go more smoothly when the moon is in a particular sign, just as other activities are more difficult to accomplish. Scheduling things accordingly could prevent a lot of frustration. You don't have to become a complete "lunatic" (ancient meaning, "one ruled by the moon") to benefit from its positive vibes, but simply go with the flow. Keep in mind, however, that the moon's effect will be *modified* by your sun sign, so be sure to check out your individual daily prediction. For instance, for *any* sun sign, the days when the moon is in that sign should bring a surge of energy. Whether you handle that energy positively or negatively is up to you.

Here's a rundown of the moods of the moon and the human activities that go with them.

When the Moon Is in Aries There is a very *physical* tone to this day. People may be throwing their weight around in more ways than one. Impatience, independent action, and quick tempers can sprout up all over the place. The good news is that most people will be feeling rather decisive, so some things can be completed. The bad news is that decisions may be totally unilateral; what *you* want may be exactly what someone else *doesn't* want. Similarly, people may be invading each other's territories; "keep off the grass" signs won't mean much today. Rule-breaking is the order of the day, and so are the consequences that go along with it. However, if there's a big mountain to scale, today's the day to begin the climb. If there's a formidable task that requires a lot of get-up-and-go to accomplish, today's the day to plunge in with both feet. If there's something you've been hesitating to tell someone, today you'll get the nerve to say it, but it may be difficult to be tactful. Try, anyway. On the up side, people will be feeling in the mood for some fun and frolic—practical jokes are very "moon in Aries." Even the boss may get in the spirit of things. It's a good day to:

Make a sale	Sharpen knives
Do heavy housework	Stop worrying
Do some baking	Make a clean break
Start a diet	Start an exercise class
Buy a lottery ticket	Do something on your own
Get a haircut	Try a new recipe
Have your eyes checked	Throw a last-minute party

When the Moon Is in Taurus Today, the amber light goes on, and people start to proceed with more caution. Rather than being adventurous, most people will feel like sticking with routine tasks. It is not a good day to try something new. In this more conservative mood, people will tend to hold on to what they have; don't try to borrow money from a friend today. Concentrate on making your own money grow, instead. Speaking of increase, this is an excellent day to "make your garden grow" in every sense of the phrase. Along with a quieter mood of the day, you may feel like pampering yourself a bit; allow yourself at least one luxury. Chocoholics, beware, however; this is a day for food binges and all forms of dietary excess. Creature comforts are a lot on everyone's mind; in fact, it may be difficult to crawl out of that comfortable bed in the morning. And more than a few people will be crawling back into it fairly early—with their favorite person. Sexual cravings are high on the list of "moon moods" today. Enjoy!

It's a good day to:

Put something off until tomorrow	Put up preserves
Buy clothes or jewelry	Have a massage
Get your teeth filled	Start singing lessons
Start a savings account	Sell high on the market
Stick to your guns	Buy a plant
Buy candy	Buy real estate
Stay home and watch television	Hug somebody

When the Moon Is in Gemini There's a touch more energy in the air today, and people will begin moving around a lot more. For some, there will be a lot of nervous energy and the scattery feeling that goes along with it; don't force yourself to concentrate if you can avoid it. It's a day to make connections—call, write, or bump into both new and old friends. Wits are generally sharp today, and people could be cracking jokes all around you. On the other hand, they may also be spilling some secrets. Gossip is easy to start today, and it could spread like wildfire. Mind your mouth! Anything requiring manual dexterity can easily get done today; even those who are usually clumsy may find they have nimble fingers. The tendency today is to do things quickly, if a bit superficially. If there are a couple of things that require a once-over-lightly treatment, get them out of the way now. If you haven't been invited to a party, give your own—or at least plan to get together with some buddies for a little socializing; the time is definitely right.

It's a good day to:

Get your hair cut	Use your hands
Join a club	Pay bills
Have a tooth pulled	Eat out
Sign up for a new course	Take a walk/drive
Send a letter	Call your brother/sister
Try something new	Tell a fib
Learn a language	Do two things at once

When the Moon Is in Cancer In Cancer, the moon is in her very own sign—and you'll know it. All those "moon" characteristics—like changeableness, sensitivity, and the desire for security—will be heightened. Cancers, of course, will feel it most strongly; and the other water signs, Scorpio and Pisces, may be even moodier than usual. The general tendency today is to do things that make you feel comfortable and feel good. For some, that means eating a lot of food; for others, it could be hitting the bottle a bit. People tend to feel a bit sorry for themselves during the transit of the moon through Cancer. When two people who live together are both feeling that way, the result can be a rather touchy day—and evening. As much as you want the comfort of others, you are better off on your own and working off those anxious feelings by yourself. Not for safety, but for comfort's sake, the best place to go today is no farther than your own backyard. You'll probably be feeling very stay-at-home anyway. However, it's an excellent day for memories. Reminisce with somebody you love, or get out that old photo album by yourself. You might find yourself shedding a tear or two, but it's all in a good cause.

It's a good day to:

Bake something delicious	Hug your children
Buy something old	Take care of somebody
Put up preserves	Go without makeup
Buy property	Call your mother
Start a habit	Buy something for the house
Plant something	Entertain at home
Pamper yourself	Give your hair a treatment

When the Moon Is in Leo Today, everyone feels like "coming out of the woodwork." Just as Cancer moon makes you want to hide, Leo moon makes you want to get out there and be seen. Nothing but the best will do on this day, so it could be a rather expensive one. Most people will be more generous than usual—both with their money and their affections; many a new romance has started under a Leo moon. Leo is also one of the more playful signs, so a lot of you will be in the mood for fun and games. Eating out is very Leo moon—and so is picking up the check. Today, you may have to fight for it. However, the boss may be a lot stricter than usual, and even those with nobody to "boss" will try to push somebody around. If you've got children, today you will appreciate them very much—no matter what they do. Most people find themselves reaching for the newest thing in the closet under this transit of the moon. If they don't have anything new to wear, they'll probably go out and buy it—on credit. No matter what time of the year it is, you'll be looking for a little sunshine or at least a warm place. On the beaches or by the fireplaces are where most people would like to be today—wishing life were one long vacation.

It's a good day to:

Borrow money	Buy jewelry
Get a new hairstyle	Invest in the market
Start building something	Do something creative

Follow a hunch
Steal the spotlight
Be brave
Be waited on
Prepare a gourmet meal
Dress up
Kiss somebody new

When the Moon Is in Virgo   Now it's back to work, and back to reality. There's a sharp distinction between the Virgo moon mood and what precedes it, so you may shock yourself. Perhaps by deciding it's really time to get organized and then actually *doing* it. On the home front it's a great day to rearrange all those sloppy closets and cupboards. On the job, you couldn't pick a better time to wrestle with that nasty detail work you've been avoiding. However, all is not good news under Virgo moon. For one thing, by contrast to Leo moon's generosity, people will be positively stingy today—both with their money and their love. Even the best of situations could deteriorate today when one or the other of the involved parties decides to point out the other's flaws. Your best course under the Virgo moon is to check that impulse to criticize. People can become highly self-critical during this transit, too. One extreme example of the going-over some people can give themselves during a Virgo moon is to develop mysterious maladies or to discover aches and pains they never felt before. Not to worry; they'll be all better by the time the moon moves into the next sign. Virgo moon is also inspection time, so the boss may be particularly sensitive to messy desks today and sloppiness in general. Keep things buttoned up and tidy for best results.

It's a good time to:

Start a diet
Get a physical
Bake bread
Quit smoking
Buy a pet
Try to do without something
Buy health food
Start a new job
Sew or mend something
Read a good book
Get a complete makeover
Call your maiden aunt
Feel like a martyr
Do a puzzle

When the Moon Is in Libra   Now it's time to kiss and make up. Any relationships that suffered from the ragged nerves of Virgo moon time can be nicely patched up today. Pleasantries should be easy for one and all. In fact, even people who are normally rather gruff should smile a bit more today. Libra moon is one of the most social of moon periods; meeting and greeting should be prevalent activities. Most people will want to put their best foot forward, too, so the impulse to dress up and look your best may come upon you. You may feel rather self-indulgent as well; hard work is not as compatible with the Libra moon period as rest and relaxation are. It's definitely a time of togetherness, so even habitual loners may be looking for company. Most people will feel they need people—possibly one special person. Romance blossoms under the Libra moon in its purest form. It's not so much sex people want now as romantic love and companionship. No one's actually made a count, but it's a fair bet that more flowers get sent under the Libra moon than at any other time. Physical beauty is also highly important, so Libra moon is a great one under which to get yourself a whole new look or to redo anything that needs it. Something that's off-balance will bother you more at this time.

It's a good day to:

Be tactful	Forgive and forget
Redecorate	Add color to your life
Give a party	Luxuriate
Fall in love	Sign up for a dance class
Join a singing group	Buy a stereo
Buy something beautiful	Buy a down comforter
Try a new makeup	Learn about wine

When the Moon Is in Scorpio Things could easily get heavy today, and the tendency will be to go to extremes. Haters will hate more; lovers will love more passionately and physically. The sex drive is stimulated in many people during this transit of the moon. With all those intense emotions flying around, it's not surprising that people easily get hot under the collar—and/or imagine that somebody is out to get them. However, there is an up side to the Scorpio moon, and that is the extra jot of will power it gives the most weak-willed people. If you've got to dig in your heels and clench your teeth to get something done, today's the day you will be able to do it. People *endure* a lot under the Scorpio moon. The only problem is that they may develop some resentment toward those they believe should be enduring with them. However, the tendency is to keep silent. In spite of the intense emotionalism of the Scorpio moon, there isn't a lot of outright complaining. People will let the pressure build up inside of them and then burst out into violent rages. If your temper isn't good under the best of circumstances, control it during the Scorpio moon, by all means. It's also a time when people tend to feel a bit claustrophobic; a good walk in the fresh air can work wonders at this time.

It's a good day to:

See a psychiatrist
Buy a house
Open a secret bank account
Make a firm decision
Do your taxes
Throw away what you don't need
Do some strenuous exercise

Have good sex
Face up to a crisis
Read a good mystery
Take body-building
Get a prescription filled
Buy life insurance
Change your life

When the Moon Is in Sagittarius Things definitely lighten up when the moon moves into Sagittarius—and people loosen up, too. In fact, one danger under this moon is getting too relaxed—with your diet, your money, or your generous spirits. Moderation is not the mood of the day, so you may have to force it on yourself. It is not a good time to try to stop smoking—or to stop doing anything self-indulgent. There's definitely a "live and let live" attitude in the air when the moon is in Sagittarius, so bad relations should be easily improved. A spirit of good will is pervasive, as well as a lighthearted attitude. One thing that means is that even normally conservative people will be willing to take chances; those for whom a more liberal outlook is a natural state of affairs could really go too far out on a limb. If you gamble, bet *only* what you can afford to lose today. The place everyone will want to be today is outdoors. In fact, more than one person will simply disappear from the scene to do something either adventurous or relaxing. It's an excellent day to think big, but you may find the follow-through a bit difficult. The big picture is what's easiest to see right now; leave the fine brush strokes for another time. Enjoy the spirit of fun and generosity that should be in the air.

It's a good day to:

Make a long-distance call	Go to church
Plan a trip	Enjoy a hobby
Buy a dog (or a horse)	Learn a new language
Contribute to a wildlife-foundation	Do something charitable
	Borrow money
Try a new approach	Run away from it all
Sell anything to anybody	Get a bigger place
Try your luck/feel lucky	

When the Moon Is in Capricorn In sharp contrast to the "easy come, easy go" feeling of the Sagittarius moon, the moon in Capricorn brings on a much more serious mood. You could call it the "workaholic's moon," and even those whose work style is less intense will find themselves wanting to get a lot done. It's important to *accomplish something* when the moon is in Capricorn, if you are to feel comfortable. Most people want to tread only on solid ground at this time, so there could be a bit of distrust in the air. No one wants to waste time—and least of all on things or people from whom they are not likely to derive some kind of benefit. Another curious facet of the Capricorn moon mood is a tendency to feel older and more serious; some lighter types dislike the feeling so much they will go out of their way to look young. It's the kind of day that matronly secretary in the office is likely to appear in something rather frilly. People can really handle things under the Capricorn moon too; endurance is *very* Capricorn. That means those who exercise will work out harder and longer; those who normally do not push themselves will do at least a little self-prodding. A good image is paramount to many people when the moon is in this sign, and the tendency is for people to be quite status conscious. Self-control is the order of the day, in every respect.

It's a good day to:

Start a new job	Make a list
Buy antiques	Keep your money

Buy anything for investment	Go to the dentist
Wear anything with a good label on it	Start a diet
	Work late
Bet on a favorite	Ask for repayment of a debt
Go to the chiropractor	
Buy insurance	Clean house

When the Moon Is in Aquarius When the moon moves into the sign of Aquarius from the sign of Capricorn, it's as if somebody took the cork out of the bottle. Suddenly, the rather repressed mood bursts into a desire for change—a *need* for change. This is one of those days when people tend to make rash moves like quit a dull job, call it quits with a clinging person, throw out everything in their closet and start all over again. Reaching this point is easy to do under the Aquarian moon. However, it's usually very positive. What's important at this time is to try something new, not just get rid of something old. Some people decide to experiment with a new recipe, a new lover, or a new hair style. It's the kind of day when a woman with long hair will decide to get a crew cut. On the relationship side, the mood now is one of brotherly love and friendship rather than highly charged sexual encounters. Wanting to be with friends and feeling like part of a group is what's important now. No one is a stranger under the Aquarian moon, and talking to people on the street is very common. The thing to be careful of under this moon is doing something irreparable—like finally telling the boss what you really think of him. He/she could easily decide that it's time for a change of personnel.

It's a good day to:

Do something kinky	Buy/wear something crazy
Try a new food	Color your hair
Do something friendly	Contribute to a charity
Start flying lessons	Move to a new place
Do something impulsive	Buy a television/stereo
Join a club	Make a new friend
Make a speculative investment	Be fair

When the Moon Is in Pisces This is a time when people wear their hearts on their sleeves and feel *very* vulnerable. There's a lot of ultrasensitivity under the Pisces moon, and a lot of crying on shoulders—if you can find one that isn't already occupied. Mixed in with the emotionalism is a real feeling of empathy with others; now's the time people feel that everyone is in the same boat. However, it may be a bit difficult to keep things afloat today, because there isn't a lot of firm direction from anyone or anything. It's confusion time, and even the clearest of messages can get a little garbled. Indecisiveness will spread like the plague, so don't expect to get any clear-cut answers today. Creative people get more creative under the Pisces moon, and anyone could feel just a bit poetic. Romantic relationships are heavenly under the Pisces moon as long as they don't get out of control. Keeping certain other things under control—like drinking and other forms of escapism—is a wise precaution, too. The most satisfying and least dangerous escape is to hold hands with someone you love while you watch a real tearjerker movie. Lots of people call in sick under the Pisces moon, and there's a good reason: Most people don't like to cry in public.

It's a good day to:

Put on weight	Write a poem
Fall in love	Take in a stray dog or cat
Develop ESP	Visit the sick
Find God	See a therapist
Buy flowers or perfume	Stay home and read
Swear off something	Pamper yourself
Get hooked on something	Buy a camera

6

Venus and Mars

Love and Sex
Peace and War
Cooperating and Competing

Next to your sun sign, your moon sign, and your rising sign, the positions of Venus and Mars in your horoscope are probably the most important indicators of your personal psychology. This is because Venus shows your affectional nature and Mars shows your sexual nature. To put it another way, *Venus shows your wants and needs in romantic love while Mars shows your sexual style and your manner of expressing it.*

In a broader sense, Venus and Mars are the principles of peace and war. Venus wants to cooperate and relate to others, to share life experiences. Mars is totally concerned with self and getting what you want. Everybody's got a Venus and Mars in their horoscope because every human being has to both live with others and assert him-/herself. It's all a matter of degree. If you want to, you can think of Venus as the "higher" side of human relationships; Mars the "lower." However, you've got to keep in mind that—like all other opposites in the universe—both *cooperating* and competing are necessary if the world is to continue going round.

Because Venus has to do with the need to share, the sign in which it is placed will tell a lot about how you attract people you want to share with. It will also show what attracts you to others. Beyond the love arena, the position of Venus in your horoscope shows your attitudes toward money and personal possessions, creature comforts, and things of beauty. Venus is "feminine" in nature, and women tend to relate to their Venus sign more than men. But for *both* sexes, it is an available energy.

The good side of Venus is:
Sharing, beautifying, peacemaking
The bad side is:
acquisitiveness, self-indulgence, laziness

Because the position of Mars shows how you go about getting what you want, it will tell a lot about your personal drive—how *much* you want what you want. It is the desire principle, and will indicate just how passionate your passions are. Ambition, assertiveness, and anger are just a few steps away from each other, so Mars will also reveal what makes you angry or what gets you going. The planet Mars is "masculine" in nature—highly so—and men will find it easier to get in touch with their Mars energy. However, every woman's got a Mars too, and sooner or later a woman's Mars energy will present itself.

The "good" side of Mars is:
Dynamic energy, courage, sexual drive
The "bad" side is:
manipulation, cowardice, sexual abuse

No matter what area of life you are relating these planets to, it is useful to think of them in sexual terms, and of our human sexual organs. Venus is open and receptive; Mars thrusts forward and penetrates. Because we normally attract someone or are attracted to someone before we get sexually involved, Venus energy precedes Mars energy. In other words, Venus shows how *receptive* you are; Mars shows how *active* you are. Venus also has a lot to do with our ideas and images of romance, our romantic fantasies, while Mars is an indicator of sexual fantasies—which may or may not be acted out, depending on the individual's degree of inhibition.

Just as some combinations of people can coexist in constant harmony while others are in constant conflict,

Venus and Mars in an individual person can work well together, or at cross-purposes. When your Venus doesn't get along well with your Mars, you've got a problem. Sometimes a sexual problem, but always an inner conflict. How can you tell if your Venus and Mars are "friends" or "foes"? First, by looking up the positions of your personal Mars and Venus in the charts provided at the end of this chapter, reading the descriptions of those planets in the signs they fall in for you. But, just to make things a bit clearer, here's a rundown of easy Mars/Venus relationships and difficult ones. (By the way, you can also apply this principle in comparing your Venus/Mars positions to those of someone else, as well.)

Venus and Mars are "at war" when:

- One is in a fire sign, and one is in an earth sign. Here you've got a conflict between the practical and the experimental sides of yourself.
- One is in a fire sign and one is in a water sign. One part of you says "let's do it"; the other side says, "I might get hurt," so you might be stalled.
- One is in an earth sign and one is in an air sign. Air likes to think about things a little; earth needs to know it will work. Once again, it may hold you back.
- One is in an air sign and one is in a water sign. Yours is a conflict between the mental relationship and the emotional one; you may find it hard to decide what you want.

Venus and Mars are on good terms when:

- One is in a fire sign, one is in an air sign.
- One is in an earth sign and one is in a water sign.
- Both are in the same element.

Venus and Mars in The Signs

Venus in Aries (fire element)

While this position of Venus in a man or a woman indicates the kind of person who falls in love impulsively, both sexes want to be conquered, when they have Venus in Aries. They may be outrageously flirtatious, but can lead others on a merry chase before they give in. There is a tendency to look for trouble when Venus is in ths position; actually, it is excitement Venus in Aries people crave. Their personal likes and dislikes will be quite clearly defined, and they will be vocal about them. In matters of taste, there is less refinement than when Venus is in a softer sign. Both the males and the females may play up their sexuality in the way they dress; they like very loud things like rock music and bright colors. There is also an impish charm in these people and a tendency to play love games. The *real* goal is to be swept away by a romantic lover who lives up to a mediaeval code of chivalry and/or chastity.

Mars in Aries (fire element)

This is a highly competitive position for Mars; people with Mars in Aries leave no doubt about the fact that they want it, and they want it *now*—whatever "it" is. Mars in Aries can cut through a lot of life's red tape. When it comes to courtship, Mars in Aries people are equally able to disregard the small talk and get right down to business. However, this position of Mars often makes for a rather selfish lover—one who is so concerned with getting that he/she doesn't do an awful lot of giving. Mars in Aries people are likely to turn off as quickly as they turn on. Passion burns brightly, but is often short-lived. They are highly independent and likely to leave if a romantic partner gets too possessive or demanding. Mars in Aries is also always ready for a fight, so relationships are a bit stormy.

Venus in Taurus (earth element)

This is a highly sensual position for Venus to be in. People with Venus in Taurus are turned on by sweet words and soft music—and any form of touching. They like all kinds of nice and beautiful things, and will be attracted by someone who dresses well and has expensive taste. Venus in Taurus people can be a little self-indulgent, but in the main their desire is to make the object of their affection comfortable. And they will do it in very tangible ways; Venus in Taurus people of both sexes like to do things for others. When someone with Venus in Taurus is attracted, he/she is loyal. Love does not come in a flash, as it does with Venus in Aries people, but when it comes, it usually stays. At least as far as the person with Venus in Taurus is concerned. These people are generally so devoted that a breakup is extremely unsettling. You can always make a Venus in Taurus person happy with candy or flowers. The best kind of love feels good, tastes good, looks good, and smells good.

Mars in Taurus (earth element)

This Mars can express itself as ambition with a definite direction—or as controlled sexuality. Mars in Taurus people of both sexes can appear rather lazy, but actually their slow movements are usually on a deliberate course. Some people with Mars in Taurus are really looking for a safe position in a job or with a partner. Their manner of sexuality is highly sensual though they may be slow to get aroused. When a Mars in Taurus person enters into an affair, however, there is usually the intention to make it a long and serious one. These people are certainly capable of quick affairs, but they generally prefer a comfortable relationship where they do not constantly have to keep proving their love. There is a certain giving quality to Mars in Taurus, and the men are exceptionally considerate lovers. The women are fairly passive, but passionate and giving when they get going.

Venus in Gemini

Venus in Gemini people of both sexes tend to be turned on more by *talk* than by physical stimulation. Relationships have to have a mental dimension in order for them to get involved. In fact, Venus in Gemini people are likely to make better friends than lovers. When their affections *are* engaged, the connection is likely to be a little tenuous, and the Venus in Gemini's feelings may not run as deep as his/her partner's. Fickleness is a reality with these people— they like a lot of changes, and that goes for people as well as environments. Job-hopping is a trait of Venus in Gemini, and so is a constant changing of the guard in their romantic lives. However, Venus in Gemini people make wonderful romantic partners, because they are really *interested* in the people they get involved with. Never tell a Venus in Gemini person to "shut up and make love"; he/she will be very likely to shut the door on the relationship.

Mars in Gemini

Mars in Gemini people assert themselves rather erratically; there isn't a lot of staying power, in jobs or in relationships. The "alternating current" of Mars in Gemini energy makes for a rather on again, off again sexual life. People with Mars in this position are capable of having a number of purely mental relationships in between their sexual ones. These are the kind of people who talk their way into things, including a job and someone's bed. Their approach is a bit on the delicate side, and one may wonder when the Mars in Gemini person is really going to get started. However, once their passion is aroused, Mars in Gemini people like a lot of variety; sex can get quite original with these people. The tendency to bore easily goes both for their attitudes toward their sexual partners and the manner in which they have sex. Both sexes are real charmers, however, and sometimes get their way in a rather devious manner.

Venus in Cancer (water element)

The overriding thing that people with Venus in Cancer want is *security*, really the emotional kind, but since a secure home base goes along with their needs, the material kind is important too. Venus in Cancer people can be highly traditional in their romantic values— home, mother, and apple pie are symbols of the things that turn these people on. If you want to engage the emotions of a Venus in Cancer person, all you have to do is look as if you *need* somebody— preferably a mother. Venus in Cancer people need to be needed, but sometimes can go overboard by totally taking over the other person's life. With Venus in this sign, people respond strongly to all kinds of romantic things, from the card that says "I love you" to a little token of affection for no special occasion. However, Venus in Cancer people are highly self-protective, so you first have to break down their natural reserve and fear of getting hurt. Once you do, you won't find a more faithful lover. Except perhaps Taurus.

Mars in Cancer (water element)

Mars in Cancer people can sneak up on you when they've decided they want you; their approach is a bit sideways, like the locomotion of the crab that is the Cancer symbol. They are soft and subtle lovers and said by some to be among the best sexual partners in the zodiac. However, as sensitive and understanding as they tend to be in the sexual area, they can be overly possessive with people they love, and even turn rather cruel when they are rejected. Cancer is a water sign, and it is as if that water starts boiling—invisibly—then the lid totally pops off when the explosion comes. Mars in Cancer people tend to be a little blind to their sexual/ambition drive and can even pretend to themselves that it doesn't exist. For this reason, they make formidable enemies, because while they look as if they are asking for peace they are really preparing for battle.

Venus in Leo (fire element)

There's a pretty simple way to get a Venus in Leo person to like you. Give him/her a lot of attention—*positive* attention. Venus in Leo people do want love, but they want admiration and adulation to come along with it. A bit like Venus in Aries, Venus in Leo wants a *courtly* lover—someone who will swear absolute loyalty. When it's a Leo sun sign person who also has Venus in Leo, you've got the absolute monarch of them all. Venus in Leo also goes only for the best, and is attracted to what looks expensive or rewarding—in both jobs and people. Venus in Leo expects you to dress and look your best, no matter what the circumstances. It is not a "casual" Venus. Demonstrations of love are very important, too. Words are great, of course, and so is a lot of hugging and the rest of the physical love spectrum. However, candy—or some other tangible token of affection—is expected. Venus in Leo has fierce pride, so if you even slip once and appear not to *respect* this person, he/she is likely to brush you off—with a very grand gesture of course.

Mars in Leo (fire element)

Speaking of grand gestures, Mars in Leo wrote the book. This kind of person is the one who will lavish the object of his/her affection with all kinds of luxurious things. Mars in Leo is a real showy person and expects to be appreciated for it. Both the males and the females are aggressive about going after what they want, and once they are happily ensconced—with a lover or a job—they are loyal and steady. However, the down side of the Mars in Leo position is a violent temper: a *really* violent temper. Both sexes can get quite physical in expressing anger. This is the position of the female who throws plates and the man who slaps his faithless lover on the cheek. Mars in Leo is unrelentingly honest—and will expect you to be too. One devious move, and it's over

Venus in Virgo (earth element)

Venus in Virgo wants a love that *works*. Pure sex or romance may appeal to Virgo's desire for the unadulterated, but there's got to be an element of the practical in it too. People with Venus in Virgo often actually fall in love with their jobs faster than they do with people. When Venus is in the sign, you often find the dedicated, loyal, "number two" person who spends a lifetime catering to the needs of a powerful boss. He/she is likely to be just a little bit in love with that boss too. As for sex, the Venus in Virgo person has a very healthy attitude toward it—possibly too healthy in the sense that it is sometimes regarded as an excellent form of exercise. Venus in Virgo people are not really cold—in fact, when they love someone they can't do enough for them, particularly in attending to their physical comfort. The problem is that this position of Venus makes a person overly analytical in determining what he/she wants. If the Venus in Virgo person keeps his/her mouth shut, and doesn't openly criticize, there is a much better possibility that he/she will make good, solid relationships.

Mars in Virgo (earth element)

Virgo's inventive sexuality is one of the best-kept secrets in the zodiac; Mars in Virgo turns out some of the most experimental and skillful lovers of all. That is, if you can attract one of these people in the first place. Mars in Virgo people are far from promiscuous; in fact, their standards are likely to be a bit too high. They are constantly questioning their *own* desires and drives, picking them apart instead of acting upon them. Mars in Virgo is ideal for success in just about any job or profession. With any sun sign, it adds to the ability to cooly analyze problems and solve them with a reasonable amount of dispatch. When it comes to romantic involvement, this is not one of the more "romantic" Mars positions (unless the sun sign is Libra). You may feel as if your Mars in Virgo lover is checking you over first for anything that might turn him/her off. This is the sign that usually says "let's shower together" before he/she says "let's go to bed."

Venus in Libra (air element)

First off, remember that when the planet Venus is in Libra, it's in its "home sign." When it comes to beauty, harmony, and balance, Venus in Libra people want it all. When Venus is in Libra, the most attractive things in life are the *nicest*—people, places, jobs, clothes, you name it. Venus in Libra people want it nice, but they also want it *easy*. In fact, this sometimes "cold" position of Venus can make for a person who marries for status or money. If you look comfortable in every sense of the word, you've got a shot at attracting that Venus in Libra person who catches your eye. And he/she will, because this position of Venus usually confers a great-looking body. Even if the Venus in Libra person loves or marries for convenience, he/she gives an awful lot in return. Once you've engaged his/her love the Venus in Libra person considers you the best, the most beautiful/handsome, and the brightest person in the universe and will treat you accordingly.

Mars in Libra (air element)

This position of Mars often makes for a passive/aggressive type of individual—a specific psychological pattern. The Mars in Libra person rarely goes directly after what he/she wants, but more or less lingers in front of it, waiting for the other person to make the right move. Mars in Libra people don't get hired as quickly as other types because they don't seem to *care* enough about whether or not they get the job. When it comes to love, Mars in Libra can be quite frustrating. You really don't know what's going on here—does or doesn't he/she want to get involved? This is also a rather "refined" position for brash Mars. Mars in Libra people usually have excellent manners, and never appear to get ruffled. They will just sit and smile while you rant and rave. Suddenly, however, they can turn on their heel and walk out the door. The technique Mars in Libra people use to go about making their subtle conquests is *talk*—but it can easily fool you because it seems so casual.

Venus in Scorpio (water element)

A lot of people with sun sign Scorpio have Venus in Scorpio too; (one's Venus sign is often one's sun sign because Venus is so close to the sun in the solar system). These double-whammy Scorpios are extraordinarily intense in all their emotional needs, but anyone with Venus in Scorpio is going to be touched by the madness of this intense sign. The curious paradox is that Venus in Scorpio people are either totally *turned on* by someone or something—or totally *turned off*. There are very few halfway deals in their lives. Venus in Scorpio can also be highly manipulative, adjusting his/her emotions to suit other needs—like money. When Venus is in Scorpio, people are attracted to what seems mysterious, dangerous, or hard-to-get. They love puzzles, and can be a bit of a puzzle themselves to prospective romantic partners. When they do get involved, however, they have a great deal of staying power—emotionally at least. They can fairly easily separate their physical *actions* from their mental states, however.

Mars in Scorpio (water element)

People with Mars in Scorpio have a very strong "energy field" surrounding them; you can almost see it and feel it. What they want, they want passionately—and will seek in no uncertain terms. They are equally positive about what they *don't* want—so you will know whether you've got a shot with them right away. No waiting with *this* aggressive sign. The legendary supersexuality of Scorpio is real with Mars in Scorpio people. However, they may use their sexual power to control other people and situations. And, if they are rejected against their will (which doesn't happen too often) they are capable of the worst kind of venomous reactions, Jealous lovers who are violent to their former partners are a parody of the Mars in Scorpio type of intensity. One way Mars in Scorpio people can hurt or simply tease others is by withholding their love—and their physical passion. They have great powers of self-control.

Venus in Sagittarius (fire element)

People with Venus in the restless, mobile sign of the Centaur often get the reputation for being fickle, and there is more than a grain of truth in that label. But the reason a Venus in Sagittarius person may move around or not become committed is that he/she is so vulnerable to deceit and dishonesty. As the saying goes, "once burned, twice shy," and openhearted, friendly Sagittarius is likely to get burned very early in life. When Venus in Sagittarius people do get involved, they are absolutely delightful to love. Broadminded, unpossessive, full of fun, they really want to enjoy romance. Sagittarius is also a very intellectual sign, so in order to get Venus in Sagittarius people to stick with you for a while, you've got to keep them interested. Sex is great, but sex with talk is even greater for these people. Venus in Sagittarius is also highly idealistic, so you've got to be a higher type to appeal to someone with Venus in this sign. Love is gallantry and honor and all those things that are so hard to find in life.

Mars in Sagittarius (fire element)

Sagittarius is a sign that thinks in global terms, so when Mars is in the sign of Sagittarius, you find a person who wants it all—and often has to be satisfied with nothing. People with Mars in Sagittarius assert themselves bluntly and get right to the point. However, they tend to be so optimistic in their expectations that they may just as quickly decide they have made a mistake. Better luck next love. Mars in Sagittarius doesn't deliberately hurt people; this sign is kind to all—both animals and humans. Their sexual nature can also be rather "animalistic" because this is a lusty sign, and so fond of all outdoor sports that they often want to do it anywhere, anytime. One way Mars in Sagittarius people get to your heart is through your sense of humor; they really know how to make people laugh. It is a powerful weapon in their professional lives too; it's hard to fire someone who is such a delight to have around—even if he/she isn't around that much. The big problem with Mars in Sagittarius people is that they sometimes don't want to take responsibility for their own actions, and lay things on other people. Even if Mars in Sagittarius is the one to break things up, he/she will somehow or other get you to believe that it's *your* fault.

Venus in Capricorn (earth element)

Appearances count a lot to Venus in Capricorn people—in every sense of the word. In order to appeal to them, you've got to look solid and substantial—and fairly rich as well. Because there is a natural reserve to Capricorn, people with Venus in this sign will dislike public displays of affection; the cooler you are in your approach, the better. Their public image and their private one are not too far apart, either. Not that Venus in Capricorn isn't normal; he/she can be quite passionate in bed. But very, very *serious*, too. If you mistake this sign's sober approach to life for coldness, you will not be the first person who has. Once again, like those with Venus in Virgo, Venus in Capricorn is attracted to *practical* people—people who can really work for them in one way or another. While some do actually consciously go after a financially comfortable marital situation, what the vast majority will settle for is someone who is willing to help handle a lot of the more serious aspects of life. Male or female, Venus in Capricorn people want you to be *useful*. Unfortunately, some people with Venus in this sign have such a low sense of self-worth, that they will try to buy love—or sell it—because they don't feel anyone will accept them for what they are.

Mars in Capricorn (earth element)

Mars in Capricorn people always want to know the rules before they enter the game; they assert themselves with extreme caution. However, when they *know* what they want, they have incredible powers to help them get it. One is patience; Mars in Capricorn can wait very well. Another thing they have going for them is self-control; their timing is excellent because they can hold themselves back when they want to. All this makes for a rather sexually confusing type, and sometimes one who is sexually confused. Mars in Capricorn people can go without sex for amazing lengths of time if nothing seems worth the effort. When they do go for it, their approach can be extremely lusty and earthy, as befits the earth element of Capricorn. Even more than someone with Mars in Scorpio, the person with Mars in Capricorn can be a user. In love or business, he/she can easily fake it to get the carrot on the end of the stick. Then, before you know it, the person who seemed so hot for you has now turned stone cold. Sad, but true.

Venus in Aquarius (air element)

The best way to attract someone with Venus in Aquarius is to be a bit unconventional; these people love anyone or anything that is off-beat. However, you may find that you are considered a specimen rather than a romantic partner—or at least that's how it's likely to feel. People with Venus in Aquarius seem to have a real problem with deep involvement; often they really *want* it, but somehow or other their deepest wells of emotion are very difficult to tap.

Their habitual reaction to love is often "easy come, easy go." Are they cruel people? Generally not, and often Venus in Aquarius people suffer a lot from their difficulty with feeling. They will rarely tell you, however, because there is a real need for distance there. And distance is what they seek in one-on-one relationships. If you become possessive with, or jealous of a person with Venus in Aquarius, you will lose him/her very quickly. As with some of the other mental signs like Gemini and Libra, you have got to keep the affair or the marriage *interesting* in one way or another. This is a Venus position that often likes kinky sex, porno movies, and other forms of artificial stimulation. However, they usually don't care enough about sex-for-the-sake-of-sex to be unfaithful.

Mars in Aquarius (air element)

When Mars is in this erratic sign, people tend to go through periods of feast and famine, largely because they can fluctuate between being extremely assertive and sure about what they want or totally inactive. During the latter periods you could actually call the Mars in Aquarius person lazy. In love, the Mars in Aquarius person tends to go after the unusual or difficult; involvements with people who are already attached are quite common. In many cases it is because the Mars in Aquarius person really is terribly afraid of deep involvement. There is a detachment about Mars in Aquarius people that sometimes works against permanent attachment to people or professional situations. Mars in Aquarius really prefers to go it alone. Perhaps the reason is that they always want to be free to experiment with the new. In sex, the Mars in Aquarius person is hung up on technique; he/she likes intelligent sex, and sometimes wants to prove how clever he/she is via this rather bizarre route.

Venus in Pisces (water element)

For people with Venus in Pisces, what's attractive is often bound up with some kind of sacrifice. This is the position of Venus that leads to martyrdom of all kinds. Some Venus in Pisces people find it impossible to get involved with anything or anyone normal and healthy; their instinctive need is to care for the lame and needy. Therefore, many Venus in Pisces people are rather easily taken advantage of by unscrupulous types who use them or take them for all they're worth. By the same token, Venus in Pisces people can put a real *drain* on the object of their affections—demanding more and more proofs of undying love, soulful demonstrations, sometimes even more tangible support. However, in the broadest, most universal sense of the word, Pisces is the "best" position for Venus as it represents the principle of *true love*. True love is totally unselfish, totally self-sacrificing. Though few normal mortals are capable of such "divine" love, Venus in Pisces people come closest to being able to make it. On the more mundane side, people wth Venus in Pisces are attracted by all kinds of sentimental and often impractical things. They will love you most if you spend your last penny on a bouquet of violets rather than bread for the table. So what? You'll just live on love.

Mars in Pisces *(water element)*

Mars in Pisces people can easily lose their way; the sign of Pisces is not stable enough for the aggressive energy of Mars, so Mars in Pisces people tend to scatter their energies in too many places. On the other hand, they are the most subtle and devious people in the zodiac when it comes to going after what they really *do* want. Their come-on is usually to be rather weak and helpless. Both the males and the females snare you by making you think they really *need* you. There's a lot of poetry to Mars in Pisces people, so the start of an affair is likely to be all moonlight and roses. However, you may find that once you are entangled, you can't get yourself out when you want out. Mars in Pisces people have a way of snarling you up in their webs of erratic energy. Just when they've agreed that you should go, they'll become helpless again and make you feel you have to stay. However, Mars in Pisces people do offer a very wonderful kind of love—soft, sensitive, and caring. The object of their desires is often someone similar or someone involved with art or music in some way. However, Pisces types are best off hooking up with a strong partner—someone who can keep their Mars energy on a straight and even course. The best part of Mars in Pisces people is that they are rarely, if ever, cold.

VENUS SIGN 1910–1975

	Aries	Taurus	Gemini	Cancer	Leo	Virgo
1910	5/7-6/3	6/4-6/29	6/30-7/24	7/25-8/18	8/19-9/12	9/13-10/6
1911	2/28-3/23	3/24-4/17	4/18-5/12	5/13-6/8	6/9-7/7	7/8-11/8
1912	4/13-5/6	5/7-5/31	6/1-6/24	6/24-7/18	7/19-8/12	8/13-9/5
1913	2/3-3/6 5/2-5/30	3/7-5/1 5/31-7/7	7/8-8/5	8/6-8/31	9/1-9/26	9/27-10/20
1914	3/14-4/6	4/7-5/1	5/2-5/25	5/26-6/19	6/20-7/15	7/16-8/10
1915	4/27-5/21	5/22-6/15	6/16-7/10	7/11-8/3	8/4-8/28	8/29-9/21
1916	2/14-3/9	3/10-4/5	4/6-5/5	5/6-9/8	9/9-10/7	10/8-11/2
1917	3/29-4/21	4/22-5/15	5/16-6/9	6/10-7/3	7/4-7/28	7/29-8/21
1918	5/7-6/2	6/3-6/28	6/29-7/24	7/25-8/18	8/19-9/11	9/12-10/5
1919	2/27-3/22	3/23-4/16	4/17-5/12	5/13-6/7	6/8-7/7	7/8-11/8
1920	4/12-5/6	5/7-5/30	5/31-6/23	6/24-7/18	7/19-8/11	8/12-9/4
1921	2/3-3/6 4/26-6/1	3/7-4/25 6/2-7/7	7/8-8/5	8/6-8/31	9/1-9/25	9/26-10/20
1922	3/13-4/6	4/7-4/30	5/1-5/25	5/26-6/19	6/20-7/14	7/15-8/9
1923	4/27-5/21	5/22-6/14	6/15-7/9	7/10-8/3	8/4-8/27	8/28-9/20
1924	2/13-3/8	3/9-4/4	4/5-5/5	5/6-9/8	9/9-10/7	10/8-11/12
1925	3/28-4/20	4/21-5/15	5/16-6/8	6/9-7/3	7/4-7/27	7/28-8/21
1926	5/7-6/2	6/3-6/28	6/29-7/23	7/24-8/17	8/18-9/11	9/12-10/5
1927	2/27-3/22	3/23-4/16	4/17-5/11	5/12-6/7	6/8-7/7	7/8-11/9
1928	4/12-5/5	5/6-5/29	5/30-6/23	6/24-7/17	7/18-8/11	8/12-9/4
1929	2/3-3/7 4/20-6/2	3/8-4/19 6/3-7/7	7/8-8/4	8/5-8/30	8/31-9/25	9/26-10/19
1930	3/13-4/5	4/6-4/30	5/1-5/24	5/25-6/18	6/19-7/14	7/15-8/9
1931	4/26-5/20	5/21-6/13	6/14-7/8	7/9-8/2	8/3-8/26	8/27-9/19

VENUS SIGN 1910–1975

Libra	Scorpio	Sagittarius	Capricorn	Aquarius	Pisces
10/7-10/30	10/31-11/23	11/24-12/17	12/18-12/31	1/1-1/15	1/16-1/28
				1/29-4/4	4/5-5/6
11/19-12/8	12/9-12/31		1/1-1/10	1/11-2/2	2/3-2/27
9/6-9/30	1/1-1/4	1/5-1/29	1/30-2/23	2/24-3/18	3/19-4/12
	10/1-10/24	10/25-11/17	11/18-12/12	12/13-12/31	
10/21-11/13	11/14-12/7	12/8-12/31		1/1-1/6	1/7-2/2
8/11-9/6	9/7-10/9	10/10-12/5	1/1-1/24	1/25-2/17	2/18-3/13
	12/6-12/30	12/31			
9/22-10/15	10/16-11/8	1/1-2/6	2/7-3/6	3/7-4/1	4/2-4/26
		11/9-12/2	12/3-12/26	12/27-12/31	
11/3-11/27	11/28-12/21	12/22-12/31		1/1-1/19	1/20-2/13
8/22-9/16	9/17-10/11	1/1-1/14	1/15-2/7	2/8-3/4	3/5-3/28
		10/12-11/6	11/7-12/5	12/6-12/31	
10/6-10/29	10/30-11/22	11/23-12/16	12/17-12/31	1/1-4/5	4/6-5/6
11/9-12/8	12/9-12/31		1/1-1/9	1/10-2/2	2/3-2/26
9/5-9/30	1/1-1/3	1/4-1/28	1/29-2/22	2/23-3/18	3/19-4/11
	9/31-10/23	10/24-11/17	11/18-12/11	12/12-12/31	
10/21-11/13	11/14-12/7	12/8-12/31		1/1-1/6	1/7-2/2
8/10-9/6	9/7-10/10	10/11-11/28	1/1-1/24	1/25-2/16	2/17-3/12
	11/29-12/31				
9/21-10/14	1/1	1/2-2/6	2/7-3/5	3/6-3/31	4/1-4/26
	10/15-11/7	11/8-12/1	12/2-12/25	12/26-12/31	
11/3-11/26	11/27-12/21	12/22-12/31		1/1-1/19	1/20-2/12
8/22-9/15	9/16-10/11	1/1-1/14	1/15-2/7	2/8-3/3	3/4-3/27
		10-12/11-6	11/7-12/5	12/6-12/31	
10/6-10/29	10/30-11/22	11/23-12/16	12/17-12/31	1/1-4/5	4/6-5/6
11/10-12/8	12/9-12/31	1/1-1/7	1/8	1/9-2/1	2/2-2/26
9/5-9/28	1/1-1/3	1/4-1/28	1/29-2/22	2/23-3/17	3/18-4/11
	9/29-10/23	10/24-11/16	11/17-12/11	12/12-12/31	
10/20-11/12	11/13-12/6	12/7-12/30	12/31	1/1-1/5	1/6-2/2
8/10-9/6	9/7-10/11	10/12-11/21	1/1-1/23	1/24-2/16	2/17-3/12
	11/22-12/31				
9/20-10/13	1/1-1/3	1/4-2/6	2/7-3/4	3/5-3/31	4/1-4/25
	10/14-11/6	11/7-11/30	12/1-12/24	12/25-12/31	

VENUS SIGN 1910–1975

	Aries	Taurus	Gemini	Cancer	Leo	Virgo
1932	2/12-3/8	3/9-4/3	4/4-5/5 7/13-7/27	5/6-7/12 7/28-9/8	9/9-10/6	10/7-11/1
1933	3/27-4/19	4/20-5/28	5/29-6/8	6/9-7/2	7/3-7/26	7/27-8/20
1934	5/6-6/1	6/2-6/27	6/28-7/22	7/23-8/16	8/17-9/10	9/11-10/4
1935	2/26-3/21	3/22-4/15	4/16-5/10	5/11-6/6	6/7-7/6	7/7-11/8
1936	4/11-5/4	5/5-5/28	5/29-6/22	6/23-7/16	7/17-8/10	8/11-9/4
1937	2/2-3/8 4/14-6/3	3/9-4/17 6/4-7/6	7/7-8/3	8/4-8/29	8/30-9/24	9/25-10/18
1938	3/12-4/4	4/5-4/28	4/29-5/23	5/24-6/18	6/19-7/13	7/14-8/8
1939	4-25/5/19	5/20-6/13	6/14-7/8	7/9-8/1	8/2-8/25	8/26-9/19
1940	2/12-3/7	3/8-4/3	4/4-5/5 7/5-7/31	5/6-7/4 8/1-9/8	9/9-10/5	10/6-10/31
1941	3/27-4/19	4/20-5/13	5/14-6/6	6/7-6/1	7/2-7/26	7/27-8/20
1942	5/6-6/1	6/2-6/26	6/27-7/22	7/23-8/16	8/17-9/9	9/10-10/3
1943	2/25-3/20	3/21-4/14	4/15-5/10	5/11-6/6	6/7-7/6	7/7-11/8
1944	4-10/5-3	5/4-5/28	5/29-6/21	6/22-7/16	7/17-8/9	8/10-9/2
1945	2/2-3/10 4/7-6/3	3/11-4/6 6/4-7/6	7/7-8/3	8/4-8/29	8/30-9/23	9/24-10/18
1946	3/11-4/4	4/5-4/28	4/29-5/23	5/24-6/17	6/18-7/12	7/13-8/8
1947	4/25-5/19	5/20-6/12	6/13-7/7	7/8-8/1	8/2-8/25	8/26-9/18
1948	2/11-3/7	3/8-4/3	4/4-5/6 6/29-8/2	5/7-6/28 8/3-9/7	9/8-10/5	10/6-10/31
1949	3/26-4/19	4/20-5/13	5/14-6/6	6/7-6/30	7/1-7/25	7/26-8/19
1950	5/5-5/31	6/1-6/26	6/27-7/21	7/22-8/15	8/16-9/9	9/10-10/3
1951	2/25-3/21	3/22-4/15	4/16-5/10	5/11-6/6	6/7-7/7	7/8-11/9
1952	4/10-5/4	5/5-5/28	5/29-6/21	6/22-7/16	7/17-8/9	8/10-9/3
1953	2/2-3/13 4/1-6/5	3/4-3/31 6/6-7/7	7/8-8/3	8/4-8/29	8/30-9/24	9/25-10/18

VENUS SIGN 1910–1975

Libra	Scorpio	Sagittarius	Capricorn	Aquarius	Pisces
11/2-11/25	11/26-12/20	12/21-12/31		1/1-1/18	1/19-2/11
8/21-9/14	9/15-10/10	1/1-1/13	1/14-2/6	2/7-3/2	3/3-3/26
		10/11-11/5	11/6-12/4	12/5-12/31	
10/5-10/28	10/29-11/21	11/22-12/15	12/16-12/31	1/1-4/5	4/6-5/5
11/9-12/7	12/8-12/31		1/1-1/7	1/8-1/31	2/1-2/25
9/5-9/27	1/1-1/2	1/3-1/27	1/28-2/21	2/22-3/16	3/17-4/10
	9/28-10/22	10/23-11/15	11/16-12/10	12/11-12/31	
10/19-11/11	11/12-12/5	12/6-12/29	12/30-12/31	1/1-1/5	1/6-2/1
8/9-9/6	9/7-10/13	10/14-11/14	1/1-1/22	1/23-2/15	2/16-3/11
	11/15-12/31				
9/20-10/13	1/1-1/3	1/4-2/5	2/6-3/4	3/5-3/30	3/31-4/24
	10/14-11/6	11/7-11/30	12/1-12/24	12/25-12/31	
11/1-11/25	11/26-12/19	12/20-12/31		1/1-1/18	1/19-2/11
8/21-9/14	9/15-10/9	1/1-1/12	1/13-2/5	2/6-3/1	3/2-3/26
		10/10-11/5	11/6-12/4	12/5-12/31	
10/4-10/27	10/28-11/20	11/21-12/14	12/15-12/31	1/1-4/4	4/6-5/5
11/9-12/7	12/8-12/31		1/1-1/7	1/8-1/31	2/1-2/24
9/3-9/27	1/1-1/2	1/3-1/27	1/28-2/20	2/21-3/16	3/17-4/9
	9/28-10/21	10/22-11/15	11/16-12/10	12/11-12/31	
10/19-11/11	11/12-12/5	12/6-12/29	12/30-12/31	1/1-1/4	1/5-2/1
8/9-9/6	9/7-10/15	10/16-11/7	1/1-1/21	1/22-2/14	2/15-3/10
	11/8-12/31				
9/19-10/12	1/1-1/4	1/5-2/5	2/6-3/4	3/5-3/29	3/30-4/24
	10/13-11/5	11/6-11/29	11/30-12/23	12/24-12/31	
11/1-1/25	11/26-12/19	12/20-12/31		1/1-1/17	1/18-2/10
8/20-9/14	9/15-10/9	1/1-1/12	1/13-2/5	2/6-3/1	3/2-3/25
		10/10-11/5	11/6-12/5	12/6-12/31	
10/4-10/27	10/28-11/20	11/21-12/13	12/14-12/31	1/1-4/5	4/6-5/4
11/10-12/7	12/8-12/31		1/1-1/7	1/8-1/31	2/1-2/24
9/4-9/27	1/1-1/2	1/3-1/27	1/28-2/20	2/21-3/16	3/17-4/9
	9/28-10/21	10/22-11/15	11/16-12/10	12/11-12/31	
10/19-11/11	11/12-12/5	12/6-12/29	12/30-12/31	1/1-1/5	1/6-2/1

VENUS SIGN 1910–1975

	Aries	Taurus	Gemini	Cancer	Leo	Virgo
1954	3/12-4/4	4/5-4/28	4/29-5/23	5/24-6/17	6/18-7/13	7/14-8/8
1955	4/25-5/19	5/20-6/13	6/14-7/7	7/8-8/1	8/2-8/25	8/26-9/18
1956	2/12-3/7	3/8-4/4	4/5-5/7 6:24-8/4	5/8-6/23 8/5-9/8	9/9-10/5	10/6-10/31
1957	3-26/4-19	4/20-5/13	5/14-6/6	6/7-7/1	7/2-7/26	7/27-8/19
1958	5-6/5-31	6/1-6/26	6/27-7/22	7/23-8/15	8/16-9/9	9/10-10/3
1959	2-25/3-20	3/21-4/14	4/15-5/10	5/11-6/6	6/7-7/8 9/21-9/24	7/9-9/20 9/25-11/9
1960	4-10/5-3	5/4-5/28	5/29-6/21	6/22-7/15	7/16-8/9	8/10-9/2
1961	2-3/6-5	6/6-7/7	7/8-8/3	8/4-8/29	8/30-9/23	9/24-10/17
1962	3/11-4/3	4/4-4/28	4/29-5/22	5/23-6/17	6/18-7/12	7/13-8/8
1963	4/24-5/18	5/19-6/12	6/13-7/7	7/8-7/31	8/1-8/25	8/26-9/18
1964	2/11-3/7	3/8-4/4	4/5-5/9 6/18-8/5	5/10-6/17 8/6-9/8	9/9-10/5	10/6-10/31
1965	3/26-4/18	4/19-5/12	5/13-6/6	6/7-6/30	7/1-7/25	7/26-8/19
1966	5/6-6/31	6/1-6/26	6/27-7/21	7/22-8/15	8/16-9/8	9/9-10/2
1967	2/24-3/20	3/21-4/14	4/15-5/10	5/11-6/6	6/7-7/8 9/10-10/1	7/9-9/9 10/2-11/9
1968	4/9-5/3	5/4-5/27	5/28-6/20	6/21-7/15	7/16-8/8	8/9-9/2
1969	2/3-6/6	6/7-7/6	7/7-8/3	8/4-8/28	8/29-9/22	9/23-10/17
1970	3/11-4/3	4/4-4/27	4/28-5/22	5/23-6/16	6/17-7/12	7/13-8/8
1971	4/24-5/18	5/19-6/12	6/13-7/6	7/7-7/31	8/1-8/24	8/25-9/17
1972	2/11-3/7	3/8-4/3	4/4-5/10 6/12-8/6	5/11-6/11 8/7-9/8	9/9-10/5	10/6-10/30
1973	3/25-4/18	4/18-5/12	5/13-6/5	6/6-6/29	7/1-7/25	7/26-8/19
1974						
1975	5/5-5/31 2/24-3/20	6/1-6/25 3/21-4/13	6/26-7/21 4/14-5/9	7/22-8/14 5/10-6/6	8/15-9/8 6/7-7/9 9/3-10/4	9/9-10/2 7/10-9/2 10/5-11/9

VENUS SIGN 1910–1975

Libra	Scorpio	Sagittarius	Capricorn	Aquarius	Pisces
8/9-9/6	9/7-10/22	10/23-10/27	1/1-1/22	1/23-2/15	2/16-3/11
	10/28-12/31				
9/19-10/13	1/1-1/6	1/7-2/5	2/6-3/4	3/5-3/30	3/31-4/24
	10/14-11/5	11/6-11/30	12/1-12/24	12/25-12/31	
11/1-11/25	11/26-12/19	12/20-12/31		1/1-1/17	1/18-2/11
8/20-9/14	9/15-10/9	1/1-1/12	1/13-2/5	2/6-3/1	3/2-3/25
		10/10-11/5	11/6-12/16	12/7-12/31	
10/4-10/27	10/28-11/20	11/21-12/14	12/15-12/31	1/1-4/6	4/7-5/5
11/10-12/7	12/8-12/31		1/1-1/7	1/8-1/31	2/1-2/24
9/3-9/26	1/1-1/2	1/3-1/27	1/28-2/20	2/21-3/15	3/16-4/9
	9/27-10/21	10/22-11/15	11/16-12/10	12/11-12/31	
10/18-11/11	11/12-12/4	12/5-12/28	12/29-12/31	1/1-1/5	1/6-2/2
8/9-9/6	9/7-12/31		1/1-1/21	1/22-2/14	2/15-3/10
9/19-10/12	1/1-1/6	1/7-2/5	2/6-3/4	3/5-3/29	3/30-4/23
	10/13-11/5	11/6-11/29	11/30-12/23	12/24-12/31	
11/1-11/24	11/25-12/19	12/20-12/31		1/1-1/16	1/17-2/10
8/20-9/13	9/14-10/9	1/1-1/12	1/13-2/5	2/6-3/1	3/2-3/25
		10/10-11/5	11/6-12/7	12/8-12/31	
10/3-10/26	10/27-11/19	11/20-12/13	2/7-2/25	1/1-2/6	4/7-5/5
			12/14-12/31	2/26-4/6	
11/10-12/7	12/8-12/23		1/1-1/6	1/7-1/30	1/31-2/23
9/3-9/26	1/1	1/2-1/26	1/27-2/20	2/21-3/15	3/16-4/8
	9/27-10/21	10/22-11/14	11/15-12/9	12/10-12/31	
10/18-11/10	11/11-12/4	12/5-12/28	12/29-12/31	1/1-1/4	1/5-2/2
8/9-9/7	9/8-12/31		1/1-1/21	1/22-2/14	2/15-3/10
9/18-10/11	1/1-1/7	1/8-2/5	2/6-3/4	3/5-3/29	3/30-4/23
	10/12-11/5	11/6-11/29	11/30-12/23	12/24-12/31	
	11/25-12/18	12/19-12/31		1/1-1/16	1/17-2/10
10/31-11/24					
8/20-9/13		1/1-1/12	1/13-2/4	2/5-2/28	3/1-3/24
		10/9-11/5	11/6-12/7	12/8-12/31	
			1/30-2/28	1/1-1/29	
10/3-10/26	10/27-11/19	11/20-12/13	12/14-12/31	3/1-4/6	4/7-5/4
			1/1-1/6	1/7-1/30	1/31-2/23
11/10-12/7	12/8-12/31				

MARS SIGN 1910–1975

	Jan.	Feb.	Mar.	Apr.	May	June	July	Aug.	Sept.	Oct.	Nov.	Dec.
1910	AR	TA	GE	GE	CA	CA	LE	VI	VI	LI	SC	SC
1911	SA	CP	AQ	AQ	PI	AR	TA	TA	GE	GE	GE	TA
1912	TA	GE	GE	CA	CA	LE	LE	VI	LI	LI	SC	SA
1913	CP	CP	AQ	PI	AR	AR	TA	GE	CA	CA	CA	CA
1914	CA	CA	CA	CA	LE	LE	VI	LI	LI	SC	SA	SA
1915	CP	AQ	PI	PI	AR	TA	GE	GE	CA	LE	LE	LE
1916	LE	LE	LE	LE	LE	VI	VI	LI	SC	SC	SA	CP
1917	AQ	AQ	PI	AR	TA	VI	GE	CA	LE	LE	SA	VI
1918	LI	LI	VI	VI	VI	VI	LI	LI	SC	SA	VI	CP
1919	AQ	PI	AR	TA	GE	CA	CA	LE	VI	VI	CP	LI
1920	LI	SC	SC	SC	LI	LI	SC	SC	SA	SA	LI	AQ
1921	PI	AR	AR	TA	GE	GE	CA	LE	LE	VI	CP	LI
1922	SC	SC	SA	SA	SA	SA	SA	SA	CP	CP	LI	AQ
1923	PI	AR	TA	TA	GE	CA	CA	LE	VI	VI	LI	SC
1924	SC	SA	CP	CP	AQ	AQ	PI	PI	AQ	AQ	PI	PI
1925	AR	TA	TA	GE	CA	CA	LE	VI	VI	LI	SC	SC
1926	SA	CP	CP	AQ	PI	AR	AR	TA	VI	TA	TA	TA
1927	TA	TA	GE	GE	CA	LE	LE	VI	LI	LI	SC	SA
1928	SA	SA	AQ	PI	PI	AR	TA	GE	GE	CA	CA	CA

76

MARS SIGN 1910–1975

	Jan.	Feb.	Mar.	Apr.	May	June	July	Aug.	Sept.	Oct.	Nov.	Dec.
1929	GE	GE	CA	CA	LE	LE	VI	VI	LI	SC	SC	SA
1930	CP	AQ	AQ	PI	AR	TA	GE	GE	CA	CA	LE	LE
1931	LE	LE	CA	LE	LE	VI	VI	LI	LI	SC	SA	CP
1932	CP	AQ	PI	AR	TA	TA	GE	CA	CA	LE	VI	VI
1933	VI	VI	VI	VI	VI	VI	LI	LI	LI	SA	SA	CP
1934	AQ	PI	AR	AR	TA	GE	GE	CA	LE	LE	VI	LI
1935	LI	LI	LI	LI	LI	LI	LI	SC	SC	SA	VI	AQ
1936	PI	PI	AR	TA	GE	GE	CA	LE	LE	VI	LI	LI
1937	SC	SC	SA	SA	SC	SC	SC	SA	SA	CP	AQ	AQ
1938	PI	AR	TA	TA	GE	CA	CA	LE	VI	VI	LI	SC
1939	SC	SA	SA	CP	CP	AQ	AQ	CP	CP	VI	LI	PI
1940	AR	AR	TA	GE	GE	CA	LE	LE	VI	VI	LI	SC
1941	SA	SA	CP	AQ	AQ	PI	AR	AR	AR	AR	AR	AR
1942	TA	TA	TA	GE	CA	LE	LE	VI	VI	LI	SC	SC
1943	SA	CP	CP	CP	AR	AR	TA	TA	GE	GE	GE	GE
1944	GE	GE	GE	GE	CA	LE	VI	VI	LI	SC	SC	SA
1945	CP	AQ	AQ	AQ	PI	AR	AR	CP	CA	CA	LE	LE
1946	CA	CA	CA	CA	LE	TA	TA	LI	LI	SC	SA	SA
1947	CP	AQ	PI	AR	AR	TA	GE	CA	CA	LE	LE	VI

77

MARS SIGN 1910–1975

	Jan.	Feb.	Mar.	Apr.	May	June	July	Aug.	Sept.	Oct.	Nov.	Dec.
1948	VI	LE	LE	LE	LE	VI	VI	LI	SC	SC	SA	CP
1949	AQ	PI	PI	AR	TA	GE	GE	CA	LE	LE	VI	VI
1950	LI	LI	LI	VI	VI	LI	LI	SC	SA	SA	CP	CP
1951	AQ	PI	AR	TA	TA	GE	CA	CA	LE	VI	VI	LI
1952	LI	SC	SC	SC	SC	SC	SC	SC	LE	CP	CP	LI
1953	AR	AR	AR	TA	GE	GE	CA	LE	VI	VI	LI	AQ
1954	SC	SA	SA	CP	CP	CP	SA	SA	CP	CP	AQ	LI
1955	PI	AR	TA	GE	GE	CA	LE	LE	VI	LI	LI	PI
1956	SA	SA	CP	AQ	AQ	PI	PI	PI	PI	PI	SC	SC
1957	AR	TA	TA	GE	CA	CA	AR	VI	VI	LI	SC	AR
1958	SA	CP	CP	AQ	PI	AR	AR	TA	TA	GE	TA	SC
1959	TA	GE	GE	CA	CA	LE	LE	VI	LI	LI	SC	TA
1960	CP	CP	AQ	PI	AR	LE	TA	GE	GE	CA	SC	SA
1961	CA	CA	CA	CA	CA	TA	VI	VI	LI	CA	CA	CA
1962	CP	AQ	PI	PI	AR	VI	GE	GE	CA	SC	SA	SA
1963	LE	LE	LE	LE	LE	TA	VI	LI	SC	LE	LE	LE
1964	AQ	AQ	PI	AR	AR	VI	VI	CA	CA	SC	SA	CP
1965	VI	VI	VI	VI	VI	VI	VI	LI	LE	SA	VI	VI
1966	AQ	PI	AR	AR	TA	GE	CA	CA	LE	VI	VI	LI

MARS SIGN 1910–1975

	Jan.	Feb.	Mar.	Apr.	May	June	July	Aug.	Sept.	Oct.	Nov.	Dec.
1967	LI	SC	SC	LI	LI	LI	LI	SC	SA	SA	CP	AQ
1968	PI	PI	AR	TA	GE	GE	CA	LE	LE	VI	LI	LI
1969	SC	SC	SA	SA	SA	SA	SA	SA	SA	CP	AQ	PI
1970	PI	AR	TA	TA	GE	CA	CA	LE	VI	VI	LI	SC
1971	SC	SA	CP	CP	AQ	AQ	AQ	AQ	AQ	AQ	PI	PI
1972	AR	TA	TA	GE	CA	CA	LE	LE	VI	LI	SC	SC
1973	SA	CP	CP	AQ	PI	PI	AR	TA	TA	TA	AR	AR
1974	TA	TA	GE	GE	CA	LE	LE	VI	LI	LI	SC	SA
1975	SA	CP	AQ	PI	PI	AR	TA	GE	GE	GE	CA	GE

AR—Aries
TA—Taurus
GE—Gemini
CA—Cancer

LE—Leo
VI—Virgo
LI—Libra
SC—Scorpio

SA—Sagittarius
CP—Capricorn
AQ—Aquarius
PI—Pisces

9

The Planets As "Stars"

The Astrological Cast of Characters in Order of Their Appearance

As you learned in the chapter "Defining Terms," the planets are the *sine qua non* of astrology—the factor without which there would be no such study. It is the placement of the planets in the signs of the zodiac that give those signs meaning in human terms, and the placement of the planets in an individual horoscope that "spell out" that individual's character/personality. As for forecasting, it is the movement (transits) of the planets throughout our lifetime that activate one part of our chart or another and bring out certain life conditions.

Those planets are moving bodies and not "stars" in the astrological sense, though they are sometimes referred to with that word. In Shakespeare's play, *Julius Caesar*, Cassius, one of the conspirators, states, "The fault, dear Brutus, is not in our stars but in ourselves that we are underlings." Shakespeare (Cassius) actually knew what he was talking about because astrology was part and parcel of daily life in Elizabethan times when the play was written, as well as in Caesar's ancient Rome. However, Shakespeare seems to have preferred "stars" as a more poetic word than "planets." He also was right about another thing: The "stars" (planets) don't push people around unless you let them. The key is to understand the role each planet plays in your basic astrological makeup through your natal chart and to get to know yourself via this ancient and pragmatic science. Then you will better understand how the transits of the different planets are most likely to affect you.

Though the planets are not stars by astronomical definition (except for the sun), they do play the starring roles in the great cosmic drama that is acted out every day of our lives, and has been since the beginning of life on earth. There are other heavenly bodies—like the asteroids—that play supporting roles, but most astrologers take the Big Ten into consideration when they do a chart or a personal forecast: the sun, the moon, Mercury, Venus, Mars, Jupiter, Saturn, Uranus, Neptune, and Pluto. (Some of these planets, like the Moon, Venus, and Mars, are touched on in other parts of this book, and you may want to read those sections to get a better understanding of their characteristics.)

Each planet rules one or more signs of the zodiac—i.e., is very closely associated with that sign or signs. The one that rules your sun sign is your own personal planet, so to speak, and its description will fill in more of the background of your sign.

The following is a rundown of the planetary cast of characters, presented in their order of appearance, their actual position in our solar system As you know, the sun is the center of our solar system, and the orbits of the planets form rings around it. Looking at the planets this way underscores the fact that the *closer* planets influence us much more strongly as individuals. Planets farther out in the solar system are not only farther away, they also move much more slowly. While a transit of the moon lasts two days, for instance, a transit of Uranus (which takes eighty-four years to circle the zodiac) may influence your life for many months. However, even with these distant planets, their position in a specific *house* of your own horoscope will greatly influence your astrological makeup.

The Sun

Vital Statistics: 864,000 miles in diameter; average distance from earth, 93 million miles; gaseous nature. Appears to circle the zodiac in 365 days.

Rules: The sign of Leo
Fourth period of life: ages 23 to 41
Role: The true "star" ... the male lead ... the doer ... the activator.
Facts and Foibles: The position of the sun in anyone's horoscope is the central fact about that person, astrologically speaking. Your sun sign is your core—your individuality. It is your ego in the best sense of the word, the part of you that moves you in a certain life direction. No matter what your sun sign is, true self-development means developing the highest potential of that sign. People really grow into their sun signs as they mature, and the sun symbolically governs that stage of life (23 to 41) at which we are (or should be) mature individuals who are concerned with creating something in our own right. The sun is considered a masculine planet, because it is the fiery, animating force of life. We are meant to *express* our sun sign; those who do not can literally have a lifeless quality about them.

Those born under the sign of Leo have been said to be favored because of their rulership by the most important "planet" of them all. In ancient times, the sun was often the chief deity and was worshipped for its extraordinary power. It was recognized that without the sun, life on earth could not exist, and the dimming of its light via an eclipse was a terrifying experience for early civilizations that recognized their dependence upon its warmth and vitalizing nature. Whether or not Leo is a special sign is debatable, but there is no doubt that there is a tendency in some Leo sun sign people to become overly self-centered. Perhaps even unconsciously, they sense that it is a heady destiny to be ruled by the sun, but they are unable to handle its tremendous energies properly.

The Moon

Vital Statistics: 238,857 miles from the earth; 2,160 miles in diameter (one-fourth earth's size). Revolves around the earth (circles the zodiac) in about 27 ½ days
Rules: The sign of cancer
The first four years of human life

Role: The leading lady ... the "feeler" ... the mother ... the reactor.

Facts and Foibles: The moon is not exactly a planet, either; it is a satellite of our own planet, earth. However, it is the largest satellite with respect to its parent planet anywhere in the solar system that we know of. It has a tremendous gravitational pull, which is demonstrated on earth by the changing of the tides and other natural phenomena.

The moon has no light of its own, and we can see it shining only because it reflects the sun. Therefore, the moon is considered a *receptive* or "feminine" planet, rather than an active one like the sun. The moon in mythology has always been a woman—often the "Great Mother" to ancient peoples who saw the sun as the "Great Father." Accordingly, the moon rules the first four years of human life, when we are totally dependent on our mothers, and the motherly sign of Cancer, which is closely associated with nurturing and growth. In an individual horoscope, the position of the moon indicates our ability to feel and to respond emotionally. It is our impressionability and sensitivity, i.e., our subjective rather than our objective sign. The moon reacts to experience and remembers it. All our memories are stored in our subconscious, which is the part of the human psyche the moon signifies. In a sense, as the moon rules the night, it rules our dark or hidden side. As it takes some time for us to develop or grow into our sun sign, the moon sign manifests itself much more strongly in young children than the sun sign does. The moon represents the instinctual nature connected with infantile responses; our moon sign acts from habit, often without thinking.

Mercury

Vital Statistics: 36 million miles away from the sun; 2,900 miles in diameter; orbits sun at 108,000 miles per hour; goes through zodiac in 88 days.

Rules: The signs of Gemini and Virgo
Age of curiosity: 4 through 14

Role: The young male lead ... the observer ... the messenger ... the communicator.

Facts and Foibles: Mercury is the hottest, quickest, and smallest of the planets, and is closest to the sun. It is so closely associated with the sun in an astronomical sense, that Mercury is very often in the same sign as the sun in a natal chart. In any horoscope, it is never more than two signs away from your sun sign.

In ancient times Mercury was regarded as the sun's messenger, and the gods with whom it was associated always had some kind of communicating function. In Egypt, Mercury was Thoth—scribe to the gods, keeper of the divine books. The Greeks called him Hermes, the messenger; the Romans renamed him Mercury, but assigned similar functions. Hermes/Mercury always had a golden tongue, and was regarded as the great persuader. Quickness and deftness also associate Mercury with all kinds of human skills requiring manual and mental dexterity.

Mercury has a double role to play as ruler of the signs of Gemini and Virgo. In a sense, Mercury is two-faced; the communicative side in Gemini, his precise specialist side in Virgo. No matter what your sun sign is, in your horoscope Mercury symbolizes your style of thinking and communicating—not so much how intelligent you are as how you tend to put things together mentally.

Mercury is a very human planet, and has a very human foible; occasionally he gets things all mixed up and causes a lot of trouble. About three times a year, for about three weeks at a time, Mercury seems to be going *backwards*. (That appearance is caused by the varying rates of speed of various planets—like two trains traveling in the same direction that can seem as if they are traveling in two different directions.) During these periods Mercury is said to be *retrograde*, it is known to cause problems in all kinds of human interactions. People get the wrong message, or don't get it at all. People who are supposed to meet on a street corner never find each other. Trains and planes are missed, luggage is lost, orders simply never get transmitted or seem to vanish in thin air. There has been quite a bit of research on Mercury retrograde, and it all proves out. Even if people don't know *why* retrograde Mercury

makes things go wrong, they sure know it does. In 1986 Mercury will be retrograde during these periods:
  March 7 through March 30.
  July 9 through August 3.
  November 2 through November 22.

Venus

Vital Statistics: 67.2 million miles from the sun; 26 million to 160 million miles from earth; approximately the same size and volume as earth. Goes through all twelve signs of the zodiac in about 225 days.
Rules: The signs of Taurus and Libra
             Period of developing sexuality: ages 14 to 21
Role: The young, nubile female lead . . . the love interest . . . the artist.
Facts and Foibles: Like Mercury, Venus follows the sun very closely, so in anyone's horoscope it is never very far away from your sun sign. Symbolically, Venus represents your capacity to love and relate, and the capacity to appreciate beauty. In ancient myth, Venus was seen as the daughter of the moon, a feminine planet associated with many of the earthly things traditionally associated with women: the providing of food and shelter, the beautifying of the home, the harmonizing of opposites and settler of strife. Venus is a peaceful planet in every sense of the word. Aphrodite to the Greeks, Venus to the Romans, this goddess/planet was seen as the bounteous giver of life's gifts and pleasures—the personification of beauty. She is supposed to inspire us with the desire for both material and spiritual growth.

Like Mercury, Venus has two faces, but, strangely, one rules a feminine sign, Taurus, and one rules a masculine sign, Libra. In Taurus, Venus shows her earthier side, more concerned with creature comforts, sex, and material prosperity. In Libra, a more refined Venus shines forth as the graceful "hostess," the one who beautifies things and relates to others.

Though most Libra males are quite virile, their rulership by the planet Venus often manifests itself in extremely good looks and a great appreciation of beauty. The virile male hairdresser or interior decorator is the personification of this side of Venus. Because Venus seeks peace rather than war, harmony rather than discord, she rules lawyers, mediators, and arbitrators.

Since Venus rules one feminine earth sign and one masculine air sign, she is sometimes seen as a symbol for the fact that all things in the universe can be made to work in harmony—even the incompatible elements of air (Libra) and earth (Taurus) and the often antagonistic principles of male and female—in real life as in astrology. Divorce courts come under the rulership of Venus.

Mars

Vital Statistics: 14 million miles from the sun; 35 million miles from earth; 10 percent of earth's size; circles the zodiac in about 687 days.

Rules: The sign of Aries
Ages 42 to 56

Role: The virile male antagonist . . . the lover . . . the warrior.

Facts and foibles: Mars is a rather small planet and has sometimes been called "Earth's little brother." However, since ancient times Mars has been attributed with great powers—possibly because of its fiery red color. Even the earliest peoples associated Mars with strife and sex and a warriorlike attitude. In fact, Mars has had a rather bad reputation in astrology and was sometimes known as the "lesser malefic." But some groups assigned Mars another role and gave him a different dimension. The Egyptians called Mars Artes, and connected him with personal creative expression; to the Hebrews he played a similar role. When you think about it, sex, strife, and creative expression are only a few steps away from each other. Certainly, the act of procreation is a creative one, as it gives new life. War and strife are divisive, but often a new order comes out of them as well.

Mars is pure masculine energy—sometimes a bit rough, but always determined. In a personal horoscope, the sign position of Mars tells how you tend to assert yourself, how aggressive you are likely to be when going after what you want, even how much you will want it. Mars is our desire nature. (See the chapter on Venus and Mars to find out more about Mars in your own horoscope.) As the god of war, Mars is associated with courage and bravery, traits that are available to the Aries sun sign person if he/she cares to develop them. Mars is moral courage too, and the Mars-ruled Aries sun sign person at his/her best will never desert a cause or a person—no matter how rough the going gets.

About once every two years Mars returns to the same place it occupied on the day of your birth; to astrologers this is known as the "Mars return." It is a period of time during which one can make great strides, because Mars is stimulating that area of the natal chart connected with taking on the world. People often feel a great surge of energy during their Mars return, but if that energy is not directed in a productive channel, it can cause a lot of problems in relationships. You are far better taking out your Mars return aggressiveness on another job or another creative project rather than another person.

Jupiter

Vital Statistics: Largest planet in the solar system, 318 times larger than earth; 365 million to 600 million miles from earth; gaseous nature; circles the zodiac in about 12 years.
Rules: The sign of Sagittarius
   Ages 57 to 68
Role: The hero ... the "father confessor" ... the one who saves the day.
Facts and Foibles: From earliest times, Jupiter was assigned a role in the "cosmic drama" almost as important as that of the sun. Huge and luminous, Jupiter was easily visible to the naked eye eons before the age of the telescope. The sun may have been god in the all-encompassing sense, but Jupiter was *the* god who could make things happen, even interfere in human affairs if he was needed. And he has always been a "good guy." The Hindus, whose roots lie in antiquity, call him Vishnu, the preserver. To the Greeks, he was Zeus, the god

who reigned supreme on Mount Olympus; he became Jupiter under the Romans. The important thing about this masculine god-planet is that it has always been very godly but very human at the same time. Zeus frequently came down from Mount Olympus to bestow his favors on people—particularly women who caught his fancy (causing his wife Hera to become jealous). Jupiter-Zeus is the god who keeps one foot in heaven and one foot firmly planted on the earth. Since the planet itself is large and impressive-looking, it has always been associated with benevolence and expansiveness. Our English word "jovial" has its roots in the name Jove, by which name Jupiter was sometimes called.

Joviality is one of the characteristics that is available to people born under the sign of Sagittarius, which Jupiter rules. Some Sagittarians are jovial, they spend all their money and all their energy on making life one long party.

But Jupiter has a serious side, too. Jupiter is associated with the divine law, and the ability to make that law known to men on earth. The higher Sagittarian, ruled by Jupiter, has a sense of this mission, and often takes the real-life role of priest-missionary or teacher of higher studies. While Venus and Libra, the sign Venus rules, are associated with the *practice* of law, Jupiter and Sagittarius are connected with the *making* and *interpretation* of laws.

Saturn

Vital Statistics: 75,000 miles in diameter, 95 times as big as earth; 886 million miles from the sun; takes 29 years to circle the zodiac.
Rules: The sign of Capricorn
            Ages 68 on
Role: The "older man" . . . the taskmaster . . . the disciplining father.
Facts and Foibles: Like Jupiter, Saturn is so large it can be seen with the naked eye from earth and was watched carefully by early peoples. It was quickly observed that certain transits of Saturn brought trials and troubles on earth and so the planet earned itself the name of the

"greater malefic" by the time astrologers had begun to record their findings. Is Saturn really a "bad guy" as so many astrology books will tell you? There is no question that Saturn represents the principle of limitation; when you go too far out on a limb or get over expansive, Saturn is always there to teach you that there are rules and restrictions. However, as Saturn also represents the principle of contraction, this planet can and does bring periods of time in which we can consolidate our forces and make a secure place for ourselves in this world.

Saturn is also sometimes called the "lord of Karma." Translated into human terms, that means that Saturn represents our inevitable responsibilities, our "fated" duties in this world. Once again, there is a positive side. When Saturn is strongly placed in an individual's chart, that individual is exceptionally able to handle responsibility and achieve worldly success. As ruler of the sign of Capricorn, Saturn brings to that sign an extraordinary talent for working long and hard as well as reaping the material rewards that come with dedication to a task.

Kronos (or Chronos) was the ancient Greek god who is generally regarded as the prototype for Saturn's particular personality or role, and his story sheds a lot of light on the perceptions of this planet. Kronos was born to the very highest ancient god, Ouranos, and to the original earth mother, Ge. Kronos got a little carried away with this position and overthrew his father (castrating him) to take over the throne. When Kronos was told one of his own children would do the same to him, he swallowed them all—except Zeus, who was miraculously saved and became the "avenger." Later on, Zeus banished Kronos into exile. We know Kronos as Father Time—that shadowy old man who reminds us that it's later than we think. Kronos/Saturn also cautions against runaway ambitions, which is often punished by a downfall like his.

One of the most fascinating aspects of Saturn is that it is an uncannily accurate cosmic clock. Taking about 29 years to make a full circle of the zodiac, Saturn returns to the same place it occupied in your horoscope at your birth when you are about 29 years old. The "Saturn return" is regarded by astrologers as the true end of childhood (astrology is kind to us weak mortals by giving us more time to "grow up" than conventional earthly wisdom does). When Saturn begins to creep up on us in our late twenties, we generally begin to feel that it's time to settle down and do something big in the way of taking on earthly responsibility. Many people go through a "life crisis" at this time, because they feel the push that Saturn is giving them, but have trouble knowing what to do about it. Many, many people resolve the dilemma by getting married, buying a home, having a child, or getting divorced. The point is that it is time to *do something decisive* and to take responsibility for our own lives and actions. There are an incredible number of "Saturn return babies" because having a child is probably the most joyful as well as the biggest responsibility a person can assume.

On its second return—at about the human age of 58—people are generally ready to start relaxing their responsibilities and enjoying the fruits of their labors. It is a wise precaution to make ready for the second Saturn return, because just as Saturn tells us we have to *work*, he also tells us when it is time to *stop* working. But remain a productive human being, with real interests and the wherewithal to pursue them.

Uranus

Vital Statistics: 1.7 billion miles from earth; 29,300 miles in diameter, 15 times larger than earth; takes 84 years to circle the zodiac; has an erratic orbit.
Rules: The sign of Aquarius
          Teenagers
Role: The rebel ... the home-wrecker ... the visionary.
Facts and Foibles: Uranus is the first of the "modern" planets, i.e., those unknown to the ancients, and only discovered via the telescope. Uranus, the first planet to be discovered in this manner, was thus a shock to both astronomers and astrologers. Both groups believed the orbit of Saturn defined the limits of our solar system,

and both had to revise their thinking at this discovery. Astrologers took things in their stride by calling Uranus a "planet of the higher octave" and interpreting it as a breakthrough from the realm of purely earthly influences (with Saturn as the dividing line) to the "cosmic" or "higher" order of things. They decided that Uranus—an unconventional planet in many respects—must be the ruler of the quirky sign of Aquarius (which had been formerly ruled by Saturn). In a way it is uncanny that the sudden discovery of Uranus in 1781 heralded all the breakthrough discoveries of the 19th and 20th centuries. In a sense, Uranus ushered in the modern world; it also rules our current Age of Aquarius. As that age (approximately 2000 years long) will continue to shock us with discovery after discovery, it hopefully will also bring us the sense of brotherhood of humanity that is the hallmark of the sign of Aquarius.

As Uranus takes 84 years to circle the zodiac, it stays in each sign about seven years. (It is currently about two-thirds of the way through the sign of Sagittarius.) Whatever Uranus touches as it transits a person's natal chart gets a real jolt. Sometimes very suddenly. Uranus hates the status quo and almost always shakes it up. That means that a lot of changes take place when Uranus comes along, but for most people those changes are eventually positive ones. Uranus gets you out of whatever rut you happen to be in and does it quite forcefully. However, those who resist the changes Uranus "suggests" can cause themselves a lot of trouble. If you aren't willing to bend, Uranus can really "break you up."

Uranus is appropriately associated with the teen years, during which young people are often in a state of rebellion. However, here too, it is a *necessary* fact of life that people must eventually rebel against the strictures of childhood in order to become separate individual human beings. Uranus is associated not only with teenagers, but also with many of the things that represent their rebellion, like rock music, blaring radios, and all that goes with them. In essence, Uranus is the symbol of the electronic modern world.

Neptune

Vital Statistics: 2.6 billion miles from earth; 2.7 billion miles from the sun; takes about 165 years to circle the zodiac.

Rules: The sign of Pisces
No specific age.

Role: The fascinating stranger ... the poet ... the one who confuses the issue... the dreamer of great dreams.

Facts and Foibles: As it is difficult to get a handle on people heavily influenced by Neptune (like Pisceans), it took astronomers a while to figure out what Neptune really was. At first they observed nothing but some rather weird abberations in the orbit of Uranus as they began to plot that planet's orbit. In the early 1840s, some of them proved mathematically that there *must* be another planet out there, although it couldn't be seen. Finally, using all the data at hand, a German astronomer spotted Neptune in 1846.

There is a rather "sneaky" character to Neptune, but what this nebulous planet really symbolizes is the love that passes all understanding, the all-encompassing universal love that is virtually impossible for mortals to feel and give. Venus represents two-way love, the sharing kind. Neptune's love goes only in one direction. Neptune gives in a sense of self-sacrifice, and takes nothing in return.

There is evidence that even though no one really *saw* Neptune until 1846, the ancients knew all about its principles, and embodied them in the mythical figure of Poseidon (later called Neptune), the lord of the seas, master of the deep. When you think that more than three-quarters of the earth's surface is covered by water, you realize that Neptune was pretty important in the overall scheme of things. In fact, according to the Greeks, when the universe was created, it was divided among Zeus-Jupiter, who took the heavens, Hades-Pluto who took the underworld, and Poseidon-Neptune who took the oceans.

Just as water is difficult to contain, it is difficult for many people to get in touch with Neptune's higher qualities in their own charts. Water is soul and spirit, metaphysically speaking, so Neptune should make us aspire to much higher things. Not only universal love, but poetry, music and art in its purest forms. However, what Neptune touches in most people's natal charts often turns into an area of confusion rather than creativity. Neptune rules liquid in all its forms and, unfortunately, some people react to Neptune's confusing vibes by turning to alcohol or drugs. For many drug and alcohol abusers, however, the real goal of their vice is to attain a kind of "cosmic consciousness" which is the real realm of Neptune.

Since Neptune takes 165 years to circle the zodiac, it stays in one sign for 13 years or more. Therefore, it is the zodiacal *sign* Neptune makes to the "personal planets" in your chart that really count. People positively influenced by Neptune make the true artists and poets of this world—as well as the visionaries who interpret its meaning in more philosophical and metaphysical terms.

Pluto

Vital Statistics: 3,666 billion miles from the sun; takes about 242 years to circle the zodiac.
Rules: The sign of Scorpio
       Prenatal
Role: The "heavy" . . . the transformer . . . the tragic hero.
Facts and Foibles: As you will note, Pluto is a little light on vital statistics. That's because this immensely distant planet, only discovered in 1930, has yet to reveal some of its secrets to astronomers. Like Neptune, it was discovered only because of the erratic nature of the orbit of Uranus. But, even when Pluto was conclusively sighted in 1930, its small size relative to its extremely strong gravitational pull didn't make sense to astronomers. Either Pluto is much larger than we now think or it is so dense that it exerts a force much greater than its size should account for.

Either way, there's no doubt that Pluto represents *power*. In fact, many astrologers connect the discovery of Pluto with the discovery by man of the extraordinary power in matter itself—the power of the atom. As with Neptune, Pluto's "realm" had been staked out in myth and astrology long before its actual discovery. Pluto is Hades, lord of the underworld—the place of darkness that all men fear. However, since most older religions regard life and death as a cycle, Pluto represents rebirth as well. We die only to be reborn. One of the symbols for Pluto is the Phoenix that rises triumphantly from its own ashes. Pluto—and the sign of Scorpio that it rules—hold onto their secrets, but have an incredible power to endure and triumph over life's circumstances. The extremes of life and death that Pluto/Scorpio is associated with connect neatly with the extremism of this astrological sign. "Plutonic" Scorpios often regard the world as totally black and white, with very few grays in between. They can also be the "best" of people, like reformers and religious leaders, or the "worst" of people, like criminals and those who manipulate others for their own purposes.

10

Astrotrivia

How Do You Rate in the Best Game in Town?

The ancient art of astrology is loaded with bits and pieces of miscellaneous information—all of it fascinating, and some of it more useful than you may think. For instance, did you know that every zodiac sign has a special day of the week and certain colors assigned to it? And, how good are you at guessing sun signs of celebrities—those larger-than-life models of sun signs in the flesh? The Astrotrivia that follows is partly in quiz form, partly in short-take astrological facts. In the first part, you can test your own astrological perceptivity; in the second, you can add a lot to your fund of astrological information—and maybe even learn a few things, you can use in your daily life.

Astrotrivia Part I
Sun Signs of the Rich and Famous

Try to answer the following questions yourself; if you're stumped you'll find the answers on page 103–104.

1. What famous stripper and the famous actress who played her mother in a Broadway show have the sign of Capricorn in common?

2. What two show biz buddies—who run in the same pack—are both Sagittarians?

3. What do these people have in common: Joseph Stalin, Richard Nixon, Herman Goering, Al Capone, and Mao Tse Tung?

4. What two handsome male movie stars, both known for their progressive ideas, have the same sun sign? And, what is it?

5. What highly Scorpionic actor had an on-again, off-again lifetime romance with a glamourous Pisces actress?

6. What two female tennis pros are both athletic Sagittarians?

7. What U.S. president had a "show-me-I'm-from-Missouri" personality, and what was his sun sign?

8. What two famous "lonely hearts" columnists get their soft Cancerian shoulders cried on all the time?

9. What two "greats" of American popular music were both thoroughly American, and both born on the Fourth of July?

10. Under what sign were these warrior peacemakers all born: Dwight D. Eisenhower, David Ben Gurion, Jimmy Carter, Mohandus Ghandi, and Eleanor Roosevelt?

11. What anti-American villainess of World War II was born on the Fourth of July?

12. What sun sign do these people have in common: Oscar Wilde, Truman Capote, and Gore Vidal?

13. What two famous rock stars—one early, one late—were born not only under the same sign, but on the same day?

14. Which of the following is/was not a Scorpio?
    Charles Manson   Robert Kennedy
    Bo Derek   Pablo Picasso
    Katherine Hepburn   Indira Ghandi
    Princess Grace   Johnny Carson
    Henry Kissinger   Billy Graham

15. All of the following were born under the two most musical signs of the zodiac. What are they?

Judy Collins	Michael Jackson
Barbra Steisand	George Gershwin
Stevie Wonder	Luciano Pavarotti
Fred Astaire	Paul Simon
Irving Berlin	Julie Andrews
Bing Crosby	Anthony Newly
Beverly Sills	John Lennon
Bobby Darin	Guiseppe Verdi

16. All the following ladies of the stage and screen are masters of their craft. Which craftsman-like sun sign were they all born under?

Lauren Bacall	Celeste Holm
Anne Bancroft	Greer Garson
Ingrid Bergman	Twiggy
Greta Garbo	Jo Ann Worley
Sophia Loren	Claudette Colbert
Lilly Tomlin	Raquel Welch

17. What sun sign do the following famous rebels and rule-breakers have in common: Marlon Brando, Warren Beatty, Eddie Murphy, Charlie Chaplin, Hugh Hefner?

18. What sun sign do these medical and research geniuses have in common: Madame Curie, Jonas Salk, Christian Bernard?

19. What present-day famous Leo "princess" lived in Camelot with her Gemini "prince"?

20. What two great ballet stars were both born in the same country, and share the graceful sun sign, Pisces?

Answers on p. 103–104

Astrotrivia Part II
More Celebrity Sun Sign Lore

Just a handful of the many, many stage/screen-struck Leos:

Robert DeNiro	Julia Child
Mike Jagger	Arlene Dahl
Lucille Ball	Alfred Hitchcock
Dustin Hoffman	Mae West
Cecil B. Demille	George Bernard Shaw
John Derek	Dino D. Laurentis
Mike Douglas	Robert Mitchum
Robert Redford	Peter O'Toole
Jason Robards Jr.	Roman Polanski
Esther Williams	Jill St. John
Stanley Kubrick	Robert Taylor
Shelly Winters	Keenan Wynn

And here are some Leos who make/made the international scene their stage:

Fidel Castro	Henry Ford
Jackie Onassis	Alex Haley
Coco Chanel	Lawrence of Arabia
Benito Mussolini	Mata Hari
Rasputin	Napoleon
Neil Armstrong	Andy Warhol
Mike Conners	

Librans are often lovely, like Catherine Deneuve and Brigitte Bardot. Barbara Walters is the ultimate "cool" Libra.

Cancer is the second fame sign, because Cancer rules the public. Cancers who have made it somehow or other are:

Bill Cosby	Ringo Starr
Jimmy Cagney	John Glenn
Ernest Hemingway	Arthur Ashe
Gerald Ford	The Mayo brothers (of the Mayo clinic)

Some outspoken, inventive Aquarians whose opinions have not always been popular, but were always ahead of their time:

Norman Mailer
Charles Darwin
Jules Verne
Ayn Rand
Galileo

Ralph Nader
Thomas Edison
Betty Friedan
Vanessa Redgrave
Franklin D. Roosevelt

Astrotrivia Part III
Fascinating Facts About the Signs

Here are the colors that, by tradition, match each of the signs of the zodiac:

1. Aries: bright red, scarlet, magenta

2. Taurus: pastels in most shades, especially pink and turquoise

3. Gemini: beiges and light gray

4. Cancer: shimmery and irridescent shades of gray and silver; anything luminous

5. Leo: bright golds and yellows

6. Virgo: dark navy, brown, gray

7. Libra: cloudy pales, especially blue-green

8. Scorpio: murky colors, especially blood red and black

9. Sagittarius: rich blues, purples, greens

10. Capricorn: black, "no-color" colors

11. Aquarius: checks, stripes, patterns, electric blue

12. Pisces: deep lilac, mauve, sea green

Each Sign/Planet owns a day of the week:

Sunday = Sun/Leo

Monday = Moon/Cancer

Tuesday = Mars/Aries, Mars/Scorpio

Wednesday = Mercury/Gemini, Mercury/Virgo

Thursday = Jupiter/Sagittarius, Neptune/Pisces

Friday = Venus/Taurus, Venus/Libra

Saturday = Saturn/Capricorn, Saturn/Aquarius

(Since there are only seven days and twelve signs, some of the signs double up. Also, since the ancients only knew seven planets, there are only enough days to match seven of the ten planets we now recognize.)

Astrotrivia Part IV
Where Do You Belong?

Each sign is said to have certain places where it belongs. Long ago, the world was divided up according to astrological tradition, so there are certain countries, cities, and areas that have the vibrations of certain signs. Tradition divides up other kinds of spaces, too, as you will see.

- *Aries places:* In the world: Birmingham, Oldman, Leicester, and Blackburn, *England* ... Florence, Naples, Verona and Padua *Italy* ... Marseilles and Burgundy *France* ... *Denmark, Germany, Palestine, Syria, Japan.*

    Anywhere: sheepfolds, forges, tool houses, fireplaces, on sandy soil, kilns, ceilings, fire houses, emergency rooms.

- *Taurus places:* In the world: Dublin, *Ireland* ... Mantua, Parma, Palermo, *Italy* ... St. Louis, *U.S.A.* ... *The Greek Islands, Asia Minor,* the *Caucasus.*

    Anywhere: banks, dairies, pastures, shady places, corn fields, middle rooms of houses, altars, maypoles.

- *Gemini places:* In the world: San Francisco, *U.S.A.* ... London and Plymouth, *England* ... Bruges, *Belgium* ... Versailles and Louvaine, *France* ... Nurenburg, *Germany* ... *Lower Egypt, Armenia, Wales.*

    Anywhere: buildings with pillars, bookcases, hills and mountains, upper back rooms, graineries.

- *Cancer places:* In the world; St. Andrews, *Scotland* ... Amsterdam, *Holland* ... New York City, *U.S.A.* ... Stockholm, *Sweden* ... Genoa, Venice, Milan, *Italy* ... *Paraguay, North and West Africa.*

Anywhere: lakes and brooks, salt marshes, pubs, kitchens, cellars, corner houses facing north.

- *Sagittarius places:* In the world: Avignon, *France* ... Stuttgart, Cologne, *Germany* ... Nottingham, Sheffield, Bradford, *England* ... Provence, *France* ... *Hungary, Arabia, Tuscany.*

  Anywhere: highest place around, topmost room in house, stables for racing horses, obelisks, places near fire, where incense is burned.

- *Capricorn places:* In the world: Brussels, *Belgium* ... Port Said, *Egypt* ... *India, Afghanistan, Mexico, Lithuania, Orkney Islands, Macedonia.*

  Anywhere: vaults, convents, thick forests, gates and hinges, old trees, jails, cattle barns, door knockers, game preserves.

- *Aquarius places:* In the world: Brighton and Trent, *England* ... Salszburg, *Austria* ... Hamburg, *Germany* ... the Piedmont, *Italy* ... *Prussia, Red Russia, Westphalia.*

  Anywhere: buses, bridges, ladders, garages, airplanes, power transmitters, fountains, springs and streams, sleds, ice caps.

- *Pisces places:* In the world; Alexandria, *Egypt* ... Seville, *Spain* ... Southport, Lancaster, Bournemouth, Tiverton, *England* ... *Portugal, Calabria, Normandy, Sahara.*

  Anywhere: fish ponds, oceans, oil fields, submarines, séances, flooded areas, bars, aquariums, boat yards, swimming pools, hospitals.

- *Leo Places:* In the world: Rome, Ravenna, *Italy* ... Bath, Bristol, Portsmouth, Blackpool, *England* ... Philadelphia, Chicago, *U.S.A.* ... *Bohemia, Sicily, the Alps, Damascus.*

  Anywhere: wild animal preserves, deserts and forests, castles, furnaces, gold mines, porches, forts.

- *Virgo places:* In the world: Paris, Lyons, Toulouse, *France* ... Boston, Los Angeles, *U.S.A.* ... Heidelberg, *Germany* ... *Turkey, West Indies, Brazil, Silesia, Switzerland.*

  Anywhere: pantries, restaurants, refrigerators, medicine cabinets, desks, malt houses.

- *Libra places:* In the world: Dover, Liverpool, Newcastle, *England* . . . Messina, *Italy* . . . Halifax, *Nova Scotia* . . . China, Norway, The Transvaal, the Barbary coast.

    Anywhere: windmills, wood sheds, harbors, tops of mountains, garrets and lofts, guest rooms, tops of dressers, domed buildings.
- *Scorpio places:* In the world: Copenhagen, *Denmark* . . . Leeds, Nottingham, *England* . . . Johannesburg, *South Africa* . . . Burma, *India* . . . Tibet, North China, Argentina.

    Anywhere: junk yards, meat markets, laboratories, low gardens and streams, vineyards, deepest part of ocean.

Astrotrivia Part V
Which Animal Best Suits You?

Each sign is said to have an affinity with certain kinds of pets. Here's the rundown.

Aries: No animal that needs a lot of taking care of; but if Aries has one pet, he/she will usually have two, so the animals can take care of each other.

Taurus: Almost any kind of soft, warm creature. Taurus is a great nature lover, so even a skunk would be welcome.

Gemini: Anything with fascinating habits, like bees or ants, or anything that talks, like a parrot or a minah bird.

Cancer: Anything in need of a mother is welcome in Cancer's house, no matter how sloppy or in need of care.

Leo: Cats, of course, preferably with good breeding. Peacocks or anything with bright colors or plumage are fine too.

Virgo: Cats are preferable, because they are clean animals, but any animal in distress brings out Virgo's warmth.

Libra: This sign would just as soon do without, but if a pet is preferred, it's the perfectly groomed poodle or other refined breed of dog or cat.

Scorpio: This sign goes for rather dangerous pets, such as snakes, or anything with a sting. Basically, animals are creatures to be observed, not coddled.

Sagittarius: Horses—at home or at the race track. Any very large dog in the city, almost anything of immense size in the country.

Capricorn: Capricorns *need* pets to help pull them out of their frequent depressions. The friendliest kind of animals are the best bet, like sheepdogs.

Aquarius: This sign needs a very smart animal, so is picky about the breed of dog or cat. Actually, birds are preferable to this cool sign.

Pisces: Many people born under this sign will take in any stray that strays into their path, no matter how scraggly or ugly. They often put animals before humans in their scheme of things.

Astrotrivia Part I answers

1. Gypsy Rose Lee and Ethel Merman (who played Gypsy's mother in *Gypsy*).
2. Frank Sinatra and Sammie Davis, Jr.
3. They were all born under the calculating sign of Capricorn.
4. Paul Newman and Alan Alda were both born under the sign of Aquarius.
5. Richard Burton was the Scorpio; Liz Taylor the Pisces.
6. Billie Jean King and Chris Evert.
7. Harry S. Truman, a Taurus.
8. Abigail Van Buren ("Dear Abby") and Ann Landers.

9. George M. Cohan ("Yankee Doodle Dandy") and Louis "Satchmo" Armstrong.
10. Libra.
11. Tokyo Rose.
12. Libra.
13. Elvis Presley and David Bowie (January 5—Capricorn).
14. Henry Kissinger. He's a wily Gemini, but he could easily fool you, because his moon sign is Scorpio.
15. The column on the left are Taureans; those on the right are Librans.
16. Virgo.
17. Aries.
18. Scorpio.
19. Jackie Kennedy Onassis is a Leo; John F. Kennedy was a Gemini.
20. Rudolph Nureyev and Vaslav Nijinsky.

11
Sun Sign Changes. 1920–1975

If you were born "on the cusp" (very near the end or the beginning of a sign) you can find out what your sign really is by using the chart that follows. Many people do not realize that the sun does not "change signs" on the same day every year—or, for that matter, at the same time. For this reason the chart of sun sign changes is calculated to the minute.

How to Use the Chart

Locate your year of birth, then the month in which you were born. Let's say you were born in April of 1942. In the box for that month and year you will see

20–Tau
12:30 P.M.

That means if you are born *after* 12:30 p.m. on April 20 in 1942, you are a Taurus. If you were born before that date and time, your sun sign is the preceding one, Aries.

In this chart (as well as in the rising-sign chart) the signs are abbreviated as follows:

Ar = Aries
Tau = Taurus
Gem = Gemini
Can = Cancer
Leo = Leo
Vir = Virgo
Lib = Libra
Sc = Scorpio

Sag = Sagittarius
Cap = Capricorn
Aq = Aquarius
Pis = Pisces

NOTE: All times given in the sun sign changes chart are Eastern Standard. You must correct for daylight savings time (subtract one hour) and for time zone. For Central Standard Time subtract one hour; for Mountain Standard Time subtract two hours; for Pacific Standard Time subtract three hours.

	1920	1921	1922	1923	1924	1925	1926	1927	1928	1929
Jan	21–Aq 4:05 am	20–Aq 8:55 am	20–Aq 2:48 pm	20–Aq 8:35 pm	21–Aq 2:29 am	20–Aq 8:20 am	20–Aq 2:13 pm	20–Aq 8:12 pm	21–Aq 1:57 am	20–Aq 7:42 am
Feb	19–Pis 5:29 pm	18–Pis 11:21 pm	19–Pis 5:16 am	19–Pis 11:00 am	19–Pis 4:51 pm	18–Pis 11:43 pm	18–Pis 4:35 am	19–Pis 10:35 am	19–Pis 4:20 pm	18–Pis 10:07 pm
Mar	20–Ar 5:00 pm	20–Ar 10:51 pm	21–Ar 4:49 am	21–Ar 10:29 am	20–Ar 4:20 pm	20–Ar 11:13 pm	21–Ar 4:01 am	21–Ar 11:59 am	20–Ar 3:44 pm	20–Ar 9:35 pm
Apr	20–Tau 4:39 pm	20–Tau 10:32 pm	20–Tau 4:29 am	20–Tau 10:06 pm	20–Tau 3:59 am	20–Tau 10:51 pm	20–Tau 3:36 pm	20–Tau 9:32 pm	20–Tau 3:17 am	20–Tau 9:11 am
May	21–Gem 4:22 am	21–Gem 10:17 am	21–Gem 9:11 pm	22–Gem 9:45 pm	21–Gem 3:41 am	21–Gem 10:33 pm	21–Gem 3:15 pm	21–Gem 9:08 pm	21–Gem 2:53 am	21–Gem 8:48 am
June	21–Can 12:40 pm	21–Can 6:36 pm	22–Can 12:27 am	22–Can 6:03 am	21–Can 12:noon	21–Can 5:50 pm	21–Can 5:21 am	22–Can 9:08 pm	21–Can 11:07 am	21–Can 5:01 pm
July	22–Leo 11:40 pm	23–Leo 5:31 am	23–Leo 11:20 am	23–Leo 5:01 pm	22–Leo 11:58 pm	23–Leo 4:45 am	23–Leo 10:25 am	23–Leo 4:17 am	22–Leo 11:02 pm	23–Leo 3:54 am
Aug	23–Vir 6:22 am	23–Vir 12:15 pm	23–Vir 6:04 pm	23–Vir 11:52 pm	23–Vir 5:48 am	23–Vir 11:33 am	23–Vir 5:14 pm	23–Vir 11:06 pm	23–Vir 4:53 am	23–Vir 10:41 am
Sept	23–Lib 3:25 am	23–Lib 11:20 am	23–Lib 5:10 am	23–Lib 9:04 am	23–Lib 2:58 am	23–Lib 8:43 am	23–Lib 2:25 pm	23–Lib 8:17 pm	23–Lib 2:36 am	23–Lib 7:52 am
Oct	23–Sc 12:31 pm	23–Sc 6:03 pm	23–Sc 11:53 pm	24–Sc 5:51 am	23–Sc 11:44 am	23–Sc 5:31 pm	23–Sc 11:18 pm	24–Sc 5:07 am	23–Sc 10:55 am	23–Sc 4:41 pm
Nov	22–Sag 9:15 am	22–Sag 3:21 pm	22–Sag 8:55 pm	23–Sag 2:54 am	22–Sag 8:46 am	22–Sag 2:36 pm	22–Sag 8:28 pm	23–Sag 2:14 am	22–Sag 8:00 am	22–Sag 1:48 pm
Dec	21–Cap 10:17 pm	22–Cap 4:08 am	22–Cap 9:57 am	22–Cap 3:53 pm	21–Cap 10:45 pm	22–Cap 3:37 am	22–Cap 9:34 am	22–cap 3:18 pm	21–Cap 9:04 pm	22–Cap 2:53 am

	1930	1931	1932	1933	1934	1935	1936	1937	1938	1939
Jan	20–Aq	21–Aq	20–Aq	20–Aq	20–Aq	20–Aq	21–Aq	20–Aq	20–Aq	20–Aq
	1:33 pm	7:18 pm	1:07 am	6:53 am	10:37 am	6:29 pm	12:12am	6:01 am	11:59 am	5:51 pm
Feb	19–Pis	19–Pis	19–Pis	19–Pis	19–Pis	19–Pis	19–Pis	18–Pis	19–Pis	19–Pis
	4:00 am	9:06 am	3:29 pm	9:16 pm	3:02 am	8:52 am	2:33 pm	3:21 pm	2:20 am	8:10 pm
Mar	21–Ar	21–Ar	20–Ar	21–Ar	21–Ar	21–Ar	20–Ar	20–Ar	21–Ar	21–Ar
	3:30 am	9:40 am	2:54 pm	8:43 pm	2:28 am	8:19 am	1:58 pm	7:45 pm	1:43 am	7:29 am
Apr	20–Tau	20–Tau	20–Tau	20–Tau	20–Tau	20–Tau	20–Tau	20–Tau	20–Tau	20–Tau
	3:06 pm	8:40 pm	2:28 am	8:19 am	2:00 pm	7:50 pm	1:31 am	7:20 am	1:15 pm	6:55 pm
May	21–Gem	21–Gem	21–Gem	21–Gem	21–Gem	21–Gem	21–Gem	21–Gem	21–Gem	21–Gem
	2:42 pm	8:15 pm	2:07 am	7:57 am	1:35 pm	7:25 pm	1:08 am	6:57 am	12:51 pm	6:27 pm
June	21–Can	23–Can	21–Can	21–Can	21–Can	22–Can	21–Can	21–Can	21–Can	22–Can
	11:53 pm	4:28 am	10:23 am	4:12 pm	9:48 pm	3:32 am	9:22 am	3:12 pm	9:04 pm	2:40 am
July	23–Leo	23–Leo	22–Leo	23–Leo	23–Leo	23–Leo	22–Leo	23–Leo	23–Leo	23–Leo
	10:42 am	3:21 pm	9:18 pm	3:06 am	8:42 am	2:33 pm	8:18 am	2:07 am	7:57 am	1:37 pm
Aug	23–Vir	23–Vir	23–Vir	23–Vir	23–Vir	23–Vir	23–Vir	23–Vir	23–Vir	23–Vir
	4:27 pm	10:10 pm	4:06 am	9:53 am	3:32 pm	9:24 pm	3:11 am	8:58 am	2:46 pm	8:31 pm
Sept	23–Lib	23–Lib	23–Lib	23–Lib	23–Lib	23–Lib	23–Lib	23–Lib	23–Lib	23–Lib
	1:35 pm	7:23 pm	1:16 am	7:01 am	10:45 am	6:38 pm	12:26 am	6:13 am	12:noon	5:50 pm
Oct	23–Sc	24–Sc	23–Sc	23–Sc	23–Sc	24–Sc	23–Sc	23–Sc	23–Sc	24–Sc
	11:25 pm	4:15 am	10:04 am	3:48 pm	9:35 pm	3:29 am	10:18 am	3:06 pm	8:54 pm	2:46 am
Nov	22–Sag	23–Sag	22–Sag	22–Sag	22–Sag	23–Sag	22–Sag	22–Sag	22–Sag	22–Sag
	7:34 pm	1:25 am	7:10 am	10:53 am	6:44 pm	12:35 am	6:25 pm	12:17 pm	6:06 pm	11:59 pm
Dec	22–Cap	22–Cap	21–Cap	22–Cap	22–Cap	22–Cap	21–Cap	22–Cap	22–Cap	22–Cap
	8:40 am	2:30 pm	8:14 pm	1:58 am	5:49 pm	1:37 am	7:27 pm	1:22 am	7:13 am	1:05 pm

	1940	1941	1942	1943	1944	1945	1946	1947	1948
Jan	20–Aq 11:44 pm	20–Aq 5:34 am	20–Aq 11:16 am	20–Aq 5:20 pm	20–Aq 11:09 pm	20–Aq 4:55 am	20–Aq 10:44 am	20–Aq 4:23 pm	20–Aq 10:18 pm
Feb	19–Pis 2:04 pm	18–Pis 7:59 pm	19–Pis 1:39 am	19–Pis 7:41 am	19–Pis 1:28 pm	18–Pis 7:15 pm	19–Pis 1:10 am	19–Pis 6:53 am	19–Pis 12:37 pm
Mar	20–Ar 1:24 pm	20–Ar 7:21 pm	21–Ar 1:03 am	21–Ar 7:03 am	21–Ar 12:49 pm	20–Ar 6:38 pm	21–Ar 12:34 am	21–Ar 6:13 am	20–Ar 11:57 am
Apr	20–Tau 12:51 am	20–Tau 6:51 am	20–Tau 12:30 pm	20–Tau 6:32 pm	20–Tau 12:18 am	20–Tau 6:08 am	20–Tau 12:03 pm	20–Tau 5:40 pm	19–Tau 11:25 pm
May	21–Gem 12:23 am	21–Gem 6:23 am	21–Gem 12:01 pm	21–Gem 6:03 pm	20–Gem 11:51 pm	22–Gem 5:41 am	21–Gem 1:34 am	21–Gem 5:04 pm	20–Gem 10:58 pm
June	21–Can 8:37 am	21–Can 2:33 am	21–Can 8:08 pm	22–Can 2:13 am	21–Can 9:03 am	21–Can 1:52 pm	21–Can 7:45 pm	22–Can 1:19 am	21–Can 7:11 am
July	22–Leo 7:34 pm	23–Leo 1:26 am	23–Leo 6:59 am	23–Leo 1:05 pm	22–Leo 6:55 pm	23–Leo 12:48 am	23–Leo 6:37 am	23–Leo 12:12 pm	22–Leo 6:06 pm
Aug	23–Vir 2:21 am	23–Vir 8:30 am	23–Vir 1:50 pm	23–Vir 7:55 pm	23–Vir 1:47 am	23–Vir 7:36 am	23–Vir 1:23 pm	23–Vir 7:09 pm	23–Vir 1:03 am
Sept	22–Lib 11:46 pm	23–Lib 5:33 am	23–Lib 11:10 am	23–Lib 5:12 pm	22–Lib 11:02 pm	23–Lib 4:50 am	23–Lib 10:41 am	23–Lib 4:29 pm	22–Lib 10:22 pm
Oct	23–Sc 8:39 am	23–Sc 2:22 pm	22–Sc 8:01 pm	24–Sc 2:09 am	23–Sc 7:57 am	20–Sc 1:45 pm	23–Sc 7:37 pm	24–Sc 1:27 am	23–Sc 7:19 am
Nov	22–Sag 5:49 am	22–Sag 11:38 am	22–Sag 5:23 pm	22–Sag 11:22 pm	22–Sag 5:09 am	22–Sag 10:56 am	22–Sag 4:47 pm	22–Sag 10:38 pm	22–Sag 4:29 am
Dec	21–Cap 6:55 pm	22–Cap 12:44 am	22–Cap 6:31 am	22–Cap 12:30 pm	21–Cap 6:15 pm	22–Cap 12:04 am	22–Cap 5:54 am	22–Cap 11:44 am	21–Cap 5:23 pm

	1949	1950	1951	1952	1953	1954	1955	1956	1957
Jan	20—Aq 4:11 am	20—Aq 10:00 am	20—Aq 3:53 pm	20—Aq 9:38 pm	20—Aq 3:22 am	20—Aq 9:14 am	20—Aq 3:03 pm	20—Aq 8:49 pm	20—Aq 2:43 am
Feb	18—Pis 6:27 pm	19—Pis 12:16 am	19—Pis 6:10 am	19—Pis 11:57 am	18—Pis 5:41 pm	19—Pis 11:33 pm	19—Pis 5:19 am	19—Pis 11:05 am	18—Pis 5:01 pm
Mar	20—Ar 5:49 pm	20—Ar 11:30 pm	21—Ar 5:26 am	20—Ar 11:14 am	20—Ar 5:01 pm	20—Ar 10:54 pm	21—Ar 4:36 am	20—Ar 10:21 am	20—Ar 4:17 pm
Apr	20—Tau 5:18 am	20—Tau 11:00 am	20—Tau 4:49 pm	20—Tau 10:37 pm	20—Tau 4:26 am	20—Tau 10:20 am	20—Tau 3:58 pm	19—Tau 9:44 pm	20—Tau 3:45 am
May	21—Gem 4:51 am	21—Gem 10:27 am	21—Gem 4:15 pm	20—Gem 10:04 pm	21—Gem 3:53 am	21—Gem 9:48 am	21—Gem 3:25 pm	20—Gem 9:13 pm	21—Gem 3:09 am
June	21—Can 1:03 pm	21—Can 6:37 pm	22—Can 12:25 am	21—Can 6:13 am	21—Can 12:noon	21—Can 5:55 pm	21—Can 11:32 pm	21—Can 5:24 am	21—Can 11:21 am
July	22—Leo 1:58 pm	23—Leo 5:30 am	23—Leo 11:29 am	22—Leo 5:05 pm	22—Leo 10:53 pm	23—Leo 4:45 am	23—Leo 10:25 am	22—Leo 4:20 pm	22—Leo 10:13 pm
Aug	23—Vir 6:49 pm	23—Vir 12:24 pm	23—Vir 6:22 pm	23—Vir 12:03 am	23—Vir 5:46 am	23—Vir 11:37 am	23—Vir 5:19 pm	22—Vir 11:15 pm	23—Vir 5:07 am
Sept	23—Lib 4:05 am	23—Lib 9:44 am	23—Lib 3:38 pm	22—Lib 9:24 am	23—Lib 3:07 pm	23—Lib 8:56 am	23—Lib 2:42 pm	22—Lib 8:30 pm	23—Lib 2:27 am
Oct	23—Sc 1:04 pm	23—Sc 6:48 pm	23—Sc 12:37 am	23—Sc 6:22 am	23—Sc 12:07 pm	23—Sc 5:58 pm	22—Sc 11:44 pm	23—Sc 5:35 am	23—Sc 11:33 am
Nov	22—Sag 10:17 am	22—Sag 4:03 pm	22—Sag 9:52 pm	22—Sag 3:36 am	22—Sag 9:23 am	22—Sag 3:14 pm	22—Sag 9:02 pm	22—Sag 2:51 am	22—Sag 8:45 am
Dec	21—Cap 11:24 pm	22—Cap 5:14 am	22—Cap 11:01 am	21—Cap 4:44 pm	21—Cap 10:22 pm	22—Cap 4:25 am	22—Cap 10:12 am	21—Cap 4:00 pm	21—Cap 9:49 pm

	1958	1959	1960	1961	1962	1963	1964	1965	1966
Jan	20–Aq 2:20 pm	20–Aq 2:20 am	20–Aq 8:11 pm	20–Aq 2:02 am	20–Aq 7:49 am	20–Aq 1:55 pm	19–Aq 7:43 pm	20–Aq 1:30 am	20–Aq 8:21 am
Feb	18–Pis	19–Pis 4:38 am	19–Pis 10:26 am	18–Pis 6:27 pm	18–Pis 10:16 am	19–Pis 4:09 am	19–Pis 10:25 am	18–Pis 3:49 pm	18–Pis 9:39 pm
Mar	20–Ar 10:49 pm	21–Ar 3:55 am	20–Ar 9:43 am	20–Ar 5:27 am	20–Ar 9:30 pm	21–Ar 3:20 am	20–Ar 9:43 am	20–Ar 3:05 pm	20–Ar 8:53 pm
Apr	20–Tau 10:06 am	20–Tau 3:17 pm	20–Tau 10:06 pm	20–Tau 2:33 am	20–Tau 8:51 am	20–Tau 2:37 pm	19–Tau 9:00 pm	20–Tau 2:27 am	20–Tau 8:12 am
May	20–Gem 9:28 am	21–Gem 2:38 pm	20–Gem 8:33 pm	21–Gem 1:51 am	21–Gem 8:17 am	21–Gem 1:59 pm	20–Gem 8:33 pm	21–Gem 1:27 am	21–Gem 7:33 am
June	21–Can 8:52 am	21–Can	21–Can 4:43 am	21–Can 10:12 am	21–Can 4:24 pm	21–Can 11:04 pm	21–Can 4:43 am	21–Can 9:56 am	21–Can 3:33 pm
July	23–Leo 4:57 pm	23–Leo 10:50 pm	22–Leo 5:38 pm	22–Leo 9:12 pm	23–Leo 3:19 am	23–Leo 9:00 am	22–Leo 3:38 pm	22–Leo 8:49 pm	23–Leo 2:24 am
Aug	23–Vir 3:51 am	23–Vir 9:45 am	22–Vir	23–Vir	23–Vir	23–Vir	22–Vir	23–Vir	23–Vir
Sept	23–Lib 10:47 pm	23–Lib 4:44 pm	22–Lib 10:35 pm	23–Lib 3:46 am	23–Lib 10:13 am	23–Lib 3:58 pm	22–Lib 10:35 pm	23–Lib 3:43 am	23–Lib 9:18 am
Oct	23–Sc 5:10 am	23–Sc 2:09 pm	23–Sc 8:00 pm	23–Sc 1:26 am	23–Sc 7:35 am	23–Sc 1:24 pm	22–Lib 8:00 pm	23–Lib 1:06 am	23–Lib 6:43 am
Nov	22–Sag 5:12 am	22–Sag 11:12 pm	22–Sag 5:03 pm	22–Sag 10:46 am	22–Sag 4:41 pm	22–Sag 11:30 pm	22–Sag 5:03 am	22–Sag 10:11 am	22–Sag 3:52 pm
Dec	22–Cap 2:30 pm	22–Cap 8:23 pm	22–Cap 2:19 am	22–Cap 8:10 am	22–Cap 2:02 pm	22–Cap 7:50 pm	22–Cap 2:19 am	22–Cap 7:30 am	22–Sag 1:15 pm
	22–Cap 3:40 am	22–Cap 9:35 am	21–Cap 5:27 pm	21–Cap 9:25 pm	22–Cap 3:15 am	22–Cap 9:02 am	21–Cap 3:27 pm	21–Cap 8:41 pm	22–Cap 2:29 pm

	1967	1968	1969	1970	1971	1972	1973	1974	1975
Jan	20–Aq 1:05 pm	20–Aq 6:54 pm	20–Aq 12:30 am	20–Aq 6:25 am	20–Aq 12:14 pm	20–Aq 6:00 pm	19–Aq 11:49 pm	20–Aq 5:47 am	20–Aq 11:37 am
Feb	19–Pis 3:25 am	19–Pis 9:11 am	18–Pis 2:47 pm	18–Pis 8:43 pm	19–Pis 2:28 am	19–Pis 8:12am	18–Pis 2:02 pm	18–Pis 8:00 pm	19–Pis 1:51 am
Mar	21–Ar 2:37 am	20–Ar 8:22 am	20–Ar 2:08 pm	20–Ar 7:59 pm	21–Ar 1:28 am	20–Ar 7:22 am	20–Ar 1:13 pm	20–Ar 7:08 pm	21–Ar 12:58 am
Apr	20–Tau 1:56 am	19–Tau 7:42 pm	20–Tau 1:18 am	20–Tau 5:16 am	20–Tau 12:54 pm	19–Tau 6:38 pm	20–Tau 12:31 am	20–Tau 5:19 am	20–Tau 12:08 pm
May	21–Gem 1:19 pm	20–Gem 7:07 pm	21–Gem 12:41 am	21–Gem 6:32 am	21–Gem 12:16 pm	20–Gem 6:00 pm	21–Gem 11:54 am	21–Gem 5:37 am	21–Gem 1:25 pm
June	21–Can 4:23 pm	21–Can 1:13 am	21–Can 6:55 am	21–Can 2:43 pm	21–Can 8:21 pm	21–Can 2:07 am	21–Can 8:01 am	21–Can 1:38 pm	21–Can 7:27 pm
July	23–Leo 8:16 am	22–Leo 2:13 pm	22–Leo 8:05 pm	23–Leo 1:38 am	23–Leo 7:15 am	22–Leo 1:03 pm	22–Leo 6:56 pm	23–Leo 12:30 am	23–Leo 7:23 am
Aug	23–Vir 3:13 pm	22–Vir 9:52 pm	23–Vir 2:35 am	23–Vir 6:35 am	23–Vir 2:16 pm	22–Vir 8:04 pm	23–Vir 1:55 am	23–Vir 7:29 am	23–Vir 1:24 pm
Sept	23–Lib 12:38 pm	22–Lib 6:26 pm	23–Lib 12:07 pm	23–Lib 5:59 am	23–Lib 11:47 am	22–Lib 5:34 pm	22–Lib 11:22 pm	23–Lib 4:59 am	23–Lib 10:56 am
Oct	23–Sc 9:44 pm	23–Sc 1:30 am	23–Sc 9:03 am	23–Sc 3:05 pm	22–Sc 8:53 pm	23–Sc 2:42 am	23–Sc 8:31 am	23–Sc 2:12 pm	23–Sc 8:07 pm
Nov	22–Sag 7:05 pm	22–Sag 12:59 am	22–Sag 6:23 am	22–Sag 12:25 pm	22–Sag 6:15 pm	22–Sag 12:04 am	22–Sag 5:55 am	22–Sag 11:39 am	22–Sag 5:32 pm
Dec	22–Cap 8:17 am	21–Cap 2:00 pm	21–Cap 7:44 pm	22–Cap 1:36 am	22–Cap 5:26 am	21–Cap 1:14 pm	21–Cap 7:09 pm	22–Cap 12:57 am	22–Cap 7:47 am

12

Libra: The Big Picture

Because the twelve signs of the zodiac represent twelve ways of being in the world, you will know more about yourself and why you tend toward certain types of behavior and attitudes by knowing more about Libra. If you read about the elements and qualities in "Defining Terms," for instance, you'll find out that you are one of the "cool," restless *air signs*, and, as one of the *cardinal signs*, you have a fair amount of initiative energy. You can "meet yourself" in the Libra prototype described in "Twelve Places At The Table," and your lovely, "artistic" planetary ruler, Venus, provides some excellent clues about the Libran style.

However, even with these broad brush strokes, your Libra portrait is still a bit abstract; to "see yourself" in totality, you need more of the background filled in. That means going back to some very important basics: your seventh-place position in the zodiac, your picture/symbol, the scales, and the "shorthand figure" or glyph that astrologers use to indicate the sign of Libra when they draw up a horoscope. In Libra, as in every other astrological sign, these three factors link together, forming a strong chain of meaning that holds together everything that is Libra.

On or about September 23, the sun reaches zero degrees Libra, and the earth briefly experiences days and nights of equal length as fall begins. The beginning of the sign Libra, the autumnal equinox, is a very important point in both the zodiac and the seasonal year.

The first half—the growing seasons of spring and summer—is over. For the next six months, the earth will be in a state of hibernation, waiting for the cycle to begin again. Now there is time to watch, to think, and to contemplate life. Similarly, the first six signs of the zodiac—Aries through Virgo—represent the growing phase of human life when all of our energies are concentrated on reaching a state of physical maturity. The sign Libra represents the turning point at which man must begin to think about other people, learn how to live in the social world, and cooperate with those people. In many senses, Libra is the perfect "social animal," not only enjoying the company of others, but actually needing others in order to survive.

One of the reasons Librans are often slapped with the label "indecisive" is that they instinctively know that, despite the fact that we are all self-centered, there *are* other people in the world who have other points of view. Librans can certainly be selfish, and many are; however, before they take self-seeking action, they go through an internal process of weighing their own wants and needs against those of others.

At the autumnal equinox, something else happens to life on earth. While nature begins to go into its long sleep, it also gives one last gorgeous display of beauty. Many consider the fall foliage turning to be the most beautiful performance the earth has to give. Similarly, the sign Libra is considered by many the most "beautiful" of all. A touch of the sign Libra in anyone's chart usually indicates a physically attractive person. But, more important to the sign's personality, the typical Libra's love of all things beautiful is a very important component of his/her makeup. It is the major reason why Librans shy away from confrontations, disputes, and other "unattractive" forms of human behavior. Unfortunately, many Librans are so determined to avoid anything "ugly" that they go through life skimming its surface.

In myth and legend, the famous scales of Libra turn up many times, though sometimes in disguise. The picture/symbol of the scales goes back to very ancient times when early man first recognized that at the autumnal equinox, the world hung in the balance between the bright seasons of growing and harvesting, and the dark seasons when the earth seemed to die. However, to the Greeks, Libra was represented as the chariot that carried Persephone—one of the many symbols of the Virgo virgin—to Hades, where her lover Pluto—the ruler of Scorpio—was lord and master. This legend of the chariot shows Libra, which falls between Virgo and Scorpio, as an agent between people, especially lovers. Librans are excellent mediators, in every sense of the word. What the Libra scales are all about, no matter what form they come in, is Libra's connection with the spirit of cooperation rather than competition, and with the reconciliation of opposites. Only by putting balanced weights on each side of the scales can you achieve a state of equilibrium—the state that people born under the sign of Libra desire so much.

Libra's glyph or shorthand symbol (see illustration) can be interpreted as a stylized representation of the scales. However, there is another interpretation that is especially pertinent to the personality of the seventh sign. The straight line below is seen as representing the world of matter, and the line above, with its raised center portion, as man attempting to reach above the world of matter to the world of spirit. In a way, the essence of Libra is the struggle for man to balance his worldly urges with his desire for higher things. In the 360-degree circle of the zodiac, Libra is the first sign in which man is said to symbolically reach beyond his isolated earthly situation and connect both with other human beings and with the divine. This split or duality is often reflected in the paradoxical nature of many Librans, who can be the most crass of human beings one moment, and the most refined the next.

13

Libra: Objectives and Obstacles

A Game Plan for Being the Most Successful Libra Under the Sun

Every astrological sign is a set of possibilities; being born under a particular sign does not guarantee you *are* or *will be* all those things that sign is capable of being. Nor would you want to. There are positive characteristics to be cultivated, as well as negative ones you can avoid or overcome. Living "à la carte"—selecting what you want from all the options available—is open to you, within the overall context of your sign.

You can, of course, order the "prix fixe" dinner, by living your life as it comes without attempting to direct it. The choice is yours, which is one good reason it is incorrect to regard your astrological destiny as preordained. You are responsible for how you embody your sign and what results from that embodiment.

Astrologically speaking, your life as a sign is a journey with a starting point, the raw, or "primitive" end of the side, and a destination, the evolved or "ideal" realization of that sign. Once again, you don't have to take the full trip; there are plenty of exits if you choose to use them. Few people are ever totally "finished." But if you at least know where you are going, and what potential booby traps lie along the way, you will be way ahead of the game.

Regard the following as a map and use it in charting

your course. The most successful way to be the best of your astrological sign is to work with it, in full knowledge of its up side and its down side. The happiest people of any astrological sign are those who aim high, and are not afraid to stretch their understanding of themselves in order to reach their goal.

Where Libra starts

Some of Libra's best traits—impartiality, a tendency to yield, and a generally pleasant nature—are some of the sign's worst traits in the "unevolved" or "primitive" Libran. Many Librans lack any "passion," i.e., someone or something that involves them completely. That is because so many things look interesting; it's more comforting to dabble than to plunge in whole-heartedly and tip the scales too far in one direction. Such Librans get a reputation for being superficial, and they really can be. They can also be inveterate flirts who never totally connect with one special human being. As a sign, Libra is so desperately in need of an "opposite number" that he/she often goes through life believing that the perfect partner is right around the next corner. In a sense many Libras live in a bland world where there are no hots or colds; Libra can be the original lukewarm personality.

Similarly, the unevolved Libra never learns to say a hearty "yes" or a determined "no." He/she will go along with something because taking the line of least resistance is the easiest path. It may not be the thing Libra really *wants* to do, but, then again, this type of Libra doesn't really know what he/she wants to do. It's a short trip from being a pliant, agreeable person to being nothing but a piece of putty that is completely molded by circumstances. Librans are often considered the most charming people under the sun—but also quite weak as well. Closely linked with the Libran tendency to go in the direction the wind is blowing is Libra's unfortunate penchant for living from moment to moment. If it looks or feels good *now*, Libra will buy it, do it, go along with it; tomorrow doesn't count. By that time, something better will have come along anyway.

Some buzz words by which you can recognize the unevolved Libra type:

Vacillating	Flirtatious
Superficial	Gullible
Indecisive	Resentful
Frivolous/wasteful	Weak
Changeable	Colorless

Where Libra can go

One of the most prized of all states of human consciousness is available to the sign of Libra: complete inner harmony, a sense of profound peace and serenity. Very few people of any sign ever reach this marvelous level—at least without drugs or some other form of consciousness-changing aid. However, evolved Librans come very close. They are accepting of everyone and everything, unflapped by adversity, offended by nothing. This kind of Libran is the one to whom "nothing human is alien." Eleanor Roosevelt is among those Librans who probably came very close to this ideal.

The finished Libra, because of this inner balance, is also able to concentrate his/her energies in a most effective way, working at full tilt for however long it takes to get something done. Then they can relax in the true sense of the word and gather forces for the next "good fight." And this kind of Libra is capable of fighting for what he/she believes in, because he/she *believes* in something. There is nothing wishy-washy about the evolved Libran; however, in shaping up to this point, he/she has also not lost that sweet temperament and willingness to please that is the Libran's birthright. They are genuinely appreciative of the good and beautiful in everyone—but also realistic enough to know that hurts and ugliness do exist. The evolved Libran is well-balanced in every sense of the word. Here are some buzz words by which you can recognize the higher Libran type:

Tactful	Gentle but firm
Happily "partnered"	Romantic
Helpful	Refined
Just/fair/impartial	Idealistic/realistic
Productive	Generous

How Libra Can Get There

Buried deep in the Libran consciousness—but accessible—is the ability to tolerate the paradoxes of the world. To be able to see the light, but understand that light only exists because there is dark. It is difficult, but it is possible for the Libran to hold opposites in his/her mind without getting confused; to *synthesize* the way preceding sign Virgo can analyze.

Librans should train themselves to use this capacity and understand it for what it is. Many Librans become rather cynical people because they are able to see that there is no absolute truth in any situation. What Libra should really do with this knowledge is turn it around and become the great arbitrator, the one who is able to reconcile opposites. When someone says dogmatically "this is so," Libra should point out that "this is also true" and help the other person see the gray areas that exist. Instead of cynicism, the Libran should develop subtlety. Libra is the polar opposite of Aries in the zodiac, and has the *reverse* of Aries' great talent for single-mindedness. Libra can be double-minded without being double-dealing. Being "fair" means more than simply giving each side its due; the real fairness Libra should develop for success is the crystal-clear mentality that comes from knowing nothing and no one is ever all bad or all good.

Potential Pitfalls

As an air sign, Libra has a "natural enemy": nerves. Many Librans find it very difficult to tolerate noise and confusion and can easily fall apart if too many tasks or too many options present themselves at one time. Thinking about all of them and trying to weigh them in the balance can be emotionally and physically exhausting. It is a paradox that the sign has the most potential to find the greatest inner peace can also suffer so badly from jangled nerves. The only solution for the naturally nervous Libra (who rarely shows it) is to develop a calming technique that he/she can apply anywhere. Deep breathing, one-point concentration, and other relaxing methods should be part of every Libran's self-education process. The minute Libra senses the warning of mental confusion, he/she should sit down and close out the world, if only momentarily. Once refreshed in mind and in spirit, Libra will then be ready to take on almost anything.

14

Pairing Off with Libra

Your Compatibility with Other Signs of the Zodiac

Since there are only twelve signs of the zodiac, it would be unusual to go through life without having to interact with each of them at one time or another. Obviously, your astrological makeup is more complex than your Libra sun sign, but there are some basic truths about how you tend to react when face to face with someone of another sun sign. If you have read "The Geometry of Relationships," you already know that being an air sign means Libra relates more easily to certain elements than to others. Now, getting more specific, you will see what the odds are on your matchups with each of the other signs, including your own.

When people talk about "relationships," they are usually referring to the romantic kind, and there is no doubt that since time immemorial love has been observed to have a great deal to do with keeping the earth revolving in its orbit. However, we also have a lot of other personal interactions—from important ones, like boss-employee and parent-child to more casual ones, like waitress-patron, cabdriver-rider, and buddy-buddy. The general "rules" that follow apply in all cases; just change the language a little and do a bit of interpretation. You will find that there is more truth than poetry in the matter of astrological compatibility.

Libra with Aries Most astrologers would label this relationship as possible, but difficult. You are polar opposites in the zodiac, and therefore come from very different places. As quick as Aries is to take action, you are as slow. When Aries says "let's go," you may say "not yet." However, as an air sign, you can be very stimulating to fire sign Aries; in fact, Aries is one of the few signs you might end up facing off with. Keep this on an intellectual level for best results.

Libra with Taurus You two share a planetary ruler, Venus. However, you represent the two very different sides of her nature. Libra is Venus' "graceful" side; Taurus is the "lusty" Venus of rough-and-tumble physical love. It is possible that in the physical area you will totally turn each other off. On the positive side, you both tend to be pragmatists who look at life with few illusions. And you both love the good life. Try this combination, you may like it!

Libra with Gemini You two could definitely put wind in each others' sails; when you meet, you will probably click instantly. However, for a deep emotional relationship, Gemini is not your best bet. Socially it will be fabulous, and you should have a marvelous time together; but when the party's over, you may find there's not much left to Gemini. For life happiness, look for more substance.

Libra with Cancer Cancer will love your gentle ways and tactful nature, and quickly figure out that he/she has nothing to fear from you. You will love Cancer's soft-spoken, soft-hearted personality. This could be an excellent long-term relationship, but there are a few cautionary notes. For one thing, there is a surprising core of inner strength in both of you, and you could eventually disagree on many matters. Resolve at the start to stay your lovely sweet selves, no matter what happens.

Libra with Leo Rip-roaring Leo could quickly tire you, even though you will be immensely attracted to this active, outgoing sign. Try to make it last long enough to get to know Leo, however, because in many ways you are made for each other. When it comes to appearances, you both love the best, and only the best. Your life together would be beautiful in at least its external aspects. And, if you let yourself, you could get totally emotionally involved with bighearted Leo.

Libra with Virgo   Both of you have a kind of inner refinement that sparks interest in each other. And you both seek a kind of perfection. However, be prepared for the fact that Virgo is a lot more hardworking than you. You may leave yourself open to Virgo's legendary criticism when you slack off, as you so love to do. Still, if you are both honest at the start about each others' little faults, it could be a beautiful relationship.

Libra with Libra   What a pair of dabblers you two are! In a romantic relationship, you could kill each other with kindness, but you might not get anywhere emotionally. Libra's got the same problems you've got, and you are not about to solve them for each other. However, you are both the soul of civility, so neither of you may have the nerve to say "it's over" when it's over. In business, there isn't enough push and pull to make anything productive happen either.

Libra with Scorpio   If you can stand Scorpio's possessive ways, this is probably the best relationship in the zodiac for you, no matter what conventional astrology books say about air sign–water sign combinations. Scorpio is the one sign that may cause you real pain, but real involvement as well. Since you both are heartbreakers in your own way, the road to a permanent relationship may be a rocky one. However, when you get there, it will be more than just fine.

Libra with Sagittarius   "Sloppy" Sagittarius could drive you crazy in some ways, but you shouldn't dismiss this relationship before you give it a chance. Sagittarius is so open-minded and accepting of people that you can't help but admire one. After all, in some ways it is a reflection of one of your own best traits. In addition to mutual admiration, you should click on the mental plane. Sagittarius will encourage you to open up and talk about your aspirations.

Libra with Capricorn   Reliable, efficient Capricorn will make you feel very comfortable, which is what you really want out of a relationship. And Capricorn will not attempt to possess you like Scorpio. You are both seekers of the beautiful, although Capricorn may be more interested in things for their monetary value than you are. All in all, you could make a lovely life together. However, if times get rough, you may have to prove your strengths to Capricorn.

Libra with Aquarius   You two could end up in a Mexican standoff—if you ever get started, that is. You are both such cool characters that it would take something major for you to touch each other emotionally. On a mental level, you are fabulous together, and Aquarius could bring out the very best in your intellect. Keep this one platonic, which is probably the way it will be anyway.

Libra with Pisces   If you two get involved with one another, it could be a mutual disaster. There is not enough sternness in either of you to form a bulwark against the harsh realities of life. However, Pisces is one of the signs that could really get to your emotional core and involve your heart once and for all. If you are both really evolved, you stand a chance of being able to give each other a world of love and cope with the real world too.

15

The Libra Sex Role Dilemma

One of the most important ways in which the twelve signs of the zodiac are divided is into "masculine" signs and "feminine" signs, and there are six of each. The reason is simple: As one sign follows the other in the zodiac, they alternate energies, much like the Yin/Yang principle of eastern philosophy. The universe is made up of opposites that complement each other: light and dark, hot and cold, black and white, hard and soft. One is not better than the other; rather, each is essential to the existence of its opposite. In other words, you can't have one without the other.

The six fire and air signs are "masculine," since fire and air are connected with *active, assertive, outgoing* energy.

Aries	Gemini
Leo	Libra
Sagittarius	Aquarius

The six water and earth signs are "feminine," because water and earth represent *reactive, inner-directed, receptive* energy.

Taurus	Cancer
Virgo	Scorpio
Capricorn	Pisces

To put it simply, *the masculine fire and air signs are positive, while the earth and water signs are negative.* To remain neutral and avoid placing a higher value on one or the other kind of energy (or sign) it is useful to think of a battery with positive and negative poles. Without both, it simply doesn't work.

Though the masculine-feminine division of the signs has nothing whatever to do with human physical sexuality or sexual preference, it has very important implications for human behavior. Bluntly put, women born into male signs can be more masculine/achieving/competitive than men born into female signs. On the other hand, men born in female signs can be more feminine/nurturing/cooperative than women born into male signs. Both men and women born into signs that match their own sex may overemphasize the behavior and attitudes connected with that gender. The "ideal" person, psychologically and metaphysically speaking, has a healthy mix of both masculine and feminine attitudes. Without at least some of both, we cannot be whole people, able to encompass and understand the total range of human emotions, desires, drives, and goals. Since none of us is perfect, just about everyone could stand a bit more gender blending. Your astrological sign offers some excellent clues about how you can accomplish that.

In some ways, Libra is the least masculine of the masculine signs—at least on the surface. This sign's gentle ways are a bit deceiving in this sense. For instance, Libra men are rarely macho types; even tough-minded warrior Dwight Eisenhower was the essence of civility in his public appearance. Libra men are a curious paradox, however; many find the dichoctomy between their masculinity (of both body and sign) and their love of beauty so overwhelming, they become homosexual in self-defense. However, the vast majority of Libra males are quite normal in their sexual preference, but suffer big problems because they really do not understand the yielding, compassionate feminine principle at all. That makes them doubly prey to the male "trap" of not being able to get in touch with the real feeling part of themselves. Libra males are notoriously cool, particularly in their relationships.

Libra women are also quite paradoxical. On the surface many are the most feminine, even flighty of creatures; however, because Libra is one of the assertive masculine signs, the female's surface softness often belies a really tough core of cold determination. The Libra sex role dilemma is clear. Both sexes have a problem with feeling and the feminine principle of physicality. The women may actually despise their more animal nature, and totally reject their natural penchant for nurturing. The men born under the sign are even farther away from that female part that is essential to the whole person. Keep these things in mind as you read the following Libra portraits and you will better understand the why of your Libra behavior.

16

The Libra Female

The Iron Hand in the Velvet Glove

One of the biggest surprises in the zodiac is the Libra woman. Usually all charm and sweetness on the outside, she appears to be the most feminine of females. In fact, many Libra women come off as the stereotypical clinging vines because they seem to need so much support from men and the world in general. However, what is operating in the Libra female is not so much the passive female side of her human nature as the basic problem of the Libran person—the tendency to think rather than act. When she does act, however, the Libra woman is swift and as calculating as the proverbial "cold, rational male." In fact, Libra women can be absolutely dangerous in their sometimes desperate desire to be perceived as tough customers rather than weak women. Much more than the Libra male, the Libra female is capable of tossing aside her Libran love of fairness when there is something she really wants.

The Libran woman is typically brought up in a father-dominated atmosphere—or at least in a situation where she saw her parents as equal antagonists. Somehow or other, possibly because daddy was at least bigger and stronger, she unconsciously decided to cast her lot (psychologically speaking) with the male rather than the female side of her personality. Underneath it all, even the most attractive Libra female doesn't believe that being a woman gives you much status or rank. And that is at the root of her life problem.

As a child, the Libra girl is generally quite docile and sweet, as long as no one pushes her. If her parents catch on to what makes her tick, they will never force her to move too quickly or to make absolute decisions between "this" and "that." The Libra girl, when presented with a hard-and-fast choice to make, will become curiously passive; what is really happening is that she is *furious* with her parents (or her teacher) and is exhibiting that infuriating kind of stubbornness known to psychiatrists as "passive aggressivity." Yelling and screaming at her only makes the Libra girl smile all the more sweetly, and continue to refuse to move. The Libra girl is often quite popular with her friends, and among the first to be singled out by the boys when their fancies first turn to thoughts of love.

As a young woman, the Libra female is a "walking time bomb." Because of her inherent politeness, she is very civil; however, underneath it all she has a lot of anger to work out. One way she does that is by carving out a pleasant spot for herself in the business or professional world, often gravitating toward jobs in the arts, or in any field, such as fashion, where she can indulge her love of the beautiful and use her fine aesthetic sense. The perfect spot for her to start is the receptionist desk, where she will soon be noticed for her marvelous way with people and her well-balanced, even-tempered ways. After that, many Libra women rocket to the top, not caring who they push out of their way in their zeal to reach the executive suite. Libra women are smart, witty, and very quick at teamwork, so, in spite of their Libran "Achilles' heel" of indecisiveness, they often handle responsibility easily.

In her personal life, however, the Libran woman does not usually fare so well. She is desperate for a partner, but often has a lot of trouble finding one who suits her. For one thing, she is extremely competitive with men, so she either decides that a potential lover is a better business partner (and treats him as such) or she winds up being contemptuous of a man when she decides he is weak. However, since she is great at hiding her keen mind behind her surface femininity it is usually a total shock to her man when she says "let's call it quits." Libra women are such paradoxes that they can cause emotional devastation to the men they get involved with. Perhaps the most traumatic thing is the fact that the Libra female appears totally unaffected by the breakup. She may even say, "let's talk about it," but her heartbroken lover will have discovered by that time that the Libran woman talks a lot about emotion, but doesn't really understand the "real thing."

As a mate, the Libra female is the perfect mistress, but not a very good housewife. If she really understands herself, she will avoid getting into a marriage where there will not be enough money to live according to her rather high standards. The Libra woman is not really mercenary, but she does not want to do any "dirty work"—at least around the house. (In business she is curiously able to handle it.) The Libra wife wants to direct a household of servants, not be servant to a household. As rational as she is and as yielding as she appears to be, the Libran woman does not last long with a man who attempts to control her. What she really wants is for the honeymoon to go on forever. In some cases that happens, and then you have the happiest of Libra women—and the most contented of husbands because his Libra wife has decided he is terrific and deserves nothing but the best from her. Since outward appearances are so important to Libra, the Libran wife will want to have a certain standing in the community; some will want it so much that they will put up with a loveless marriage in order to satisfy their desire for status. It is sad but true that behind the smiling face of many a Libra housewife/hostess, there is a rather unhappy and unfulfilled female.

As a mother, the Libra woman is sometimes a little uncomfortable. She may like the idea of children, but be a little shocked at how rough a job motherhood really is. But of course, her rational mind will tell her what needs to be done and she will do it—or get somebody else to. Most Libra mothers are not exactly pushovers, and can be rather strict; however, you will rarely find them raising their voices to get their children's attention. One unfortunate characteristic of the Libra mother is to appear to "turn off" and be silent when her children disappoint her. They can interpret this as a withdrawing of her love and suffer a lot because of it. For the contented Libra wife, her husband will also always come first, and her children will have to learn to accept that. However, many Libra women raise very happy children because they have had the benefit of a sweet-tempered, affectionate parent who never seemed to get bent out of shape, no matter what they did.

17

The Libra Male

Mr. Nice Guy

The most important thing to remember about the smiling, friendly, unflappable Libra male is that he's got a nervous system—and a rather delicate one at that. No one can walk away from a person or a situation more quickly than a Libra male who's been getting quietly but progressively more annoyed while you didn't even notice what was going on. Many people make the mistake of believing you can take advantage of the Libra man's good nature; it is true up to a point, but when that point comes and you have offended his innate sense of fairness, he will do a quick vanishing act.

Some Libra men even get the reputation for being cruel. That is usually because they have appeared so attentive and interested in someone that she assumes he is in love. He may actually have only been "in like," but his romantic ways have given the wrong impression. Libra males are generally quite witty, sometimes even brilliant; however, they usually know very little about the emotional side of life. And some just never learn. Libra men simply *love* the company of women, which also can give the wrong impression. What is really going on is that the Libra male's gentle, artistic sensibilities are more in tune with the typical female's than the typical male's. Many Librans are real men's men, but even *they* often can't find the kind of intellectual companionship with men that they can find with women. And yet, in their heart of hearts they know that "male is better." Like their Libran sisters, Libra men saw a battle of wits between their parents, and generally decided dad came off best.

As a child, the Libra boy can be a shock to his parents. For one thing, unless something interferes, he will be naturally neat and tidy; the Libran's desire to have an orderly world around him starts very early. The Libra male will also begin to match wits with his parents as a boy. Though some are mere smart alecks, many Libra boys demonstrate incredible powers of logic and the ability to reason things out when they are still quite young. You cannot say "because I said so" to a Libra boy. You've got to give him a reason *he* can accept if you expect him to accept *your* decision. And, of course, the Libra boy really wants you to make the decision, because it is so difficult for him to do so. Many parents make the mistake of thinking their Libran child is lazy when he just lies around staring into space. The real problem is that life presents too many alternatives—all of them attractive—and he can't figure out how to spend his time most pleasurably. Libran boys are also surprisingly bookish and usually fare well in school. In fact, when all else fails, the parents of a bored Libran boy can put a book in his hands and make him very happy.

As a young man, the Libra male usually starts very early on his lifetime "hobby"—collecting women. And he generally has little trouble finding agreeable specimens because he is loaded with that famous Libra charm. However, it is amazing how many Libra men marry very late or not at all; one would think that at some point the quest would end and the Libra man would find a partner. It is sad but true that many Libra men go through life seeking that other half, which they need so badly, but are never able to settle on the "perfect" mate. Why can't they make up their minds? Only a Libra man could tell you—but he won't. Few signs of the zodiac find it as difficult to get in touch with and express their feelings as Libra—and particularly the Libra male. However, any woman he gets involved with can look forward to the most glorious romantic affair; but if she makes the mistake of getting too possessive, she can ruin the whole thing.

On the job, young Libra males usually make such a good appearance that their actual performance is secondary. A Libra man can be promoted several times before anyone becomes aware of the fact that he's not only a bit lazy, he really isn't a very good executive. But he makes up in intelligence for what he lacks in persistence, and there is no one more capable to mediating a dispute than the logical, fair-minded Libran. Libra men often gravitate toward the arts or public relations careers; not only is the competition less strenuous, they are also able to display their usually excellent taste and ability to discriminate among "good," "better," and "best."

As a mate, the Libra male can be quite infuriating, for several reasons. First of all, if he is typical, he demands a lot of peace and quiet, as well as a perfectly ordered household. How will you know? The Libra male will rarely criticize his spouse in a direct manner; he is more likely to become smilingly silent—but it will be obvious that there is something wrong. Trying to right it is all the more difficult because the Libra man is so reticent about pointing out what he sees as his wife's flaws. He will do anything to avoid a scene. In more serious matters, it is even more of a problem. If his wife tries to engage him in a discussion of *her* problems with *him*, she will probably meet a stone wall. The Libra husband is rarely, if ever, deliberately cruel; he simply doesn't understand what the fuss is all about. Nor does he really care; emotions simply don't interest him. Libra men are infuriatingly unaware of their partners' needs and the results can be disastrous. When a Libra male marries, he does it out of his little-understood necessity for *completeness*. If his emotionally frustrated wife decides to leave him, what she often leaves behind is a person in search of a personality. The divorced or otherwise unattached Libra man is often called the "happy bachelor," but that is often far from the truth.

As a father, the Libra male can be curiously detached from his children. It's not that he doesn't love them, he does, but until they reach the age of reason he will find them rather boring. He may flaunt them as beautiful little people, but he won't really come into his own as a father until he can talk to them on an adult level. As logical and fair a disciplinarian as the Libra father can be, he may also expect much more grown-up responses from his children than they are able to give. However, when it comes to mediating the problems of sibling rivalry, the Libra father has no peer. When one child says "it's not fair," he will really listen and try to make sure no one takes advantage of anyone else.

18

Libra Help Wanted

Selecting a Career/Your On-the Job Style

A vitally important aspect of a successful Libra game plan is making sure you land in the "right" job or career—i.e., the one that best suits your native talents and tendencies. It is more than a truism that people perform better doing what comes naturally. There are some "natural" careers for Libra, and they have several common denominators. One major theme that runs through many Libra careers is creating balance and harmony—among people, things, and ideas. Another is the use of Libra's powers of discrimination. It is not possible to list *all* the specific jobs a Libra should do well at, but there are some "Libra images" that provide useful guidelines. Though you may not literally end up *doing* any of these things, try to conjure up an idea of what it takes to do the following jobs, and you'll have a better handle on what kind of inner resources Libra people have available to them for career success.

Hairdresser/cosmetician
Diplomatic service
Jeweler/jewelry store owner
Wine critic
Advertising artist
Public relations person

Family counselor
Insurance adjustor
Clothing manufacturer
Political strategist
Lawyer
Hotel/resort manager

Equally important to finding the best job slot for you is understanding how your Libra sun sign affects your modus operandi on the job and your potential for moving up. Every sun sign has certain success skills that can smooth and widen the career path, as well as blind spots that can cause roadblocks. The more you know about both, the better off you will be.

Because most Libra's are fairly softspoken, it is easy to forget that Libra is one of the active *cardinal* signs. That means Libra really has some excellent equipment to be a self-starter in the business world. There are many Librans who wind up in positions where their quiet voice of authority keeps projects and people moving steadily and surely. However, an equal number of people born under this sign somehow never seem to make it in terms of reaching the top of their fields. Libra's "internal monster" is the culprit: This sign's extreme desire for peace and harmony is very often counterproductive in the rough-and-tumble world of business. Confrontation comes with the executive territory, and confrontation is what Librans want to avoid at all costs. "Yes" people are rarely the ones who are singled out as promotable; they usually stay right where they are—both because they don't cause any trouble, and because they don't bring anything new and exciting to the table. Libra sun sign people usually function best in positions where their native refinement and impartiality allow them to pour oil on the troubled waters of others. Librans can be arbitrators without peer—as long as they are not involved in the dispute. Law and counseling are two other excellent choices. Librans also excell wherever a balanced eye is what's needed; decorating, graphic arts, and other related fields are obvious possibilities. However, not every Libran has the real talent for an artistic career. Such Librans should seek out fields and jobs where *teamwork* is the key to success; being a Libra may not be the one factor that catapulted Micky Mantle to success, but it certainly didn't hurt. Another prescription for Libran success is to get yourself a good manager or partner. Everything a Libra does well is done better when there's a firm anchor somewhere. Sales is a natural field for Libra, though this gentle sign may not be the type to break a new territory. However, Libra's sincere, logical approach and winning ways are often just the right prescription for bringing back the order.

With the often mistaken idea that there is less dog-eat-dog competition there, many Librans gravitate toward the fine and performing arts. It is sad but true that a lot of glorious talent goes unnoticed in this world because those who possess it don't know how to package and sell it. The world of show business is peopled with talented Librans like Julie Andrews, Charleton Heston, and Brigitte Bardot. If you are a Libra who really has the stuff of stardom, don't rely on your efforts alone to get you where you want to go. Just keep on smiling sweetly, and let someone else find an opening for you—and cut the deal, too.

19

How "Pure" a Libra Are You?

Your Moon Sign ... Your Rising Sign

No one is a "pure Libra"—or pure anything, for that matter—when it comes to astrological signs. As you will learn in "Defining Terms," there are many other factors in a horoscope that add up to the total person that is "you." Yes, there are twelve basic personality types, according to the zodiac, but within those broad groups there are almost infinite variations.

Though you are a Libra at the core and can count on the portrait of your sun sign to define you in essence, the two other horoscope factors that count most are in your personality profile: your moon sign and your rising sign. Many people know their moon sign; anyone can quickly determine it via an ephemeris. If you know your birth time at least within one hour, you can use the table in this book to find out what your rising sign is.

The Moon—Your "Dark Side"
Almost more than your sun sign, your moon sign indicates what makes you run. Most of the time, you do not know it yourself, because the moon is your subconscious ... your "dark side" not because it is bad, but because it is hidden. When the meaning of your moon sign is added to your Libra sun sign, it is a fuller picture and a better indicator of your probable

personality. Here's how a Libra sun sign mixes with each of the moon signs.

Libra sun sign/Aries moon sign Deep down inside you don't really want to be the leaner that Libra can easily be; you have a streak of independence that can't be denied. You also can come up with some very clever ideas—even startling ones! Many people find you a paradox because you tend to be all action one day, and not able to get yourself organized the next.

Libra sun sign/Taurus moon sign The easier and more pleasant life is, the better you like it; you may even be a bit self-indulgent. It's important with this combination to learn discipline. As a mate, you are marvelous—though you can be tempted to stray. You do not have the most active of imaginations, and people may have to spell things out for you.

Libra sun sign/Gemini moon sign You run the risk of being all talk and no action; you live very much in your head. Your best bet is to choose a definite path and force yourself to stick to it. You are delightful company, however, and you should be an excellent communicator. Why not put that talent to work?

Libra sun sign/Cancer moon sign Your Cancer moon drives you to achieve some kind of recognition, and should put a solid foundation under your efforts. However, sensual pleasures attract you more than they should; don't give in to those pleasure urges too often. You are an excellent listener, but could easily be taken advantage of.

Libra sun sign/Leo moon sign No matter what other talents you may not possess, you've got excellent taste, and you are always attracted to the finer things. That goes for people too. However, extravagances could keep you broke a lot of the time. This is an excellent combination for success in the arts.

Libra sun sign/Virgo moon sign You could be a more narrow-minded Libra than most, and more discriminating as well. Your Virgo moon is a great internal organizer if you listen to its promptings. Just don't go to great lengths to please others, because you could find yourself being stepped on.

Libra sun sign/Libra moon sign You are easily satisfied—often too easily. You don't demand a lot of others or of yourself. If you don't shake some reality into yourself, you could walk around in a dream world a lot of the time. Since you are easily influenced, make sure you run with the right people, i.e., those who will keep you on the track.

Libra sun sign/Scorpio moon sign Believe it or not, there are some surly Libras, and you could be one of them. The problem is that your moon sign is saying "let's go" and your sun sign is saying "not yet." You have a lot of energy and should make sure it is channeled in productive directions if you are not going to go around mad a lot of the time.

Libra sun sign/Sagittarius moon sign This is a sun/moon combination that sometimes makes for the classic runaround. You should be immensely popular, but that only complicates your problem. So many things and people look so good to you, you want to experience them all, and that's not possible. Use your wonderful imagination in some productive, constructive way.

Libra sun sign/Capricorn moon sign You are fortunate to have such a sturdy moon sign to give you a sense of direction and to keep you on course. However, you could get carried away with the material aspects of life; make sure you tend to your soul as well. You are also exceptionally competitive for a Libra, and could get a reputation for stepping on other people's toes.

Libra sun sign/Aquarius moon sign You are friend to everyone but may have difficulty zeroing in on close relationships. And there is such a thing as being *too* fairminded and impartial. You could end up giving the impression that you don't care enough to care—which is far from the truth. Cultivate some of those warm feelings, and attempt to form some solid opinions.

Libra sun sign/Pisces moon sign Unless someone tosses you a very strong anchor, you are one of those people who could simply drift from one situation to another. However, you are the kindest of souls and quite intuitive as well; you really *know* when someone needs help. Just don't go through life taking care of every stray puppy that crosses your path.

Your Rising Sign—Know Your "Cover"

The third of the "big three" astrological factors is your rising sign, which you can think of as an *overlay* to your sun sign. Although it does not carry the psychological weight your moon sign does, your rising sign is also "unconscious" because it is a mode of external behavior that comes so naturally to you that you may not be aware of it. In a sense, your rising sign is your "cover." It can never totally obscure the "real you" of your sun sign, but it can temporarily mask that sign, especially when people first meet you. Here's what happens to Libra when you lay a rising sign over "typical" Libra behavior.

Libra with Aries rising You appear to be a great deal more energetic than you really are; why not follow through on your image?

Libra with Taurus rising Even if you do not literally have dimples, you are the "dimply" type—maybe even too cute for your own good.

Libra with Gemini rising At least on the surface, you are a lot less shy than the typical Libra; you're great fun at parties.

Libra with Cancer rising This combination often creates sex appeal personified. Admit that you enjoy making a grand entrance—and enjoy it.

Libra with Leo rising Male or female, you greet people with a hearty handshake and a lot of enthusiasm; try not to overpower them.

Libra with Virgo rising You come on very quietly, and may prefer not to be noticed. Loosen up and come out of the corner for some fun.

Libra with Scorpio rising There's a lot of magnetism with this combination; you surprise people later on by being much cooler than you appear.

Libra with Sagittarius rising You are so easily distracted that you could come off as rather flaky; try to concentrate on one person at a time.

Libra with Capricorn rising You probably love being well dressed; don't let too many people notice those dollar signs in your eyes.

Libra with Aquarius rising Even though you seem a bit "kooky," you are really quite conventional. So the raised eyebrows you get might be a little confusing to you.

Libra with Pisces rising Females with this combination are sometimes pale and frail looking; the men too look as if they need vitamins. Come on a bit stronger; you can.

20

Find Your Rising Sign

It is easier than many people think to find out your rising sign. One reason is that it is based on "universal" or "sidereal" time—the measure used in space travel. To ascertain your rising sign, look through the following chart and locate the birthdate nearest your birth date; look across and locate the time nearest your birth time. Remember that if daylight saving time was in effect at your birth, you must subtract one hour from the time stated on your birth certificate. In the section for your date and time, you will find an abbreviation for the sign that was rising when you were born. For instance, if your birthdate is June 12 at 9:30 a.m., your rising sign is Leo; if you were born on the same date at 9:30 p.m., your rising sign is Capricorn.

You will notice that the *year* you were born does not affect your rising sign. However, the geographical latitude does. These tables are calculated for the middle latitudes of the United States. If you were born far to the south, it is wise to look at the sign that *follows* your rising sign as well. If you were born far to the north, check out the *previous* sign.

Rising Signs—A.M. Births

	1 AM	2 AM	3 AM	4 AM	5 AM	6 AM	7 AM	8 AM	9 AM	10 AM	11 AM	12 NOON
Jan 1	Lib	Sc	Sc	Sc	Sag	Sag	Cap	Cap	Aq	Aq	Pis	Ar
Jan 9	Lib	Sc	Sc	Sag	Sag	Sag	Cap	Cap	Aq	Aq	Ar	Tau
Jan 17	Sc	Sc	Sc	Sag	Sag	Cap	Cap	Aq	Aq	Pis	Ar	Tau
Jan 25	Sc	Sc	Sag	Sag	Sag	Cap	Cap	Aq	Pis	Ar	Tau	Tau
Feb 2	Sc	Sc	Sag	Sag	Cap	Cap	Aq	Pis	Pis	Ar	Tau	Gem
Feb 10	Sc	Sag	Sag	Sag	Cap	Cap	Aq	Pis	Ar	Tau	Tau	Gem
Feb 18	Sc	Sag	Sag	Cap	Cap	Aq	Pis	Pis	Ar	Tau	Gem	Gem
Feb 26	Sag	Sag	Sag	Cap	Aq	Aq	Pis	Ar	Tau	Tau	Gem	Gem
Mar 6	Sag	Sag	Cap	Cap	Aq	Pis	Pis	Ar	Tau	Gem	Gem	Can
Mar 14	Sag	Cap	Cap	Aq	Aq	Pis	Ar	Tau	Tau	Gem	Gem	Can
Mar 22	Sag	Cap	Cap	Aq	Pis	Ar	Ar	Tau	Gem	Gem	Can	Can
Mar 30	Cap	Cap	Aq	Pis	Pis	Ar	Tau	Tau	Gem	Can	Can	Can
Apr 7	Cap	Cap	Aq	Pis	Ar	Ar	Tau	Gem	Gem	Can	Can	Leo
Apr 14	Cap	Aq	Aq	Pis	Ar	Tau	Tau	Gem	Can	Can	Can	Leo
Apr 22	Cap	Aq	Pis	Ar	Ar	Tau	Gem	Gem	Gem	Can	Leo	Leo
Apr 30	Aq	Aq	Pis	Ar	Tau	Tau	Gem	Can	Can	Can	Leo	Leo
May 8	Aq	Pis	Ar	Ar	Tau	Gem	Gem	Can	Can	Leo	Leo	Leo
May 16	Aq	Pis	Ar	Tau	Gem	Gem	Can	Can	Can	Leo	Leo	Vir
May 24	Pis	Ar	Ar	Tau	Gem	Gem	Can	Can	Leo	Leo	Leo	Vir
June 1	Pis	Ar	Tau	Gem	Gem	Can	Can	Can	Leo	Leo	Vir	Vir
June 9	Ar	Ar	Tau	Gem	Gem	Can	Can	Leo	Leo	Leo	Vir	Vir
June 17	Ar	Tau	Gem	Gem	Can	Can	Can	Leo	Leo	Vir	Vir	Vir
June 25	Tau	Tau	Gem	Gem	Can	Can	Leo	Leo	Leo	Vir	Vir	Lib
July 3	Tau	Gem	Gem	Can	Can	Can	Leo	Leo	Vir	Vir	Vir	Lib
July 11	Tau	Gem	Gem	Can	Can	Leo	Leo	Leo	Vir	Vir	Lib	Lib
July 18	Gem	Gem	Can	Can	Can	Leo	Leo	Vir	Vir	Vir	Lib	Lib
July 26	Gem	Gem	Can	Can	Leo	Leo	Vir	Vir	Vir	Lib	Lib	Lib
Aug 3	Gem	Can	Can	Can	Leo	Leo	Vir	Vir	Vir	Lib	Lib	Sc
Aug 11	Gem	Can	Can	Leo	Leo	Leo	Vir	Vir	Lib	Lib	Lib	Sc
Aug 18	Can	Can	Can	Leo	Leo	Vir	Vir	Vir	Lib	Lib	Sc	Sc
Aug 27	Can	Can	Leo	Leo	Leo	Vir	Vir	Lib	Lib	Lib	Sc	Sc
Sept 4	Can	Can	Leo	Leo	Leo	Vir	Vir	Vir	Lib	Lib	Sc	Sc
Sept 12	Can	Leo	Leo	Leo	Vir	Vir	Lib	Lib	Lib	Sc	Sc	Sag
Sept 30	Leo	Leo	Leo	Vir	Vir	Vir	Lib	Lib	Sc	Sc	Sc	Sag
Sept 28	Leo	Leo	Leo	Vir	Vir	Lib	Lib	Lib	Sc	Sc	Sag	Sag
Oct 6	Leo	Leo	Vir	Vir	Vir	Lib	Lib	Sc	Sc	Sc	Sag	Sag
Oct 14	Leo	Vir	Vir	Vir	Lib	Lib	Lib	Sc	Sc	Sag	Sag	Cap
Oct 22	Leo	Vir	Vir	Lib	Lib	Lib	Sc	Sc	Sc	Sag	Sag	Cap
Oct 30	Vir	Vir	Vir	Lib	Lib	Sc	Sc	Sc	Sag	Sag	Cap	Cap
Nov 7	Vir	Vir	Lib	Lib	Lib	Sc	Sc	Sc	Sag	Sag	Cap	Cap
Nov 15	Vir	Vir	Lib	Lib	Sc	Sc	Sc	Sag	Sag	Cap	Cap	Aq
Nov 23	Vir	Lib	Lib	Lib	Sc	Sc	Sag	Sag	Sag	Cap	Cap	Aq
Dec 1	Vir	Lib	Lib	Sc	Sc	Sc	Sag	Sag	Cap	Cap	Aq	Aq
Dec 9	Lib	Lib	Lib	Sc	Sc	Sag	Sag	Cap	Cap	Cap	Aq	Pis
Dec 18	Lib	Lib	Sc	Sc	Sc	Sag	Sag	Cap	Cap	Aq	Aq	Pis
Dec 28	Lib	Lib	Sc	Sc	Sag	Sag	Sag	Cap	Aq	Aq	Pis	Ar

Rising Signs—P.M. Births

	1 PM	2 PM	3 PM	4 PM	5 PM	6 PM	7 PM	8 PM	9 PM	10 PM	11 PM	12 MIDNIGHT
Jan 1	Tau	Gem	Gem	Can	Can	Can	Leo	Leo	Vir	Vir	Vir	Lib
Jan 9	Tau	Gem	Gem	Can	Can	Leo	Leo	Leo	Vir	Vir	Vir	Lib
Jan 17	Gem	Gem	Can	Can	Can	Leo	Leo	Vir	Vir	Vir	Lib	Lib
Jan 25	Gem	Gem	Can	Can	Leo	Leo	Leo	Vir	Vir	Lib	Lib	Lib
Feb 2	Gem	Can	Can	Can	Leo	Leo	Vir	Vir	Vir	Lib	Lib	Sc
Feb 10	Gem	Can	Can	Leo	Leo	Leo	Vir	Vir	Lib	Lib	Lib	Sc
Feb 18	Can	Can	Can	Leo	Leo	Vir	Vir	Vir	Lib	Lib	Sc	Sc
Feb 26	Can	Can	Leo	Leo	Leo	Vir	Vir	Lib	Lib	Lib	Sc	Sc
Mar 6	Can	Leo	Leo	Leo	Vir	Vir	Vir	Lib	Lib	Sc	Sc	Sc
Mar 14	Can	Leo	Leo	Vir	Vir	Vir	Lib	Lib	Lib	Sc	Sc	Sag
Mar 22	Leo	Leo	Leo	Vir	Vir	Lib	Lib	Lib	Sc	Sc	Sc	Sag
Mar 30	Leo	Leo	Vir	Vir	Vir	Lib	Lib	Sc	Sc	Sc	Sag	Sag
Apr 7	Leo	Leo	Vir	Vir	Lib	Lib	Lib	Sc	Sc	Sc	Sag	Sag
Apr 14	Leo	Vir	Vir	Vir	Lib	Lib	Sc	Sc	Sc	Sag	Sag	Cap
Apr 22	Leo	Vir	Vir	Lib	Lib	Lib	Sc	Sc	Sc	Sag	Sag	Cap
Apr 30	Vir	Vir	Vir	Lib	Lib	Sc	Sc	Sc	Sag	Sag	Cap	Cap
May 8	Vir	Vir	Lib	Lib	Lib	Sc	Sc	Sag	Sag	Sag	Cap	Cap
May 16	Vir	Vir	Lib	Lib	Sc	Sc	Sc	Sag	Sag	Cap	Cap	Aq
May 24	Vir	Lib	Lib	Lib	Sc	Sc	Sag	Sag	Sag	Cap	Cap	Aq
June 1	Vir	Lib	Lib	Sc	Sc	Sc	Sag	Sag	Cap	Cap	Aq	Aq
June 9	Lib	Lib	Lib	Sc	Sc	Sag	Sag	Sag	Cap	Cap	Aq	Pis
June 17	Lib	Lib	Sc	Sc	Sc	Sag	Sag	Cap	Cap	Aq	Aq	Pis
June 25	Lib	Lib	Sc	Sc	Sag	Sag	Sag	Cap	Cap	Aq	Pis	Ar
July 3	Lib	Sc	Sc	Sc	Sag	Sag	Cap	Cap	Aq	Aq	Pis	Ar
July 11	Lib	Sc	Sc	Sag	Sag	Sag	Cap	Cap	Aq	Pis	Ar	Tau
July 18	Sc	Sc	Sc	Sag	Sag	Cap	Cap	Aq	Aq	Pis	Ar	Tau
July 26	Sc	Sc	Sag	Sag	Sag	Cap	Cap	Aq	Pis	Ar	Tau	Tau
Aug 3	Sc	Sc	Sag	Sag	Cap	Cap	Aq	Aq	Pis	Ar	Tau	Gem
Aug 11	Sc	Sag	Sag	Sag	Cap	Cap	Aq	Pis	Ar	Tau	Tau	Gem
Aug 18	Sc	Sag	Sag	Cap	Cap	Aq	Pis	Pis	Ar	Tau	Gem	Gem
Aug 27	Sag	Sag	Sag	Cap	Cap	Aq	Pis	Ar	Tau	Tau	Gem	Gem
Sept 4	Sag	Sag	Cap	Cap	Aq	Pis	Pis	Ar	Tau	Gem	Gem	Can
Sept 12	Sag	Sag	Cap	Aq	Aq	Pis	Ar	Tau	Tau	Gem	Gem	Can
Sept 20	Sag	Cap	Cap	Aq	Pis	Pis	Ar	Tau	Gem	Gem	Can	Can
Sept 28	Cap	Cap	Aq	Aq	Pis	Ar	Tau	Tau	Gem	Gem	Can	Can
Oct 6	Cap	Cap	Aq	Pis	Ar	Ar	Tau	Gem	Gem	Can	Can	Leo
Oct 14	Cap	Aq	Aq	Pis	Ar	Tau	Tau	Gem	Gem	Can	Can	Leo
Oct 22	Cap	Aq	Pis	Ar	Ar	Tau	Gem	Gem	Can	Can	Leo	Leo
Oct 30	Aq	Aq	Pis	Ar	Tau	Tau	Gem	Can	Can	Can	Leo	Leo
Nov 7	Aq	Aq	Pis	Ar	Tau	Tau	Gem	Can	Can	Can	Leo	Leo
Nov 15	Aq	Pis	Ar	Tau	Gem	Gem	Can	Can	Can	Leo	Leo	Vir
Nov 23	Pis	Ar	Ar	Tau	Gem	Gem	Can	Leo	Leo	Leo	Leo	Vir
Dec 1	Pis	Ar	Tau	Gem	Gem	Can	Can	Can	Leo	Leo	Vir	Vir
Dec 9	Ar	Tau	Tau	Gem	Gem	Can	Can	Leo	Leo	Leo	Vir	Vir
Dec 18	Ar	Tau	Gem	Gem	Can	Can	Can	Leo	Leo	Vir	Vir	Vir
Dec 28	Tau	Tau	Gem	Gem	Can	Can	Leo	Leo	Vir	Vir	Vir	Lib

21

Libra Astro-Outlook for 1986

This is one year you would do well to look squarely at reality and not take anything for granted. Your easygoing ways will be challenged by the course of events—but you will find yourself going in a much more positive direction. It is a time to build strong foundations for the future, in several areas of your life. In career and in love, however, it is not enough to dream beautiful dreams; you are going to have to make them come true with hard work and a keen eye for what is the best course of action.

If you are a Libra born between September 25 and September 29, your tendency to see the world through rose-colored glasses may be particularly accentuated this year. On the positive side, you will be almost "psychic," and it could serve you very well—as long as you don't get carried away by your impressions. Resolve to base your actions on facts that you have checked out carefully.

It is an excellent time to begin developing some creative ideas that have been brewing in the back of your mind for a while. You will be able to give them both practical application and the attention to detail that is required if you are to derive benefit from them.

Once again this year you will learn some lessons about the real value of money and money management. You can also profitably clear out a lot of old clutter and reduce your possessions to a much more workable level. In doing so, you will make room for some of the good things that are likely to come your way this year.

April could be a peak time, but June also looks highly romantic as well as creative. For fun and popularity, as well as travel, January, August, and October look excellent. For more details about what you are most likely to encounter in 1986, consult the day-by-day forecasts on the following pages.

22

15 Months of Day-by-Day Predictions

OCTOBER 1985

Tuesday, October 1 (Moon in Taurus) You may have been experiencing some problems with a member of the opposite sex—today those problems become a thing of the past and you begin a whole new chapter. Count your blessings for being able to make a new start. In another matter, you can get what you want—if you contact the right people. Don't be afraid to approach someone in authority; you will get a better reception than you think.

Wednesday, October 2 (Moon in Taurus) The thing that is most important to you today is being together with the person you love. In fact, you may even be able to talk over some things that have been touchy subjects lately—and now they go quite smoothly. What to do to make your home more pleasant and beautiful may be high on the list of priorities for both of you. You can come to a decision, and you can have luck with number 6.

Thursday, October 3 (Moon Taurus to Gemini 8:26 a.m.) Today, you realize you don't want much—just peace of mind and someone to love. Those things are harder to find than you think. Try to clear your mind by finding time to be alone—or alone with nature. The thinking you are doing is in a rather spiritual direction, and you need some time by yourself. Tomorrow, you will be more able to face the world.

Friday, October 4 (Moon in Gemini) You see a new path for yourself now, and you are tempted to start down it. However, it may be a bit premature. You have intense emotions about the subject, but you realize you must put your focus on what has to be done now. Don't give up your dreams; simply put them away for another day. You will get what you want someday, but not right now.

Saturday, October 5 (Moon Gemini to Cancer 8:42 p.m.) This is the part of the lunar cycle that emphasizes your standing in this world. Even if you try, you will not be able to hide today. What you should do is take advantage of this period by promoting your ideas and being your own public relations director. You know what you want now and you know you may have to make some small sacrifices to get it; but your view of the larger pictures lets you accept that. Go for it!

Sunday, October 6 (Moon in Cancer) Not all of you may be feeling as if you have to put yourself forward now. However, that may be the case with many. The time is right to exercise your initiative to be assertive and take action. Whatever course you decide to take, remember that your appearance is particularly important now. You should look bright and be bright—so as to be ready for anything. Keep an eye out for a Leo who might be gaining on you.

Monday, October 7 (Moon in Cancer) Determine which way the wind is blowing today before you venture out; you've got to be alert to details in order to be in the right place at the right time. Things can work to your advantage if you are willing to work on them a bit. Team up with a Cancer who has the same objective as you do; you may find things go a lot more easily. Whatever you do, don't rush!

Tuesday, October 8 (Moon Cancer to Leo 6:38 a.m.) This is one of those days in which you could make one of your wishes come true—as long as it is reasonably realistic. Be sure you know what you are getting into before you jump—too many challenges at one time could be a bit confusing. Try your luck with number 3.

Wednesday, October 9 (Moon in Leo) Pay attention to the facts and figures today, and little else. The only way to accomplish something is to give it your complete attention. Realize that someone may be testing you—but that you can easily pass the test. For relaxation, you might try getting involved in a community project. It may mean more work, but it's worth it.

Thursday, October 10 (Moon Leo to Virgo 1:24 p.m.) You should be communicating extremely well right now—especially with members of the opposite sex. In fact, you could be communicating so well with one of them that you fall in love; or refall in love with somebody you already know. At any rate, your feelings are revitalized. You may even decide to travel tandem—it could work out extremely well. The lucky number today is 5.

Friday, October 11 (Moon in Virgo) Once again the emphasis is on rediscovering someone you've been close to—but now feel even closer. There is an aspect of happiness and harmony about this day which little can disturb. Music may be part of the scenario, and if you do not play now, you may decide to take up an instrument. Who knows? Some hidden talent may out!

Saturday, October 12 (Moon Virgo to Libra 2:38 p.m.) Stay behind the scenes as much as possible today; you will learn more about what is going on that way. As far as your own aims are concerned, pursue them quietly—away from the prying eyes of others. It is a day in which you can accomplish much toward your personal growth and psychic development. Spend some time with yourself.

Sunday, October 13 (Moon in Libra) Now your energy shifts to high, and there are swift new developments. In fact, you could find yourself in the money! It is also a time of peak physical energy, and you can shoulder so many responsibilities, the world could literally be your oyster. Other people are noticing, so you are definitely not wasting your efforts.

Monday, October 14 (Moon Libra to Scorpio 2:50 p.m.) Your sense of inner direction is strong now, and it gives you a big lift toward a long-range goal. As long as you know where you're going, nothing or no one can stop you. With the strength that you have, your ideal can be realized. You should look good and feel good—and even make a romantic conquest. The lucky number is 9.

Tuesday, October 15 (Moon in Scorpio) You are still in a high lunar cycle, and able to accomplish a great deal. Do not be shy about stepping out and asking for what you want as well as what you need. Don't hide your light under any kind of bushel, because you have a great deal to offer. You may surprise yourself when you step into the spotlight.

Wednesday, October 16 (Moon Scorpio to Sagittarius 2:25 p.m.) Today, you may have to lie back and adopt a spirit of acceptance. You have made your wishes known; now you must wait for the response. Meanwhile, turn your thoughts to security measures at home—or the home of someone dependent upon you. Give some thought to maintaining a separate bank account for "splurging"—you will feel a little less guilty about your extravagances that way.

Thursday, October 17 (Moon in Sagittarius) It will be difficult to look at long-range things today because you will be so busy with short-term problems. A lot of things need attending to, like letters, phone calls, and visits. Your work may be annoyingly peppered with details as well. Be careful not to lose something small but important. Someone does come along and lighten the atmosphere—it could be a Sagittarian.

Friday, October 18 (Moon Sagittarius to Capricorn 3:37 p.m.) This is no time to delegate responsibility; you are the one who must do it yourself—that is, if you want the best results, which you certainly do. In this responsible frame of mind, you could inspire someone who works with you—and even attract notice in the upper echelons. Spend some time talking over common problems with a couple of rather smart people— one of whom could be a Taurus or a Scorpio.

Saturday, October 19 (Moon in Capricorn) A change comes over you today, and it could lead to a total transformation of attitude. Suddenly you don't want to go anywhere; home is the best place there is—if not literally the place, then the feeling that goes along with it. Your emotions are running high and deep, and you are grateful for love and support. The lucky number today could be 5.

Sunday, October 20 (Moon Capricorn to Aquarius 8:04 p.m.) You are still drawn to domestic things today. Whatever your age, a parent may be influential now—or at least an authority figure of some sort. You learn that you must be considerate and willing to play fair even when you are the object of some jealousy. Be your diplomatic self, and make someone realize you love him/her anyway.

Monday, October 21 (Moon in Aquarius) It is a quiet day from beginning to end—at least it should be. It will be if you realize the best posture is to lie low today, and defer to the wishes of others. Be your graceful, winning self and don't try to force anything. Even in this quiet atmosphere, something rather wonderful and possibly romantic could happen.

Tuesday, October 22 (Moon in Aquarius) Whether you want it or not, someone places greater authority in your hands today. Don't resist it! Though it is not easy to see now, great dividends will be paid to you later on. Others who know you are dependable could lean on you too much, however. Don't let that happen!

Wednesday, October 23 (Moon Aquarius to Pisces 3:35 p.m.) Put your back into completing a project so you can move on to some new things—and brighter prospects. You feel like striking out and pioneering in a certain venture; it might even be one in which you help others more than yourself. Count on someone rather sparky—possibly an Aries—for lots of cooperation. Another Libra may cross your path, and be a pleasant companion.

Thursday, October 24 (Moon in Pisces) You can make some savvy judgments today, and put a couple of points on the success side of the ledger. One of your best qualities is knowing how to give priorities to things and get done first what needs to be done first. As a result of your hard work, someone may give you an unusual opportunity to get in on the beginning of a deal. It's not a bad idea; consider it.

Friday, October 25 (Moon Pisces to Aries 2:09 p.m.) Pay particular attention to how you look today; if you don't, you will regret it when someone rather attractive crosses your path. Your general well-being should be at the top of your mind today; you may even decide that something has to be done about your diet/exercise routine. It would be good for you to think about your image and resolve to do something about it. Your efforts in this department can win raves and second glances.

Saturday, October 26 (Moon in Aries) You could be all over the lot today if you don't concentrate your efforts on one or maybe two things. In one of your many interests, it will pay to make some discreet inquiries, because you can easily snag off some bargains now. The emphasis is on quality over quantity, but that is okay with you. Think about the legal side of a certain matter in which you are getting involved; it may be more complicated than you think. Be willing to give in when someone asks you to; next time it will be your turn.

Sunday, October 27 (Moon in Aries) All kinds of agreements are up for scrutiny today; that may include your marital status. There is a testing period going on, and you should be aware of it. If you feel like you are under the gun, be straightforward with your mate or partner and say, "Let's discuss it." In fact, your best plan might be to delay everything until a better day. It is coming.

Monday, October 28 (Moon Aries to Taurus 2:11 a.m.) Today, you are easily able to resolve a dilemma you thought was virtually impossible to cope with. In fact, it goes so much better than you thought, you find yourself ending up with more than you had in the beginning. Celebrate your luck by doing something very tangible for someone you love; the relationship has been growing more intense, and you should acknowledge the fact. You may be able to come up with an ingenious solution today that surprises everyone. It shouldn't surprise you.

Tuesday, October 29 (Moon in Taurus) You can find an easier and quicker way to do things if you try. In fact, you should be something of an efficiency expert. You may find a variety of choices presented to you. Don't get so carried away that you forget to "mind the store"; someone could get ahead of you while you aren't looking. Be sure to count your change!

Wednesday, October 30 (Moon Taurus to Gemini 2:36 p.m.) Don't be afraid to experiment with a new way of doing things today; you are in an unorthodox situation so you may have to use unorthodox means to deal with it. The important thing is not to kid yourself today—remember what is at stake. Do not feel you are alone, however, because someone close to you is willing to back you up all the way—perhaps even with money.

Thursday, October 31 (Moon in Gemini) Today, you are out of a tight spot. You feel as if a whole new chapter is opening. You are on the move, and someone who thinks much like you shares his/her dreams with you. Though you feel quite independent, realize that you can make much more progress as a pair. Be ready to eliminate the things in your life that are holding you down, and to cut some ties that are outgrown now. You should feel free, and act it. The lucky number could be 8 today.

NOVEMBER 1985

Friday, November 1 (Moon in Gemini) You may get a very pleasant surprise, and it may come in the form of an unexpected gift. It brightens a day that is already rather bright on its own. You are still in the midst of change, and motivated by the urge to do new things. In a relationship matter, you are ready to talk—and it can work wonders.

Saturday, November 2 (Moon Gemini to Cancer 3:12 a.m.) As anxious as you are to contribute to the happiness of someone special, don't promise more than you can deliver. Sometimes you can get carried away with an excess of good feeling. One way to set yourself straight is to sit down and look at the budget; realize what you can do and what you can't. A Taurus could be very helpful in balancing that budget—listen carefully.

Sunday, November 3 (Moon in Cancer) Your intuition is particularly keen today, and it could allow you to "psych out" someone who seems to have plans for you. Get the jump on things, and show how good you are. Then this businesslike individual will realize how much you have to offer. You may be thinking rather lofty thoughts; you have every right to be optimistic.

Monday, November 4 (Moon Cancer to Leo 3:12 a.m.)
Be willing to stretch again today, because there are good things within your grasp. Whatever you do today, you will get feedback—and most of it positive. You should be able to get a better fix on where you stand, both in work and in love. It should make you feel good. The lucky number today is 9.

Tuesday, November 5 (Moon in Leo) You may even surprise yourself with the amount of energy you have today and how far it takes you. Don't dissipate that energy on little things, because there are some big ones that need your attention. In a relationship matter, you should take the initiative now, and make what you might consider a rather bold step. Do not fear; the time is right.

Wednesday, November 6 (Moon Leo to Virgo 9:34 p.m.) You may pull in your horns a bit today, which is all well and good. Reach inside yourself rather than out toward others; it will be much more productive. However, don't neglect someone who would welcome contact with you; you could play the good samaritan. A nice compliment could make you walk a little taller.

Thursday, November 7 (Moon in Virgo) Some days you are restless as a willow in a windstorm, and this could be one of them. Don't rush things, and don't scatter your attention—you could find yourself making a foolish error. Someone you met recently is becoming an excellent friend; cultivate this relationship. An idea you had a while ago is revived, and seems to have new life.

Friday, November 8 (Moon in Virgo) You've got to be willing to do your homework and stay on schedule. Someone is going to hold you accountable, and you want to make a good showing. Someone tells you a "secret" and it is an eye-opener! The number 4 should be lucky today.

Saturday, November 9 (Moon Virgo to Libra 1:14 a.m.) Your world is opening up now, as the moon moves into your sign. All kinds of messages may be coming in to you, and you should be ready to sort them out. One of them will lead to a total change in scene which, though sudden, is extremely clever. One of your relationships is getting a lot better—it even has the possibility of becoming permanent. Talk it over with a sensitive person—possibly a Pisces.

Sunday, November 10 (Moon in Libra) The truth and nothing but the truth will do today. If you try to skirt it, you will find yourself in trouble. However, with the way things are today, anything you do should bear good results. You are continuing to develop one of your talents.

Monday, November 11 (Moon Libra to Scorpio 1:53 a.m.) Today, it may become obvious to you why another has more credibility than you do: observe and learn something from the experience. You may be in a position where you have to become a bit more buttoned-up and able. In general, it is a low-key day, but a rather productive one. The lucky number today could be 7.

Tuesday, November 12 (Moon in Scorpio) You obviously learned your lesson, and are ready to apply it today. It pays off handsomely, and you are in a new position of power. See what can happen when you manage things better? You may find yourself the center of attention today—don't be shy.

Wednesday, November 13 (Moon Scorpio to Sagittarius 1:12 a.m.) An old problem may surface again today, but with your new knowledge you are prepared for it and can overcome things. However, it is important that you take the initiative and not leave the first move to someone else. Believe in yourself and in the fact that you can have an impact now.

Thursday, November 14 (Moon in Sagittarius) You should be revved up and ready to go, with lots of physical stamina—and sex appeal! You should be particularly attractive to other people today, as your individuality shines through. Your personal income is affected in a positive way today, even though it is in a rather unusual manner. Accept the help that someone gives you—that someone could possibly be a Leo.

Friday, November 15 (Moon Sagittarius to Capricorn 1:10 a.m.) Any judgments you make today should be based on what you see as your needs in the future. Don't sell yourself short. If you are asked to contribute something of value, you can do that in the form of ideas rather than money. Offer your excellent public relations skills. The lucky number today could be 2.

Saturday, November 16 (Moon in Capricorn) Home is a lovely place to be today, and you could be perfectly happy fixing up things the way you would like them to be. However, don't get so involved that you neglect someone who is trying to get a message across; it could be vital to the future of the relationship. If necessary, use your Libra charms to smooth over a possible "bump" and make the person smile again—it will be time very well spent. The lucky number today is 3.

Sunday, November 17 (Moon Capricorn to Aquarius 3:54 a.m.) It is possible you are considering a change of residence—for yourself or for someone else who values your opinions. Be practical in making suggestions; you sometimes go for the facade rather than the foundation. You get rather charged up by an opportunity to express yourself. It could lead to a whole new activity—possibly a sport or a hobby. Enjoy!

Monday, November 18 (Moon in Aquarius) You start out the week in excellent shape, emotionally speaking at least. You sense great forces within yourself, but you must learn how to harness them. You may be tempted to explore some new things, but you really should direct your energies toward projects you have already started. To satisfy that urge for novelty, start thinking about a travel plan, and make the sky the limit as far as destination goes.

Tuesday, November 19 (Moon Aquarius to Pisces 10:04 a.m.) You may have to come back down to earth today and realize that there is some serious work to be done. However, it needn't ruin your day, because you are bound to be involved with some very sensitive people who understand your feelings. Be careful not to speak out before you think, however; you might easily say something that could be misinterpreted. Be as clear as possible when you define terms.

Wednesday, November 20 (Moon in Pisces) Make sure everyone understands exactly where you stand today; you may have to define your terms very clearly. As things come into focus, you should feel more secure and able to concentrate on the work at hand. It may not be an altogether delightful day, but it is brightened when a decision is made in your favor. Try your luck with number 7 today.

Thursday, November 21 (Moon Pisces to Aries 8:00 p.m.) A good part of the day may be spent in finishing some rather niggling things you would rather not have to deal with. However, later on you could have an absolutely glorious time with someone you find very stimulating. For some of you, that will apply in the physical sense. Just realize that you are better off letting the other person take the lead. Indicate that you are only too happy to follow.

Friday, November 22 (Moon in Aries) Once again today, you pull out all the stops and move forward—and with great flair. Your vision allows you to tell others the best way to get from here to there. You are right, and you get the credit for it. Someone new on the scene seems to have possibilities; try to get close to this "team member."

Saturday, November 23 (Moon in Aries) Look out for yourself today, because no one else may be doing that. Though you have to go it alone, you can make great strides. The reason may be that you know exactly whom to approach to get what you want. It's nice to have contacts. Don't look so far ahead that you miss an opportunity that presents itself at your feet today.

Sunday, November 24 (Moon Aries to Taurus 8:37 a.m.) You are glad to slow down today and get some much needed R & R. The most attractive bargain you could make today is one for time. Someone may be rather annoying when he/she tries to "mother you"; don't overreact—just smile and enjoy. You may recover something sentimental you thought you had lost.

Monday, November 25 (Moon in Taurus) You could find yourself spending a lot of money you don't have if you're not careful. Is it necessary to make such a splashy impression? Be your sweet self and you won't need fancy "packaging." You may be frustrated by someone who is being very mysterious; realize that timing is important to this person. Be patient.

Tuesday, November 26 (Moon Taurus to Gemini 9:02 p.m.) Is this change really necessary, you wonder? Perhaps you would be better holding on and waiting; it is a calculated risk, but you take it. The answers will come soon enough. Don't give in to some badgering by someone who is trying to make you show your hand—it is premature.

Wednesday, November 27 (Moon in Gemini) You may be extremely sensitive today, but in a very good sense of the word. You can pick up lots of signals and "messages" from those around you. It puts you in a good position, because you know what people are thinking before they say it. Someone you talk with today has similar goals and aspirations; perhaps you two should spend more time together. It is good for you to have this kind of intimate communication with others.

Thursday, November 28 (Moon in Gemini) Some plans that have been floating around are suddenly pinned down; it's great to know exactly where you will be going, and when. If someone suggests a slight change, be receptive and diplomatic—there is both money and love riding on this. Another Libra or possibly a Taurus may come in and smooth the waters.

Friday, November 29 (Moon Gemini to Cancer 8:59 a.m.) You may have to look after your legal rights today, as someone may try to encroach on them. Just make sure you've got all your ducks in a row, and all your papers lined up today—that way you have nothing to fear. Spend some quiet time in meditation and you will get to the heart of the matter that's been bothering you.

Saturday, November 30 (Moon in Cancer) An opportunity for greater prestige may come your way, but realize that there are strings attached. It's up to you—and your sense of responsibility. Question whether you are really ready to take on more pressure. Your most intimate relationships are quite intense today; something very significant could happen in one of them.

DECEMBER 1985

Sunday, December 1 (Moon Cancer to Leo 8:04 p.m.) You may have to trim your sails a bit today, and settle down to the essential matters in your life. Though you may feel like goofing off, you really will not have the time. Though this is not an official "work day," your job or career is on your mind. Trust an instinct you have about whether to stay or to go.

Monday, December 2 (Moon in Leo) A project needs a leader, and it could be you. You are an excellent choice to work in a common cause; you know how to get people to agree. Something you did a while back now pays off—and you find yourself with a windfall. Use it wisely. One of your fondest wishes could come true.

Tuesday, December 3 (Moon in Leo) Some high-level connections expand your horizons now, and start you thinking about bigger and better things. Try to keep this broad perspective all the time. Doors that were once closed to you are now beginning to open—be sure you are ready to walk through. Team efforts are best today—as is number 9.

Wednesday, December 4 (Moon Leo to Virgo 4:38 a.m.) You may wake with some vague anxieties today. Realize that your fear of failure is all in your mind. You must get out there and sell yourself, because the emphasis is on action now. It may be difficult, but you can do it. In fact, your persistence will pay off better than you could possibly have imagined. You will get the opportunity to state your case—possibly in a romantic matter.

Thursday, December 5 (Moon in Virgo) A secret is revealed today, and you realize how foolish you were to worry. It should teach you a lesson and make you be more confident next time. You may be in the market for something of value—possibly even a new house or residence. This is a good time to get what you need; do some fast computing to see how much you can afford.

Friday, December 6 (Moon Virgo to Libra 9:44 a.m.) You don't have to wait any longer; now is the time to forge full speed ahead. Break out of the rut you've been in, and go for everything that's new and different. The only limits are the ones you place on yourself now, but as usual you must take care not to stretch yourself too thin. You may be involved with a very sparky person—possibly a Gemini. You run the risk of being overstimulated. Learn to walk before you run.

Saturday, December 7 (Moon in Libra) Today's a day you can make a marvelous impression; you are the picture of health and vitality. A look at yourself in the mirror should boost your morale—don't be critical of what you see, because others may see you differently.

Are you really ready to see a project through to its completion? Don't bite off more than you can chew, and test out your patience before you take a first step.

Sunday, December 8 (Moon Libra to Scorpio 1:05 p.m.) No matter what the weather, the sun is shining on you today. You could be singled out for congratulations; accept the compliment, but don't be smug. Others may be jealous enough of you. All kinds of changes and happenings make this a rather exciting day—you could find yourself doing something you've never done before. Try your luck with number 5 today.

Monday, December 9 (Moon in Scorpio) Today, it is others you must think of rather than yourself. In fact, you may have to give up something in order to help someone else. This sobering experience makes you focus on matters of security. Remember, you are not your only dependent. Start thinking about saving.

Tuesday, December 10 (Moon Scorpio to Sagittarius 1:11 p.m.) You've got the chance to increase your earning power greatly; be willing to make the effort. Sometimes you do not like to do your "homework," but this is one time it will pay off. Someone may try to tempt you with a get-rich scheme—realize that it is quite flimsy. There are much more solid deals available, if you look for them.

Wednesday, December 11 (Moon in Sagittarius) You don't feel like taking very much seriously today, and with luck, you won't have to. You should enjoy some light-hearted conversation, some of it with someone who surprises you—you didn't think he/she had it in him/her. Keep your eye on the mailbox today, because a significant message may be on the way. However, it could come in some other form. Stay alert!

Thursday, December 12 (Moon Sagittarius to Capricorn 1:03 p.m.) Today, you must get back to business, but you are very ready for it. A minor issue threatens to become a real bone of contention; don't let the situation get out of hand. Apply your Libran diplomacy and you will get warring factions to agree. Don't miss the subtleties of some news that arrives today. There may be more there than meets the eye.

Friday, December 13 (Moon in Capricorn) There is nothing unlucky about this day for you. In fact, you may get a lot of attention and admiration—even from members of the opposite sex. If love is not on your mind, business is where you will shine. In fact, you may go right to the top and get a chance to show how clever you really are.

Saturday, December 14 (Moon Capricorn to Aquarius 1:39 p.m.) If you are willing to wait it out, you will be the winner in the end. It may be tough to sit and watch, but realize you can't be "on" all the time. The most valuable thing you can do today is some quiet reflection—be sure to get some privacy to do it. Some lessons from the past you remember now should help you greatly in this situation.

Sunday, December 15 (Moon in Aquarius) You reach an almost perfect understanding with someone you love today; it bolsters your ego and your confidence. Knowing where you stand makes it easier for you to turn your attention to things that need doing. In fact, you may find yourself getting very wrapped up in a fascinating subject. If you feel lucky today, try your luck with number 3.

Monday, December 16 (Moon Aquarius to Pisces 6:21 p.m.) You may have to play the part of a disciplinarian, but you will temper justice with mercy; in fact, the "orders" you give are received as a message of love. Some money may be burning a hole in your pocket; why not give in to that urge to buy something new and rather elegant? You can afford it.

Tuesday, December 17 (Moon in Pisces) You get so wound up in a conversation today that it could go on endlessly. The person you talk with really stimulates your mind and your thinking. You find you have lots of questions, and that the answers are extremely enlightening. On another front, someone turns around and does you a favor in repayment for what you did not too long ago. Kindness does pay off sometimes.

Wednesday, December 18 (Moon in Pisces) A difficult situation suddenly dissolves, and you feel much freer. As you sit down to do things your way, you may have to avoid somebody who is rather meddlesome and seems to want to complicate the issue. It is really quite simple—and you can simply tell the person to butt out. The lucky number today could be 6.

Thursday, December 19 (Moon Pisces to Aries 2:55 a.m.) Your focus and energies shift to matters of partnership and relationships. You may find that you have to keep a low profile, and let others work things out their way. Realize that your time will come. As long as you are sure your rights are protected, you do not have to act at this time. However, you should be on the alert for behind-the-scenes maneuvers.

Friday, December 20 (Moon in Aries) You have an excellent chance to beat out the competition today and fulfill one of your aspirations. One reason is that a very powerful player wants to be on your team; it could possibly be a Capricorn. Whatever happens, you end up in a much stronger position than before. You might celebrate by trying your luck with number 8.

Saturday, December 21 (Moon Aries to Taurus 3:09 p.m.) You may be in the process of evaluating one of your relationships and of discovering that it could be time for a change. Don't be afraid to put things on a new footing; you don't have to be a leaner anymore. The other person should be willing to accept the fact that you are your own person now. Your interests are expanding quickly, and you could find yourself more involved in a community or charity campaign than you would like to be. Know when to call a halt.

Sunday, December 22 (Moon in Taurus) There is something you want to put into motion; the only way to get it off the ground is to be assertive and state clearly what you want to do. You may be surprised at how much backing you get from people you thought would be opposed to your idea. In fact, it turns out to be a joint transaction, and you have a partner you didn't expect. In another area, you could really stand out from the crowd today—your personality rating is very high.

Monday, December 23 (Moon in Taurus) Your money has been flowing rather freely this holiday season—all in the opposite direction from your wallet. Make sure your outgo is not exceeding your income. In another area of your life, you are in a period of transition. The best way to weather it is to adopt a spirit of acceptance. A surprising fact comes to light, and suddenly you understand things a lot better.

Tuesday, December 24 (Moon Taurus to Gemini 3:46 a.m.) You are definitely in a festive mood and full of good humor. You win a new friend by making him/her laugh about something that could be rather serious. By doing so, you give the other person a sense of perspective. Good for you. At this point in time you are able to see the big picture, and to keep long-range plans in focus. The accent is on luck today, and you might try yours with the number 3.

Wednesday, December 25 (Moon in Gemini) There is an excellent feeling to this day, and a sense of order should replace some confusion of the recent past. Because you are sincere about wanting to make a fresh start, another person responds with sincere feelings, too. Communication is excellent right now—and you should take advantage of it. Let everyone know what you are all about.

Thursday, December 26 (Moon Gemini to Cancer 3:41 p.m.) A worthy cause captures your attention and gives you an impetus to positive action. This is an excellent time to be charitable. You are not alone in your efforts—a "right-hand man" is right there at your side. Make sure you express your appreciation in some tangible manner—it could be a late Christmas gift.

Friday, December 27 (Moon in Cancer) This is a wonderful day to enjoy those new things the holidays brought your way. You should feel quite luxurious! Relax in a pleasant environment and take stock of the many good things you have. This could be a great day for a gathering of intimate friends; you should extend the warm glow of your feelings to others. Try your luck with number 6 today.

Saturday, December 28 (Moon in Cancer) Today again, you might want to spend some time just sitting back and enjoying life as it is. There will be plenty of time to think about tomorrow tomorrow. Something you hear or read is very thought-provoking and could set you on a whole new course of study. The inspiration may come from a rather analytical type—possibly a Virgo or a Pisces. For some of you, there may be a "secret rendezvous."

Sunday, December 29 (Moon Cancer to Leo 1:51 a.m.) Though it may lie deep in your subconscious, you do have an urge for power. Today, it may rise to the surface and give you the impetus to take a bold step. As you go straight to the point, you realize how easy it is to get what you want when you are assertive. A relationship may be growing a lot more intense—are you sure this is what you want? Someone grants you a wish.

Monday, December 30 (Moon in Leo) You may have to let some petty behavior roll off your back today. Jealousy may be the cause, but diplomacy is the cure. Meanwhile, a loyal friend needs some reassurance; let him/her know that you can be counted on no matter what happens. Realize that you are seen as a person of strength now. Don't let anyone down.

Tuesday, December 31 (Moon Leo to Virgo 10:06 a.m.) The year ends on a very positive note for you. Put the accent on love and friendship. As you exchange greetings and thoughts with others, you realize what an excellent variety of people people your world. If you have the opportunity to speculate today, you might try your luck with number 1. Happy New Year!

JANUARY 1986

Wednesday, January 1 (Moon in Virgo) Your best way to start out the year is with a quiet day at home with the family. If that sounds a bit dull, it is true that responsibilities to others are likely to overshadow any purely personal plans for now. To get your own gratification, you can be a key influence in straightening out family differences—if you listen to all the problems and are willing to act as counselor.

Thursday, January 2 (Moon Virgo to Libra 3:45 p.m.) Though in general this looks like a rather practical year for you, there will be times, like today, when you will be able to just get away by yourself and escape—with a film, book, or music. Even if it seems impossible, you should try. It is not a time to push yourself or to begin any new projects. Lighten your day by trying your luck with number 7.

Friday, January 3 (Moon in Libra) With the moon now fully in your sign, you should be able to at least have a sense that you have control over your circumstances. What that means is you should listen to your inner voice and make that enterprising business move you may have been considering. For others, the step you take may be as critical as proposing marriage—or at least expressing a desire for greater involvement with someone you love. A Capricorn could very well be involved in the day's activities.

Saturday, January 4 (Moon Libra to Scorpio 7:44 p.m.) Don't get upset if your sense of balance might be temporarily thrown off by the fire and dash of a certain person—possibly an Aries. The good part is that person can pave new paths for you and help you see a bigger, brighter picture. Keep your cool, and remember that the moon is still favoring you. Look ahead, and do so with optimism.

Sunday, January 5 (Moon in Scorpio) The accent today is squarely on money and possessions, as well as the creative use of your talents. It is possible you have been sweeping under the rug a possible additional source of income that will permit you to do what you want. The thing you do best may be the very thing that could bring you the most money. And the luxuries you've been eyeing. It's time for a new start! The lucky number today is 1.

Monday, January 6 (Moon Scorpio to Sagittarius 9:47 p.m.) It's possible your emotions may be reacting more than they should in relation to the circumstances. Exaggeration is the order of the day. That means you should think twice before you spend money on something sentimental; what you really should do is go to the other extreme and decide that putting something away for a rainy day is really the wisest course. Listen to a Cancer who knows how to "conserve." The lucky number today could be 2.

Tuesday, January 7 (Moon in Sagittarius) Today the moon energy makes you concerned with breaking out of your current rut—getting out and going places and doing things. Good for you! Any kind of interpersonal communication or travel is favored now. If someone invites you to a party, say yes immediately. However, don't waste any time on activity that leads you nowhere; a productive goal should be kept firmly in mind.

Wednesday, January 8 (Moon Sagittarius to Capricorn 10:42 p.m.) You don't have any problem with having ideas today, but you may experience difficulty sticking with the routine things that have to be done. Too bad! It's tough to feel "inspired" but to have to spend your time on a lot of what appear to be minor details. However, it is possible to keep yourself busy with things at hand, and to still keep your mind on the future.

Thursday, January 9 (Moon in Capricorn) Even if this day seems a bit dreary at first, it will definitely pick up later on. For one thing, a real message of love could easily come your way. For some, it could be hidden among some words that are exchanged that don't sound particularly sweet at first. Don't hesitate to reach out and question things, because you are becoming a kind of "base of operations" for those around you. They look to you for guidance.

Friday, January 10 (Moon in Capricorn) No matter what else you have to do today, your mind will be very much on home and property. Some may be embarking on a beautifying campaign. If you've thought of moving, it's an excellent day to look around—or possibly even buy or sell. Peace and harmony should reign within your own four walls. The lucky number is 6.

Saturday, January 11 (Moon Capricorn to Aquarius 12:01 a.m.) It's possible a romantic dream could be shattered now; admit that you've been a bit too idealistic about someone or some thing. Sometimes it's fun to be "in love with love," but it is a bit unrealistic. Don't force any issues today, and get your entertainment in some way that puts you on your own. Pisces would make a delightful companion.

Sunday, January 12 (Moon in Aquarius) For some, a long-term affair of the heart gets a lot hotter now. It may be that you are looking at love and life in much more practical terms. Good for you! Because you believe in yourself, you will inspire confidence in others.

For many, marriage and stability of all kinds are very much top-of-the-mind subjects. The lucky number is 8.

Monday, January 13 (Moon Aquarius to Pisces 3:39 a.m.)   You may find yourself in a face-off today—possibly with a co-worker. Don't blow it out of proportion. Keep your Libra cool, even if your sense of justice is injured a bit. Show that you are able to rise above petty issues and see the big picture. An Aries could be involved in the situation.

Tuesday, January 14 (Moon in Pisces)   Once again work is at the top of the list of things that engage your interest. Some of you may be absolutely overflowing with good ideas and new ways to make progress through new methods. If you really want to make an impression, introduce these new ideas rather subtly and slowly. You could cause some waves among those who tend to cling to the past. The lucky number is 2.

Wednesday, January 15 (Moon Pisces to Aries 11:03 a.m.)   Now you're coming into a moon phase where it is best to slow down and let others make the major decisions in your life. You'll have plenty of time for yours later on. As a matter of fact, you could use a little downtime to revive your energies and catch up on some details. Someone older—possibly a female—provides emotional support and has some valuable advice to give. Listen!

Thursday, January 16 (Moon in Aries)   It's an excellent time to meet the public—and to deal with people whose backgrounds are quite different from yours. You should be in a rather good mood, and generally out for fun. You find that you attract it in generous quantities. Be careful of acting too independently now; it's important to find a common meeting ground.

Friday, January 17 (Moon Aries to Taurus 10:14 p.m.)   Now it's time to get down to essentials. It may be necessary to follow through on a promise you made to a partner or an associate. Cooperation is the key word now; you can get to the heart of things in a personal relationship by striking a note of balance rather than by debating the issues. The lucky number is 4 today.

Saturday, January 18 (Moon in Taurus) Try to be a bit creative in your money management right now; a change might be refreshing—and rewarding. If you talk to someone who really knows the ropes, you can make a lot of progress in this area. New approaches to old problems are very much on the calendar—in both love and money. Be sure to keep your partner totally informed.

Sunday, January 19 (Moon in Taurus) Many may be feeling like blowing a little cash on a luxury item now. It may be the best way to smooth over a rather tense situation at home. You can also spend in the area of kind words and appreciation for your loved ones; they can be as welcome as a gift today. A celebration is in the wind, and you will hear of it soon.

Monday, January 20 (Moon Taurus to Gemini 11:12 a.m.) For best results, work behind the scenes today. You are particularly sensitive to the needs and desires of others now, so isolating yourself a bit will make you feel most comfortable. If you look within yourself for answers, you will gain a greater understanding of what makes you tick. The lucky number today is 7.

Tuesday, January 21 (Moon in Gemini) You have what it takes to make a big impression on someone who can make your future a lot more secure. Make sure you show it! It's important to discuss long-range plans with important people in your life, and to think about getting some special education or future training in order to meet your goals. Your lucky number is 8.

Wednesday, January 22 (Moon Gemini to Cancer 11:14 p.m.) You may be feeling very openhanded today and full of compassion for others. It's okay to be philanthropic, but do keep in mind that sometimes charity begins at home. Try to look beyond your day-by-day routine and develop some higher interests. Travel could be very much on your mind; don't limit yourself to plans you can make now. Things will be better later on. An Aries and another Libra might figure prominently.

Thursday, January 23 (Moon in Cancer) Be prepared to be in the limelight today; some honor and recognition could easily be coming your way. Put your best foot forward, because you should be full of vitality and able to attract the admiration of someone important. In your love life as well as your work life, you are likely to have "high visibility" today.

Friday, January 24 (Moon in Cancer) Don't push your ambitions too forcefully; right now, you are better off maintaining a low profile. You've got time on your side, and you don't have to push now. Use your intuition to find the best answer to a career matter; reasoning it out is not likely to work. Your lucky number is 2.

Saturday, January 25 (Moon Cancer to Leo 8:47 a.m.) You may really feel like "busting out" today. And you may have plenty of opportunity to. Your optimistic attitude should attract a variety of invitations—be sure to choose wisely! Someone new can really stimulate you and get you involved in a heated discussion. But it's all very positive. Keep your eye on a Sagittarian!

Sunday, January 26 (Moon in Leo) The full moon could make you feel a bit of sync with the world today, but you've got to get the things done that need doing. Because this full moon falls right in your sector of friends and associations, you may be tempted to drop everything in order to "party." You'll be sorry tomorrow if you don't complete a key project. The lucky number is 4.

Monday, January 27 (Moon Leo to Virgo 3:51 p.m.) There's a high possibility that you will attract an exciting member of the opposite sex now. It may be someone who wants to make a friendship much more than that—possibly something very romantic. Even if that is not your scenario, keep your lines of communication open with others. You stand to learn something of great value. A Gemini could be involved.

Tuesday, January 28 (Moon in Virgo) A rather major change in your living arrangements could be on the horizon; and the change may be of your own doing. Be sure to talk it over with yourself before you announce your plans to everyone. Tact and discretion are essential now, if you are to maintain loving feelings and harmony with those around you. For many, it's a good time to cultivate an interest in art or music.

Wednesday, January 29 (Moon Virgo to Libra 9:10 p.m.) You may find that you are your own best company today; many will be in a situation where the people they depend on are either away or otherwise occupied. However, you needn't feel deserted or rejected. By the time evening rolls around, you probably will find yourself much less alone—and much wiser because of the insights you have gained during your temporary isolation. Your lucky number is 7.

Thursday, January 30 (Moon in Libra) Now you feel very much in command, and quite comfortable with the leadership role you may be asked to play today. Now is the time to push for what you want, and to take that big step you've been thinking about. You'll get a lot of support for your plans—especially from someone you love and who loves you very much. However, remember you're in this alone basically. A Capricorn may be very important today.

Friday, January 31 (Moon in Libra) This is no time to hide your special talents. Even something you don't feel is rather important may surface now and attract the interests of others. "Self-expression" is the word for the day, and you should be able to reach a wider audience than you have recently. All in all, you should be able to look forward to a satisfying day. The lucky number is 9.

FEBRUARY 1986

Saturday, February 1 (Moon Libra to Scorpio 1:19 a.m.) Believe it or not, you can find something you lost by putting your mind to it. Intuition is the method to use. However, in other matters of money and possessions, you will not be in a particularly practical mood now. It's important to count your change now and steer clear of bargains that seem too good to be true. They probably are. A Pisces will play a key role in the day's activities.

Sunday, February 2 (Moon in Scorpio) You may find yourself rubbing shoulders with people who can help you advance your career and fatten up your bank account. People of power and position surround you now. If you show your willingness to take on extra responsibilities, you will gain confidence where it counts. The lucky number today is 8.

Monday, February 3 (Moon Scorpio to Sagittarius 4:31 a.m.) Try to rise above the petty attitudes of those around you. Better yet, expand your sphere of interest and get to know some new people. It's possible that some may get involved with a fascinating person who can help you see things in their proper perspective. It could be a foreigner—and travel may easily be involved.

Tuesday, February 4 (Moon in Sagittarius) Some can expect romantic advances from a rather dynamic and fiery person. Realize that he/she may be more interested in being dramatic than being sincere. Others should be ready to take a chance on a rather offbeat new relationship, which may involve exposure to a whole new group of people and ideas. Take a chance! Your lucky number today is 1.

Wednesday, February 5 (Moon Sagittarius to Capricorn 7:02 a.m.) Life may slow down a bit, and you may be quite glad for the change of pace. A more relaxed view of life is probably just the ticket now. It's important not to get involved in a confrontation; you may have to go along with someone else's ideas, but it is the better way. An older person could really be on your side.

Thursday, February 6 (Moon in Capricorn) Don't get involved in more things than you can handle comfortably. Realize what you have time for and what would simply cause you a lot of anxiety later on. Tackle one thing at a time! For best results, entertain at home this evening—and make it the center of good fun and warm talk.

Friday, February 7 (Moon Capricorn to Aquarius 7:35 a.m.) You can shake off those little feelings of anxiety by attending to the routine matters that may have piled up. In some cases, it may be necessary to go back to square one and start all over again. It is worth it! A Leo or an Aquarian could be particularly helpful now. Accept their help! Your lucky number today is 4.

Saturday, February 8 (Moon in Aquarius) Some may be looking for a chance to express their very warm feelings toward a member of the opposite sex. Take the bull by the horn and do it! For others, exciting changes are in the wind—possibly including a short trip. Love of all kinds could blossom now, and you could be feeling "alive, atingle, and aglow."

Sunday, February 9 (Moon Aquarius to Pisces 11:32 a.m.) For some Librans, this could be a "dream weekend." Whether it is new love or old love that you experience, there is definitely an atmosphere of peace and poetry. Even if it's just in your own soul. Some may be involved with a comfortable Taurus or a rather emotional Scorpio.

Monday, February 10 (Moon in Pisces) This is one of those days where you get a lot more by giving than you do by expecting to take. You are the one who may have to be more understanding than those around you. For some, there could be a lot of touchiness. You could transform it into something rather artistic if you try. It's important to be content to work behind the scenes. The lucky number is 7.

Tuesday, February 11 (Moon Pisces to Aries 6:21 p.m.) Hard work is again the order of the day—and without too much in the way of emotional rewards. However, if you spot an opportunity to move ahead, go right to the top. You generally have a good attitude toward authority figures, and it will help you a great deal now. A Capricorn could be in the picture.

Wednesday, February 12 (Moon in Aries) Some Librans are breaking away from the past now, and life is taking a new direction. If your "big break" isn't that dramatic, you may find that you can insist that someone else take his/her share of the load now. It will make you feel a lot more comfortable with yourself. However, it's important to use your Libran tact to make the point.

Thursday, February 13 (Moon in Aries) This is an excellent time to play a "cat and mouse game." Someone may be after you, but all you have to do is sit back and enjoy the attention. You will lose nothing by waiting. In some cases, a Leo or an Aquarian could be the important "opposite number." The lucky number today is 1.

Friday, February 14 (Moon Aries to Taurus 5:38 a.m.) If you're feeling a bit insecure about your finances, get together with someone who really knows the ropes, and shares your interest. You would be amazed at how much you can learn in one simple budget session. Many will be feeling a particularly strong need for approval and support right now. If you reach out, you can get it.

Saturday, February 15 (Moon in Taurus) A strong element of luck or timing will put you way ahead in money matters today. Resolve to put some of that profit away. In some cases, someone may be giving you bright ideas about how to increase your income; be very discriminating about how you apply what you hear. There is a strong element of physical attraction in the atmosphere of the day. Your lucky number is 3.

Sunday, February 16 (Moon Taurus to Gemini 5:17 p.m.) It's important to catch up on important details early in the day; if you don't clear the decks, you may find yourself frustrated later on when things pick up. However, for those whose plans are blocked, utilize your gain to plot your future more carefully. Keep your eye on an Aquarian!

Monday, February 17 (Moon in Gemini) Now you should feel much less restricted, and much freer to move around. It's important to be flexible now, because plans could quickly get changed. However, you will like the changes and find them very exciting. You've got a lot to learn now by trading ideas and opinions with new people. Your lucky number is 5.

Tuesday, February 18 (Moon in Gemini) You may be called upon to play the diplomat today. A difficult situation can be solved by someone's taking on more responsibility; that someone may have to be you. The subject may be family matters and get-togethers. Do something nice for those around you today.

Wednesday, February 19 (Moon Gemini to Cancer 7:39 a.m.) You may run into a difficult professional situation, but you can easily handle it if you listen to your inner voice. Try to feel what others are feeling—it's better than sulking or feeling sorry for yourself. You will get through this just fine! Your lucky number is 7.

Thursday, February 20 (Moon in Cancer)   A strong surge of ambition puts you right in the spotlight—where those who count can see you. If you want to better your standing, show how serious you are about what you are doing, and how devoted to your duties you are. Even in matters of the heart, Librans will be preferring stability to frivolity now.

Friday, February 21 (Moon Cancer to Leo 3:25 p.m.) Don't hang on to the past just for the sake of security. It is possible to move out and still feel safe. You may run across a rather off-the-wall suggestion from a rather unusual person—look at it as an extraordinary opportunity. If you look at the big picture rather than concentrating on petty details, you will get a lot further now.

Saturday, February 22 (Moon in Leo)   Now's the time to clear the decks for action. A lot of opportunities and invitations could be coming your way; the key is to be yourself rather than simply another one of the crowd. You do have original ideas, and you should express them. In fact, for some Librans, your personal magnetism could attract an exciting romance now.

Sunday, February 23 (Moon Leo to Virgo 11:58 p.m.) You will be grateful for some R&R today. Good talk, good food, and good friends are featured. However, a love partner may want to be babied, but you should go along with it for now. Next time it will be your turn to be spoiled. The lucky number is 2.

Monday, February 24 (Moon in Virgo)   Depending on your attitude, this could be a very exciting or a very frustrating day. The full moon could bring a tug of war between your wanting to socialize and your necessity to do some quiet and lonely work. The key to getting through it all is to let go of your fears and self-doubts. If you can laugh at your own foibles, you will enjoy this day.

Tuesday, February 25 (Moon in Virgo) This is a down-to-work day where a rather confidential project or matter will demand your personal attention. It's important to be very thorough—and very fair. Don't take anything for granted, because it could cause you problems later on. If you are involved with an Aquarian, listen carefully to what he/she has to say. The lucky number is 4.

Wednesday, February 26 (Moon Virgo to Libra 4:07 a.m.) Now the moon goes into your sign, and you should feel about ten feet tall. In many cases, the reason will be love, true love. Some who have felt doubts recently will have those doubts dispelled when the other person says, "I love you." For any Libra, the message today is to get out and celebrate. Keep your schedule flexible, because you never know what can happen.

Thursday, February 27 (Moon in Libra) You may feel compelled to make some changes in your environment today—or your appearance. Looking good is very much on your mind, and very possible. Some may have been neglecting themselves in order to help others—it's time to balance out the situation. Do something nice for yourself now. Whatever it is, buy it!

Friday, February 28 (Moon Libra to Scorpio 7:06 a.m.) You may be feeling rather idealistic now. Take it out by writing a poem or making a donation—but don't make any irrevocable business moves. Wait until tomorrow to start on a new project. Your lucky number today is 7.

MARCH 1986

Saturday, March 1 (Moon in Scorpio) It's a good day to pay debts and to try and figure out how to get more money. There are ways if you put your mind to it. The key is to be enterprising and to get the help of someone who has the clout to put your ideas into action In many ways, this could be a power play—for both money and an improved personal position. The lucky number is 8.

Sunday, March 2 (Moon Scorpio to Sagittarius 9:51 p.m.) Now's the time to take stock of your possessions and clear out stuff you no longer need. If you get rid of all kinds of clutter in your life, you will find yourself much freer from the past. Someone—possibly an Aries—may be pushing you into the future. He/she is right to do so.

Monday, March 3 (Moon in Sagittarius) The accent is on new ideas and dramatic ways to present them to other people. Don't be afraid to be a bit different, and to be more forceful in the way you express yourself. For some Librans, an encounter with a dynamic member of the opposite sex is on the agenda. It could lead to something very romantic. Your lucky number is 1.

Tuesday, March 4 (Moon Sagittarius to Capricorn 12:56 p.m.) You may be feeling a bit moody now, and your wisest course is to avoid any kind of encounter that could affect you. Your feelings are rather sensitive, so don't put them in the way of anything that could cause hurt. Don't worry about simply following other people's lead today. We all have days like this. In most cases, an older person or a loving family member will be there to support you.

Wednesday, March 5 (Moon in Capricorn) The storm clouds seem to disappear today, and you should be a lot sunnier and a lot more ready for adventure. It's the kind of day when even if you don't go to other people, they will come to you. Isn't it nice to be popular? A Sagittarian could be very influential in the day's activities.

Thursday, March 6 (Moon Capricorn to Aquarius 4:42 p.m.) Many Librans will find this an excellent time to think about rebuilding and restructuring lives. Even if your scenario does not include anything so major, you may want to make some changes in your immediate environment. Try to pay a lot of attention to the small details, because they are always the ones that count. It would be wise to think about security measures too in order to provide a more solid home base.

Friday, March 7 (Moon in Aquarius) Now's the time for a playful approach to life—it's the best and fastest way to attract love and romance, or simply some exciting entertainment. No matter how shy you may be, today's the day you can express yourself with a lot of feeling and creativity. Someone who talks fast and thinks fast has some answers you've been seeking. Listen carefully!

Saturday, March 8 (Moon Aquarius to Pisces 7:48 p.m.) You may have to go out of your way to be gracious today, and to accept someone else's point of view. It may not be what you really want to do, but it is the only way to create peace and harmony. Some Librans can expect an emotional encounter of the opposite sex—and it may not be all moonlight and roses. Be willing to compromise, but insist on your own rights too.

Sunday, March 9 (Moon in Pisces) Some Librans may be feeling a bit washed out now. It's time to spend some time on your health and vitality. In addition to exercise, a little self-analysis could go a long way and help you erase some doubts and fears you have. Look deep into yourself—and perhaps talk it over with a Pisces or a Virgo.

Monday, March 10 (Moon in Pisces) You may be going in a slightly new direction, particularly in your job sphere. In the long run it is a lot more profitable, though it may not seem that way now. Well-considered moves or changes are always better than spur-of-the-moment decisions. That is particularly important now. Your lucky number is 8.

Tuesday, March 11 (Moon Pisces to Aries 5:03 a.m.) You may be a bit puzzled about a current relationship, but you've got to understand it in larger terms. Instead of feeling hurt or rejected, consider where you have been dwelling on the petty differences rather than the large pluses of the relationship. Perhaps the best course is to play a waiting game now. Your lucky number is 9.

Wednesday, March 12 (Moon in Aries) Many are ready to make a new start in a relationship or partnership. However, it's important not to appear too aggressive or to take too bossy an attitude. In fact, your best course might be to let the other person make the first move. You are rather good at that anyway. Your current charisma could attract a lot of other people to you.

Thursday, March 13 (Moon Aries to Taurus 3:04 p.m.) You may need to call on an expert to help you arrange your spending and money management now. Conservative measures are the best now, and you will feel more secure if you know there's enough there for a rainy day. Your emotional needs are very much related to your financial needs. A Capricorn or a Cancer could play a key role.

Friday, March 14 (Moon in Taurus) This is not nearly as heavy a day as yesterday. In fact, you will probably want to spend money, whether you have it or not! It's okay to be a bit extravagant but don't get totally carried away—particularly by someone who constantly wears rose-colored glasses about the future. Travel may very much be a possibility.

Saturday, March 15 (Moon in Taurus) Back to the drawing board today, and to practical matters. It's an excellent time to put your accounts in order and pay some old bills. However, keep your eyes on the fine print, because someone's addition or subtraction may not be completely accurate. The lucky number today is 4.

Sunday, March 16 (Moon Taurus to Gemini 3:23 a.m.) What you need today is a change of scenery and some stimulating companionship. It should be easy to come by! In fact, a short but marvelous trip could be just the ticket. Be sure to take a camera along, because you will want to share things with others later.

Monday, March 17 (Moon in Gemini) Somebody around you has his/her nose out of joint. You are going to have to be very patient and diplomatic and take a long-range view of the situation. The real problem is that your basic philosophy of life is at odds with the other person's. One of you is going to have to adjust.

Tuesday, March 18 (Moon Gemini to Cancer 4:04 p.m.) If you could, you probably would like to get away to a desert island and hibernate now. Unfortunately, that may not be quite practical. However, do try to get some privacy if you can. There may be an important decision to make—possibly about your career—and you should be sure your head is very clear. Your lucky number is 7.

Wednesday, March 19 (Moon in Cancer) Trends are definitely moving in your favor now—both in money and in love. In fact, some may find themselves in a position of greater power or influence. Your past efforts are paying off now, and you should be proud of yourself. A Capricorn or a Cancer can understand exactly how you feel.

Thursday, March 20 (Moon in Cancer) It's time to think big—and to move in big circles. If you can, confer with top people in your field who really know what they are doing. One in particular may have aggressive ideas for your future. A lot of Librans should be willing to say good-bye to one phase of their lives and move on to another. The lucky number today is 9.

Friday, March 21 (Moon Cancer to Leo 2:38 a.m.) Some of you have been putting in a lot of time lately, and now your attention to business begins to pay off. One way it pays off is in more time for social life and self-expression. For some, a new friend enters the scene, and may seem to be the answer to a prayer. Make sure your romantic dreams have some basis in reality. Your lucky number is 1.

Saturday, March 22 (Moon in Leo) It should be a nice feeling to become a dependent again, when someone—possibly a parent—allows you to slip back into that role. Simply enjoy it and relax. Many will be catching up with family affairs and gathering with people they have not seen in a long time. Keep your intuition on alert, because it is particularly good right now.

Sunday, March 23 (Moon Leo to Virgo 9:39 a.m.) You may have to make up your mind to be cheerful today. There's a high possibility that you could react in an overly sensitive manner to what you see as a slight. A key to handling yourself is to hold on tight to your self-confidence. If you keep smiling through your tears, you will help someone else who is less fortunate than yourself and has more reason to be upset. You can be a real inspiration!

Monday, March 24 (Moon in Virgo) Keep your eyes sharp and read between the lines today. You could easily miss something. You may also have to find some imaginative ways to overcome some obstacles. A stable solid approach is needed now, and you are up to it. Routine details may occupy most of this day. Your lucky number is 4.

Tuesday, March 25 (Moon Virgo to Libra 1:22 p.m.) Something could come out of the blue and upset the balance between you and a partner today. Don't let the incident get out of proportion—and be willing to kiss and make up. The cause for tension could be a secret that inadvertently gets out of the bag. A Gemini or a Virgo could be involved.

Wednesday, March 26 (Moon in Libra) Like magic, the air clears. You can make the first move today, and be quite sure of getting what you want. Your intuition is correct, particularly about an affair of the heart. If you are into any kind of artistic expression, today's the day to pull out all the stops. You should look as great as you feel, too.

Thursday, March 27 (Moon Libra to Scorpio 3:05 p.m.) If you wish to, you can have an aura of mystery today. However, you could also feel rather alone, even in the midst of a crowd. Don't try to buy your way into someone else's favor; you are better off going your own way than using such tactics. A Pisces may be very important in the picture today.

Friday, March 28 (Moon in Scorpio) If you think it's time for a raise, ask for it today. If you have in mind buying or selling anything, today you can do it with profit. In some cases, a promotion on the job is a high possibility. Don't fight it when someone wants you to move up. Show you mean business and are able to accept responsibility.

Saturday, March 29 (Moon Scorpio to Sagittarius 4:20 p.m.) This is a day to get rid of excess baggage, in every sense of the word. The more you clear your path, the farther you can go. Don't get involved with anyone who has a limited point of view; your own horizons are getting a lot wider and you should mix and mingle only with those who inspire you. Your lucky number is 9.

Sunday, March 30 (Moon in Sagittarius) Some Librans will be a lot more bold than they usually are today. Good for you! Express your own opinions, and do not feel you have to defer to anyone else's. A lot of activity is indicated around you today, and for some a love affair could easily be heating up. No matter where you move today, you carry with you a lot of new ideas and excitement.

Monday, March 31 (Moon Sagittarius to Capricorn 6:25 p.m.) If you take a back seat to anyone else today, you will be doing it because you are rather secure in your own private world. And because you know someone is standing firmly behind you. For some Librans, a hunch could easily pay off. Don't fight it. If you have any creative talents at all, you can use them to great advantage now.

APRIL 1986

Tuesday, April 1 (Moon in Capricorn) Don't get hung up on the past; cut those ties now. If someone is moving out of your circle, realize that it is a positive step, and do not attempt to hold him/her back. Opportunities are all around you if only you will open your eyes to them. An Aries could be extremely helpful in letting you see new possibilities.

Wednesday, April 2 (Moon Capricorn to Aquarius 10:11 p.m.) Now's the time to begin that new project you've only been dreaming about till now. You should be full of inventive and creative ideas, and should not let fears about paying the rent or pleasing your critics hold you back. Someone—possibly a Leo—has the kind of flair you would like to have. Use him/her as a role model. And try your luck with number 1.

Thursday, April 3 (Moon in Aquarius) You should be particularly sensitive to the feelings of others now—including a love partner or younger family members. If you sense that they need you, take the time to show them how much you really care. Sometimes people aren't really sure of your warmth and affection because you seem to be such a "cool" character. Don't force any issues now.

Friday, April 4 (Moon in Aquarius) The accent is on parties and popularity. Some may even be traveling a bit to reach a special kind of entertainment. All should be able to light up their surroundings with good cheer, optimism, and sparkling wit. Many will find an opposite number in the form of a mentally bright person who shares your interest in new adventures. The lucky number is 3.

Saturday, April 5 (Moon Aquarius to Pisces 4:03 a.m.) Though it may not make you jump for joy, you've got to realize today that chores have piled up and need your immediate attention. Keep a steady pace and try to deal with the little things first and you will cut down a lot on the time you have to spend. By the end of the day you'll feel a lot of satisfaction—and have both the time and the desire to play a little. Maybe a lot. Enjoy!

Sunday, April 6 (Moon in Pisces) This could be a very healthy weekend, in every sense of the word. Many will be giving a lot of time and thought to the shape and state of their body and overall image. Others will feel that a change of scenery or greater physical activity may be just what the doctor ordered to get in top shape. It's possible someone may pitch in and help you today—and prove to be more than just a "buddy," in fact, a romantic interest as well.

Monday, April 7 (Moon Pisces to Aries 12:12 p.m.) Call on your inner Libra resources to play the "master diplomat" today. That means you should listen rather than talk and show people that you're interested in the good of all rather than just your own personal glory. You are up to it! For others, artistic and musical skills are accented, and should be acted on. Another Libra may be prominent in the picture.

Tuesday, April 8 (Moon in Aries) Some Librans may be in the frustrating position of being attracted to someone who is at once glamorous and unattainable. Ask yourself, "How well do I really know the person behind the mask?" Could it be that you are merely in love with love? It's an important question and possibly one that could save you a lot of heartache later on. The lucky number is 7.

Wednesday, April 9 (Moon Aries to Taurus 10:36 p.m.) Relationships of all kinds are highlighted today, and that includes your marital status. It could be that you're feeling a bit more serious and practical about love—and about love in general. It's important to follow that urge to make stronger commitments; for those whose modus operandi has been the "one-night stand," it may become clear that that just doesn't work anymore. A Capricorn may be in the picture.

Thursday, April 10 (Moon in Taurus) A change of mood may come over you, and a change of the focus of your interest. Now it is likely to be on money in all of its forms—including taxes, loans, and bills that need to be paid. Make yourself feel more comfortable by clearing up those financial obligations. However, take care not to get involved with or cosign for someone who asks you to take on a burden that is not really yours. The lucky number is 9.

Friday, April 11 (Moon in Taurus) For many, a love affair that's gotten a bit low-key may suddenly get a lot brighter as your own renewed vitality adds fuel to the fire. For others, there may be a surge of individuality and an actual physical "new look." You may find people commenting on it. Enjoy the compliments. A Leo or an Aquarian might add a lot to your day.

Saturday, April 12 (Moon Taurus to Gemini 10:51 a.m.) Get a necessary obligation out of the way early in the day—possibly a domestic project. Then spend some time on yourself and your own interests, possibly expanding them to include travel thoughts. For some, there will be a lot of nostalgia, and you may be feeling particularly sentimental. You may find yourself looking into family roots. Be sure to follow your intuitive hunches. The lucky number is 2.

Sunday, April 13 (Moon in Gemini) The proverbial fascinating stranger could really enter your life now, and help you break free of an emotional rut you've been in. Any Libra can expect to be socializing a lot more now, and meeting more new people. It is important to grab every opportunity to learn and to expand your consciousness could be the one to help you stimulate your mind.

Monday, April 14 (Moon Gemini to Cancer 11:42 p.m.) It will become obvious that a more practical approach is necessary now. What you've got to do is collect all the new facts that have been presented to you, and put them in some logical order. You must also be willing to revise your opinions so that they are more workable. Be on guard and read all the fine print. Take nothing for granted. Your lucky number is 4.

Tuesday, April 15 (Moon in Cancer) Even if you don't feel you are ready for it, you will find that you are in the spotlight now. This applies particularly to Libras who are in high visibility jobs. However, for anyone it will be easy to break free of limiting conditions, and to express yourself with greater ease to those who can help you a lot. The key thing is to remain flexible.

Wednesday, April 16 (Moon in Cancer) Good for you! You are taking a more relaxed attitude toward your ambitions, and realizing the importance of creating greater harmony in your work situation. It is possible to combine business and pleasure, and that could be particularly pleasurable now. Some may actually comment on the fact that you are loosening up. The lucky number is 6.

Thursday, April 17 (Moon Cancer to Libra 11:10 a.m.) This is not a good day to make a big decision or to take a big step in any direction. Your wisest course is to talk things over with a sympathetic friend who knows your hopes and dreams. If possible, stay away from social situations that are draining and could make you feel rather wiped out later on. Your lucky number today is 7.

Friday, April 18 (Moon in Leo) Okay, now's the time to stop talking and start acting. Now's the time you can translate your dreams into reality by displaying how much of a leader you can be. And how responsible you are willing to be. In other matters, show your loved ones that you mean business too and are willing to make strong commitments to the future. A Capricorn could be a godsend today.

Saturday, April 19 (Moon Leo to Virgo 7:24 p.m.) Today you may meet someone who will give you a lot of inspiration about what you can do in the future to make your life a lot more stimulating and rewarding. You may be a bit jealous, because this person seems to be a creative pioneer in a new field of action. Realize that it could include you. Later on, you might try to do something worthy or spend some time on a good cause.

Sunday, April 20 (Moon in Virgo) You don't just have to go along with the crowd to be popular now; as a matter of fact, you'll win more points by taking a firm and independent position. Your own personal magnetism can help you sell your ideas, because you are very much in the mood to show just how much of an individual you can be. A Leo may be very much in the picture today.

Monday, April 21 (Moon Virgo to Libra 11:50 p.m.) Yesterday's activities may have taken a lot out of you, so if possible, take some time out to catch up with yourself now. The best thing is to work behind the scenes with people who are in sync with you and attuned to your needs. However, keep your ears open, because an important secret may be entrusted to you today. Keep it! Your lucky number is 2.

Tuesday, April 22 (Moon in Libra) The moon in your sign should encourage you to take off in a new direction today. You will find that direction by following a hunch that comes to you out of the blue. You should be full of a lot of enthusiasm and be able to spread cheer wherever you go; it will help you push right through some doors that have been closed to you up to now. However, don't exhaust yourself by not knowing when to stop.

Wednesday, April 23 (Moon in Libra) You should be feeling great, but it should inspire you to feel even greater. That means, resolve to pay some attention to your general health and nutrition. You've got the self-discipline now to put new programs into action. It's easy for you to avoid extremes and to deal with things in a sensible balanced manner.

Thursday, April 24 (Moon Libra to Scorpio 1:15 a.m.) This month's full moon falls smack in that area of your chart having to do with money and financial affairs. You are particularly receptive to new ideas, so listen to some you hear, but don't act on them right now. It's important not to spend any money until you've carefully thought it out. The lucky number today is 5.

Friday, April 25 (Moon in Scorpio) Today you may focus in on where you want to spend a little cash right now. For many, it is likely to be in home improvement. Whatever you invest now, whether it be time, money, or talent, you will make things a lot more livable and harmonious. Trust your good taste now. And trust the fact that you will make someone you love happier and will be improving the potential of the relationship. The lucky number today is 6.

Saturday, April 26 (Moon Scorpio to Sagittarius 1:16 a.m.) Steer clear of people who use tricky language now or try to give you a sales message. You may be rather susceptible. In addition, there is an aura of confusion around phone calls and conversations today. No matter how simple they may seem. Be sure to get all agreements in writing and ask for a guarantee. A very subtle Pisces could be in the picture.

Sunday, April 27 (Moon in Sagittarius) For some, a romantic involvement is deepening, and could be heading for a long-term commitment. Some singles can actually expect or expect to give a proposal of marriage. Those who are already married may be considering deepening their own commitment by an addition to the family. All in all it is a rather serious but upbeat day. The lucky number is 8.

Monday, April 28 (Moon Sagittarius to Capricorn 1:51 a.m.) It is essential to tie up some loose ends now, maybe of a property deal or family project. Try to rise above petty issues and nasty little arguments to see the big picture. It's all in the interest of your long-term security. For others, this is not time to cling to the past or to narrow viewpoints. If you clear and widen your vision, there is no limit to where you can go.

Tuesday, April 29 (Moon in Capricorn) You may start out the day with a curious feeling that you want to be noticed today—and you may even decide to dress the part. In business, it is definitely a chance to get in on the ground floor of a new project. Put yourself right out front. Later on, entertain at home for best results. Love and romance could be thriving now.

Wednesday, April 30 (Moon Capricorn to Aquarius 4:06 a.m.) It is important not to force an issue today, particularly in a romantic matter. If you give it a low-key approach you give yourself the best chance of getting what you want. Many will be feeling extra sensitive today, and positively intuitive—particularly to figuring out what someone is going to say or do next. Use the ability to your advantage. The lucky number today is 2.

MAY 1986

Thursday, May 1 (Moon in Aquarius) What a great day to begin something new! It could be a project or a romance—or possibly even a creative breakthrough. Whatever you do, try to formulate an original way of packaging a familiar idea. You may have to take a chance, but it will be worth it. All Librans should strive to imprint their own style on whatever they do today. The lucky number is 1.

Friday, May 2 (Moon Aquarius to Pisces 9:30 a.m.) You may feel like going on a sentimental journey today. Your emotions will be running high and nostalgia may threaten to overwhelm you. Take out your tender feelings by nurturing someone else today, possibly in a romantic way. For some, an old flame could be rekindled. For others, a current love affair could take on a more possessive nature.

Saturday, May 3 (Moon in Pisces) You may find it rather difficult to settle down to your necessary chores today. Your urge to travel and to extend your horizon is at war with your obligations. You can reach a compromise, particularly if you maintain a light touch and a sense of humor. Team up with a Sagittarian for best and most enjoyable results.

Sunday, May 4 (Moon Pisces to Aries 8:01 p.m.) You should find it a lot easier to be practical today, and to realize that there are some solid base-building chores to be done. If you stick to a steady pace and pay a lot of attention to little details, you'll be surprised how much progress you can make by the end of the day. For some, it is important to learn the rules before you decide to break them. Your lucky number is 4.

Monday, May 5 (Moon in Aries) You may feel as if the ball is in someone else's court today, and, judging by the phase of the moon, it is. For some, it will be the marriage partner who has the upper hand. Try to reach a closer understanding with whoever shares your concerns, and be willing to take a more passive role now. You don't always have to make all the major decisions. For others, an unexpected change of scenery will be very welcome.

Tuesday, May 6 (Moon in Aries) Be willing to listen to someone else's problems today, and lend a shoulder to be "cried on." In many cases, a domestic situation has arisen that threatens to cause some waves. You can harmonize things if you indicate you are willing to carry more of the load. Some should put their artistic talents to work to beautify surroundings for everyone; it will make a lot of difference. The lucky number is 6.

Wednesday, May 7 (Moon Aries to Taurus 4:59 a.m.) It is possible that you currently have an unrealistic attitude about money. It is important to see everything clearly, and that includes your financial situation as well as other people. There really is no such thing as a bargain or getting something for nothing. Realize that what looks like an excellent opportunity could easily boomerang. Let someone else advise you, possibly a practical Virgo.

Thursday, May 8 (Moon in Taurus) You may be feeling very much in the mood for self-pampering today. There are lots of ways to make yourself feel good without going overboard. For many, a relationship will be getting more stable and more serious at the same time; it could even go in a new direction. Both money and love are well favored today, so make the most of both of them. Your lucky number is 8.

Friday, May 9 (Moon Taurus to Gemini 5:26 p.m.) Get some kind of financial transaction early in the day, and put it behind you. You are ready for new things, and should look beyond purely current matters and take an active interest in a larger world. Sometimes you tend to get too personal. Associate with people whose eyes are firmly focused on the future and not on their own navels.

Saturday, May 10 (Moon in Gemini) Your personal magnetism is particularly high today, and you can assert your individuality with ease. Some will be mingling and mixing with people from very different backgrounds, and it could be very inspiring in terms of long-range plans. Possibly even travel. Don't be afraid to be a little controversial now, you can handle it.

Sunday, May 11 (Moon in Gemini) A touchy subject may arise today, having to do with someone's religion or philosophy. It's important to be diplomatic in these matters. And you will gain much through taking a passive role and giving tactful answers to key questions. Some Librans will find that people at a distance—possibly relatives—suddenly enter the picture and change current plans. Your lucky number is 2.

Monday, May 12 (Moon Gemini to Cancer 7:18 a.m.) Working Librans start out the week on new career vistas. Some will have the opportunity to socialize with the right people now, and promote their pet ideas. Others will find themselves breaking out of an emotional rut and looking for a broader scope to show their talents. A Sagittarian or a Gemini could be eminently important now.

Tuesday, May 13 (Moon in Cancer) A very challenging assignment could be tossed in your lap today, and you should be ready to deal with it. It gives you the self to prove yourself and to make such a good showing that you can advance quickly. Others are going to have to pay attention to the rules today; if you overlook the details, you will muff the chance to do a really good job. Read all the fine print and make sure there is nothing there that can trip you up.

Wednesday, May 14 (Moon Cancer to Leo 6:15 p.m.) It looks like a fast-paced day. Be ready to keep up with events as they happen. Some Librans will be making a new and good friend—possibly on the job. Others could have what amounts to a romantic adventure. What happens after this is up to you. If a last-minute invitation comes along, grab it. Your lucky number is 5.

Thursday, May 15 (Moon in Leo) This can be a happy and fulfilling day if you don't let yourself get distracted by too many things. Concentrate on something where you can use your peacemaking abilities—or your considerable artistic talents. For some, that means decorating, cooking a good meal, or proving to those who live under your roof that harmony is possible. A Taurus or a Scorpio could play a key role, and could try your patience.

Friday, May 16 (Moon in Leo) Someone may try to hand you the proverbial line today, but if the offer appears too good to be true, you should recognize it as such. Some Scorpios should be on the alert for someone who may try to play upon your hopes and fears in order to get what they want. Others should be aware that some romantic ideas are just fantasy and just pure illusion. Don't worry, the real thing will come along.

Saturday, May 17 (Moon Leo to Virgo 3:45 a.m.) You could get a real sense of power today by manipulating events from behind the scenes; don't get carried away. You don't have to stoop to tactics you do not approve of, because only your self-doubts are holding you back now. You have real clout where you need it. A Capricorn could prove that to you. Your lucky number is 8.

Sunday, May 18 (Moon in Virgo) Take a good look at your current situation and see where you can help others as well as yourself. However, you should draw the line at helping someone who is merely using you as a crutch and not learning to walk alone. Your interference, no matter how well-intentioned, could be counterproductive. An Aries person is very in the picture, and very much a delight.

Monday, May 19 (Moon Virgo to Libra 9:41 a.m.) If you start out the day with a few little nagging doubts, they will quickly disappear and you will be able to plunge into a new phase of vigorous activity. As the moon moves into your sign, you go into "lunar high," and there is little that can hold you back. Some can expect a rather surprising approach from a member of the opposite sex; others should prepare to follow a strong hunch which could lead to excellent things. Your lucky number is 1.

Tuesday, May 20 (Moon in Libra) Be careful today because you could easily overindulge in something. The reason will be emotional insecurity, and the feeling that others are out to get you. Realize that such thoughts are ridiculous, and if necessary, seek out someone you know is on your side, and who can allay your fears. For many, home and family will be so demanding that you will not have time for such self-indulgent worrying.

Wednesday, May 21 (Moon Libra to Scorpio 12:02 p.m.) This is one of those days you may look in the mirror and decide it's time for a change. Your sense of style is very strong today, and it could lead you to change your image in some way—possibly with a new hairstyle or new clothes. In some cases, the motivation will be a party or other social event where you will be very much on display. The lucky number today is 3.

Thursday, May 22 (Moon in Scorpio) A more practical, self-disciplined mood takes over today; you may be able to clear up some debts and even be eager to put your books in order. With the emphasis on money and earnings, you may be taking a hard look at what you own and how those things can be improved. In fact, things could look a bit "shoddy" to Librans today. Good—because it will give you the impetus to do something about it.

Friday, May 23 (Moon Scorpio to Sagittarius 11:57 a.m.) During this full moon, you could easily get involved in a heated discussion of finances and spending patterns. There is definitely tension in the air over your rights versus the rights of others. An intelligent discussion is the key to putting it all into perspective. A Gemini or a Virgo could easily be involved, and you will have to do some tiptoeing around some sensitive subjects.

Saturday, May 24 (Moon in Sagittarius) Some adjustments in your life-style are definitely in order, and it is possible that you know it. In the interest of greater peace and quiet, you may have to talk with those around you about going along with new ways of doing things. Others may be entertaining at home and very much flustered about how to make things as attractive as possible. The lucky number is 6.

Sunday, May 25 (Moon Sagittarius to Capricorn 11:15 a.m.) You will be in a very giving mood today, but don't make promises you can't keep. You do want to keep up communication with someone at a distance, but realize that there are limitations to what you can do. It is important to be inspiring to others now rather than to feel sorry for yourself. A Pisces is in the picture and may tell you so.

Monday, May 26 (Moon in Capricorn) Don't be afraid to use some important connections to advance yourself on the job or to find a new job. Everybody does it! In fact, someone who knows you well is willing to give a glowing recommendation and may give it without your asking. This can be a power-packed day if you stick to the basics and remember there are fundamental things to be done. Your lucky number is 8.

Tuesday, May 27 (Moon Capricorn to Aquarius 12:00 noon) See the big picture rather than taking a limited viewpoint now. It's important and it's time to cut loose from limiting conditions and to associate yourself with people who are looking and moving forward. Some will be completing a major project and getting ready to plunge into new and demanding work. Your best partner today is another Libra.

Wednesday, May 28 (Moon in Aquarius) This is one of those times you should not hesitate to be selfish—particularly about your romantic needs. You have been doing a lot of giving and have done without much getting. Most Librans will be in the mood for attention and affection now, as well as some just plain luxurious entertainment. Don't be afraid to make bold changes, and begin building for the future. A fiery, dynamic individual could help you more than you imagine.

Thursday, May 29 (Moon Aquarius to Pisces 3:54 p.m.) If at all possible, allow yourself the luxury of being a bit lazy today. Simply slow down the pace, and enjoy food, rest, and recreation. For some, the slow pace of events may be a bit frustrating, but realize that you will gain in the long run. The lucky number today is 2.

Friday, May 30 (Moon in Pisces) You would be amazed what a bright cheerful attitude can do to improve your immediate evironment—particularly on the job. Your sociable talents will come in handy, as long as you don't use them in mere time-wasting activities. A Gemini could be a really good buddy today.

Saturday, May 31 (Moon Pisces to Aries 11:43 p.m.) You are going to be rather bogged down in practical matters around the house today. Be content to tend your own garden rather than to look for larger worlds to conquer. Your greatest satisfaction will come from basic routine tasks—and the congratulations you get for performing them well. The lucky number today is 4.

JUNE 1986

Sunday, June 1 (Moon in Aries) You'll make a better follower than a leader today. Satisfy yourself by sitting back and letting others worry about what's got to be done—and not done. For your part, enjoy rest, good food, and pleasant exercise. In some cases, you will be reminiscing about the past with someone who just loves your sentimental approach to memories. All in all, it should be an extremely pleasant day.

Monday, June 2 (Moon in Aries) You're in a great mood to meet the public today and also to deal with their problems. You win yourself a number of points today by being extremely helpful, and someone who is new to the area will be taking a liking to you. He/she wants to share your experiences, and you should be willing to do so. The lucky number today is 3.

Tuesday, June 3 (Moon Aries to Taurus 10:45 a.m.) The most constructive thing you can do today is get together with someone who shares your finances and discuss them from a practical point of view. If all goes well, it will be a mutually beneficial session, and you could even be instrumental in helping to solve a financial problem that has been bugging both of you up to now. Be willing to go back to the beginning and review things, and possibly rebuild on a whole new foundation.

Wednesday, June 4 (Moon in Taurus) Some Librans will be finding that a love affair is intensifying now. All should be in the mood for sensually satisfying experiences. A period of surprises and a change of scenery is beginning now; get ready for it! Someone you are very in tune with almost seems to have ESP as far as you are concerned. Your lucky number today is 5.

Thursday, June 5 (Moon Taurus to Gemini 11:26 p.m.) You are going to be called upon to relieve the worries of others around you. Concentrate on that in order to bring everyone back together in harmony. You may have to agree to cut your own spending on nonessential items in order to get someone else thinking what he/she wants. It is worth it.

Friday, June 6 (Moon in Gemini) This is one of those wistful days when you may feel that the grass is really greener in someone's else's location—but realize this is merely wishful thinking. You can't escape your own problems by simply running away from them. However, try to get away from the crowd and know yourself better. It will help a lot.

Saturday, June 7 (Moon in Gemini) If you're feeling stuck in a rut, consider some further training that will help you advance on the job. If you share your plans with someone higher up, the money might be forthcoming—plus a vote of confidence. For all Librans, this is a great time to think about higher learning, more travel, or the future in general. The lucky number is 8.

Sunday, June 8 (Moon Gemini to Cancer 12:16 p.m.) Don't be afraid to dream some dreams now. If you hold yourself back, by limiting yourself to the way things have been, you will not be ready for the way they could be. Put an end to indecision now, and make it a point to get on with things. A pioneering individual may be very impatient to get started with you.

Monday, June 9 (Moon in Cancer) One good idea is all you need to get started. Especially if you have the courage to go your own way and not simply be a member of the crowd. The originality that you show now can put you right in the spotlight; don't be afraid to show how independent you can be. Romance is on the agenda for some.

Tuesday, June 10 (Moon in Cancer) Many Librans are going to have to take the needs of older people into consideration now. Or others who depend on you. You may have to curtail yourself a bit recently, but remember that you have made some constructive gains. Meanwhile, you are going to have to reassure others who have had some doubts about your affections. Be as warm and loving as you can be. Your lucky number is 2.

Wednesday, June 11 (Moon Cancer to Leo 12:11 a.m.) You can really shine today—both socially and on the job. Some may find that there are too many invitations and that you can't accept them all. Enjoy yourself, but don't take on more than you can handle. It could leave your nerves a little on the frazzled side. A Sagittarian could be a boon companion. Your lucky number is 3.

Thursday, June 12 (Moon in Leo) The role you play today may not be a particularly glamorous one, but it should bring you great satisfaction in the long run. You have the chance to prove just how necessary you are to a group or organization. While you attend to routine goodies, you can think positively about playing later. Dreams only become practical realities through hard work.

Friday, June 13 (Moon Leo to Virgo 10:18 a.m.) What a relief! You are off and running again as an exciting change of pace is on the agenda. You'll be exchanging ideas and mixing and mingling with a lot of different types. For some, romance could easily be part of the scenario. The way you will recognize that special person is by keeping your eye out for the one whose mind stimulates your own. The lucky number is 5.

Saturday, June 14 (Moon in Virgo) You may feel like simply hiding away today—possibly with those you love most. For some, it could be a very romantic seclusion. For others, home may be a kind of refuge from the world—which is a bit too much with you right now. Take some time out to listen to the problems of someone who needs proof of your affection.

Sunday, June 15 (Moon Virgo to Libra 5:38 p.m.) Once again, the accent is on staying under wraps and behind the scenes. If you have to demand it, be sure to get the privacy you need to think your own thoughts and refresh yourself. For many, it should be combined with some contact with nature. Consider yourself on a "mini-vacation." Your lucky number is 7.

Monday, June 16 (Moon in Libra) Now you bounce back into the practical world and find yourself very much in command. With the moon in your sign, you are able to grab the reins and run things quite easily. It's exactly the right day to make that knee-high first move you've been thinking about on your job. Watch out for Capricorn however.

Tuesday, June 17 (Moon Libra to Scorpio 9:36 p.m.) Many will be faced with an important personal decision. You may be torn between the past and the future, and be wondering whether it's time to cut some close ties. The way to decide is to say you are only going to give yourself the best. Talk it over with an Aries who has some good ideas about what you need. The lucky number is 9.

Wednesday, June 18 (Moon in Scorpio) If you concentrated on positive thinking yesterday, new opportunities are there today. For some, they will be financial and there will be the chance to gain through some rather innovative thinking. Don't hesitate to be bold; a rather dynamic person is ready to be generous.

Thursday, June 19 (Moon Scorpio to Sagittarius 10:36 p.m.) You may pull back and be a bit more cautious today—particularly in a financial area. You may be giving a lot more weight to your future in terms of your savings and your security. However, you should not hesitate to follow through on a hunch—possibly about real estate—which could bring in some additional income. A Cancer is a wonderful person to counsel you in this regard.

Friday, June 20 (Moon in Sagittarius) Though you probably can think of a million wonderful things you would like to do, you must take care not to overdo now. You very much want to make life a lot more interesting and expansive for a lot of people, but you could short-change yourself in the long run, by running out of nervous energy. The lucky number today is 3.

Saturday, June 21 (Moon Sagittarius to Capricorn 10:00 p.m.) If you've made some plans for the day, be sure to check them before you start out. The full moon could cause you some difficulties in communication, though they are not likely to be serious ones. In all matters of accuracy, don't take anything for granted. Stick to a basic routine if possible, in spite of a temptation to break free from restrictions.

Sunday, June 22 (Moon in Capricorn) This weekend you can stay right at home and find some interesting and exciting things coming to you. For some, this could be a fast-talking member of the opposite sex with romance on his/her mind. There are some great ideas this person wants to share, and you should welcome him/her with open arms. Literally. Your lucky number is 5.

Monday, June 23 (Moon Capricorn to Aquarius 9:50 p.m.) You are going to need all the tact and diplomacy you can muster to smooth the waters today. There appear to be a number of divergent opinions in the atmosphere—possibly at your own base of operations. A gift could work wonders to bring everybody back to one point of view.

Tuesday, June 24 (Moon in Aquarius) You may be feeling very much in the mood to escape, but be sure you do it through some reasonably safe "escape route." You could easily be attracted by things that are not the best for you. Some may realize they have been expecting too much of another person and should be prepared to be compassionate.

Wednesday, June 25 (Moon in Aquarius) Someone who is right there under your nose turns out to be a stepping stone to success. It may be that he/she is willing to back you financially—or at least emotionally—in a potentially very lucrative new product or job opportunity. Make use of all the opportunities to come your way today. Your lucky number is 8.

Thursday, June 26 (Moon Aquarius to Pisces 12:12 a.m.) Two main issues dominate the day: work and health. You may find it obvious that you've got to keep your resolutions about diet, nutrition, and exercise. Many are looking at a time when their lives are going to take a demanding new direction, and perfect health is essential to your future success. Work it off with an energetic Aries.

Friday, June 27 (Moon in Pisces) You get a lot of positive feedback from co-workers today who now seem to recognize that you are really a leader. Keep on showing them what you can do by bringing a new approach to the job at hand. You will impress a superior as well, and you'll have more fun doing what you have to do. Your lucky number is 1 today.

Saturday, June 28 (Moon Pisces to Aries 6:35 a.m.) Now you're going to have to call for a time-out to catch up on personal matters. It is essential to give your mate or partner your full attention and let other people worry about other things. Let the major decisions be made by your opposite number, while you offer comfort and support. Human relations are all important today.

Sunday, June 29 (Moon in Aries) Whatever you do today will be more fun if you do it in tandem with someone you love. You should be full of wit and good humor today and make a good companion. However, do not try to be everywhere at one time. Slow down and take one thing at a time. A Sagittarian could easily lead you astray.

Monday, June 30 (Moon Aries to Taurus 4:54 p.m.) Now you will be willing to settle down to a more routine existence. As a matter of fact, you should be able to make a very positive showing with someone who has common interests with you. This applies particularly to a financial decision that must be made later in the day. Your lucky number is 4.

JULY 1986

Tuesday, July 1 (Moon in Taurus) You may be full of big ideas today, but don't go too far and overreach yourself. Your extravagant instincts are going to have to be curbed, and you should really rely on someone else to take care of money now. It's nice to be full of enthusiasm, but it's even nicer to be solid financially.

Wednesday, July 2 (Moon in Taurus) Stick to the tried and true in both money and love. What's most important now is to build a bank account with conservative spending rather than flamboyant extravagance. If you feel a bit limited, realize that it will not be for long. You will gain true satisfaction in the long run. Your lucky number is 4.

Thursday, July 3 (Moon Taurus to Gemini 5:32 a.m.) Some Librans will be setting out on a new adventure—possibly to another country. Even stay-at-homes will find there's a lot more variety on the menu. Some kind of opportunity suddenly appears during the day, and possibly originates at a distance. A Gemini or a Virgo could be key in this matter.

Friday, July 4 (Moon in Gemini) You are going to be called upon today for a peace-keeping action. Be at your most tactic and diplomatic in handling differences. Other people have some definite ideas of right and wrong; they may not coincide with your own, but you should give them the right to hold them. The lucky number is 6.

Saturday, July 5 (Moon Gemini to Cancer 6:19 p.m.) This could be one of those times you wish you could get away from it all on a desert island or other kind of private retreat. It's important to realize that many of your problems exist only in your own mind. Someone you meet during the day or the evening could give you the real slant on things and provide you with some real inspiration. If not, do your own reflecting.

Sunday, July 6 (Moon in Cancer) It's important to listen to the voice of experience now; defer to a parent or authority figure when he/she wants to discuss your ambitions. No matter what your age, you can take a more mature approach. Your mentor could be a Capricorn or a Cancer.

Monday, July 7 (Moon in Cancer) Don't start anything new today, but complete what you have begun. Many are on the move to a new level of confidence and authority, and the only person who can hold you back is yourself. It is important to free yourself of self-doubts; take a good hard look at how you have been handling things lately. The lucky number is 9.

Tuesday, July 8 (Moon Cancer to Leo 5:56 a.m.) Many will find that someone you thought was merely a buddy now turns into a sweetheart. Isn't it nice? All should step forward with confidence now into a new social situation; you should feel your best and look it too. There are ways you can make your dreams come true faster, if you will only concentrate on them.

Wednesday, July 9 (Moon in Leo) Many will be able to take a breather now and get some much needed R&R. No matter what your situation, try not to push yourself today; let someone else carry the ball. Someone has good advice, and you should not turn a deaf ear to it. Develop a spirit of acceptance now. The lucky number is 2.

Thursday, July 10 (Moon Leo to Virgo 3:50 p.m.) Direct action is what is needed now—and an opportunity to take that action will present itself early in the day. Count on your personal popularity to gain the support you need. If you have some second thoughts and self-doubts later on, realize that they are simply negative messages. It is possible to get them from oneself. Keep your sense of humor.

Friday, July 11 (Moon in Virgo) You could feel as if you are being tested now. For some, that will include a feeling that you do not know whether or not you are on the right track. If you stick to routine and take care of details, larger matters should fall into place. Share a few light moments with an Aquarian or a Leo.

Saturday, July 12 (Moon Virgo to Libra 11:40 p.m.) Some will be involved in a confidential discussion today that can throw an entirely new light on a personal relationship. In many cases, a member of the opposite sex will reveal deep feelings about you that you did not realize were there. In some way or another, you will be rejuvenated and inspired by events. Your lucky number is 5.

Sunday, July 13 (Moon in Libra) Now you are ready to meet the world on new terms, as the moon turns into your sign. Lately you've been so involved with others, that you may have neglected your own personal appearance. Do something about it today! It's an excellent time for clothes shopping and putting some new bloom on the rose.

Monday, July 14 (Moon in Libra) Today you can learn how to be alone without feeling lonely. There's nothing wrong with realizing you are a separate entity. It is important for you to get to know yourself better now. In some cases, there will be a kind of spiritual awakening now. The lucky number is 7.

Tuesday, July 15 (Moon Libra to Scorpio 4:58 a.m.) Your money sense is particularly sharp today; that means you'll know a bargain when you see one. It also means you can make gains through influential people.

If you've been thinking about asking for a raise or promotion that you truly deserve, do not hesitate to do so now. A Capricorn could play a key role.

Wednesday, July 16 (Moon in Scorpio) Now's the time to take stock of all your possessions. For some, that means cleaning out an attic, a garage, or another area that has become piled up with useless things. It will do you good psychologically, too. Many need to clear away the past and their attachment to it now. Let an independent Aries show you how.

Thursday, July 17 (Moon Scorpio to Sagittarius 7:34 a.m.) The accent is on action, adventure, and a rather bold move that could attract attention to you. You may want to do something deliberately to impress someone new in your immediate environment. All Librans should prepare for a rather unique experience now. It could come from any quarter. You lucky number is 1.

Friday, July 18 (Moon in Sagittarius) You may feel an impulse to phone or otherwise reach that close friend or relative who has been out of touch recently. Believe it or not, this person is thinking about you too. If you feel there is ESP operating, you are probably right. In all matters, act on your hunches now because they are very valid. Let a Cancer or a Capricorn keep you from going too far.

Saturday, July 19 (Moon Sagittarius to Capricorn 8:10 a.m.) You may feel very much in need of a life; that means you should accept an invitation that comes your way. Even if it doesn't sound very interesting, you can be assured of meeting some very bright people who share your interest. It should be a lighthearted day, so make the most of it. The lucky number is 3.

Sunday, July 20 (Moon in Capricorn) You probably feel like sticking close to home today, and that is exactly what you should be doing. A slow, steady pace will aid you in accomplishing things that have piled up.

Take some time too to check out security measures and fix up some small things that could be large repairs later on.

Monday, July 21 (Moon Capricorn to Aquarius 8:17 a.m.) A full moon emphasizes changes that are very basic. In some cases, they can have to do with one's residence or other base of operations. However, in other cases they are purely psychological. Be willing to communicate your needs and desires; if you don't, people will never be aware of them. Some will feel a pull between conflicting demands of personal and professional life. You can find a creative solution.

Tuesday, July 22 (Moon in Aquarius) It is possible that a young person will require your attention; be patient and show that you understand. If you have to plan a family celebration, realize it is possible to please everybody and still please yourself. For some, a romantic attachment is getting stronger. The lucky number is 6.

Wednesday, July 23 (Moon Aquarius to Pisces 9:59 a.m.) Some Librans may be in a puzzling interpersonal situation. However, the mystery will clear up as you look at the other person realistically. Your expectations may simply be too high; remember that no one is perfect. Enjoy some escapist entertainment, but keep it constructive.

Thursday, July 24 (Moon in Pisces) You can really shine at the job today. And you can expect some favorable attention from higher up. Many Librans should be able to transform dreams into something real now; a Capricorn could be a great help in doing this.

Friday, July 25 (Moon Pisces to Aries 3:02 p.m.) Though you may feel like taking care of yourself, you are going to have to take care of others today—in one way or another. You should be ready to make personal sacrifices for the good of all, but draw the line at carrying a burden somebody else should rightly carry. And be aware of others who become too dependent on you. The lucky number is 9.

Saturday, July 26 (Moon in Aries) No matter what you think about it, a romantic relationship seems destined to take on new meaning. For some, it could mean a long-term commitment such as marriage. If you are in the mood to make the first move, don't. It would be wiser to leave that to the other person. A Leo person could figure prominently in any Libra scenario today.

Sunday, July 27 (Moon in Aries) It's possible that the pace has been a bit too quick, so it should be a relief to slow down. Take time out to enjoy your home surroundings and possibly even some domestic chores. Someone close to you needs your attention and your advice; be as generous as you can be. And try not to be impatient, though it may be difficult. Your lucky number is 2.

Monday, July 28 (Moon Aries to Taurus 12:11 a.m.) A lot of good things could come your way today—including a lot of generosity. For some, it will take the form of gifts and possibly an invitation to travel. However, don't try to experience all the possible experiences, because you could totally wear yourself out. Be very discriminating in what you choose to do. Avoid a Gemini who may not be the best influence in the world now.

Tuesday, July 29 (Moon in Taurus) Don't be afraid to dig deep for answers where matters of money and finance are concerned. It is your right. There may be any number of practical matters and basic tasks that require your personal attention today. Don't get discouraged! Some of you should be thinking about making a budget—and sticking to it. You must build a solid foundation now in order to take off in the future.

Wednesday, July 30 (Moon Taurus to Gemini 12:19 p.m.) If you get some nitty-gritty things out of the way early in the day, you should be ready for the lighter, brighter mood that will prevail later on. Some Librans will be really expanding their horizons—possibly by meeting a fascinating person from a totally different background. In other cases, a romantic communication is featured. Your lucky number is 5.

Thursday, July 31 (Moon in Gemini) You will be in the mood for lots of stimulation today—and luxurious surroundings. For those on vacation, it will be easier to find that atmosphere. For stay-at-homes, cultivate your own interesting atmosphere with music—or possibly a visit to a museum or a gallery. It's a good day to let your creative juices flow. Another Libran would be an excellent companion.

AUGUST 1986

Friday, August 1 (Moon in Gemini) This is a day when you could say a rather "business-as-usual" atmosphere prevails. Spend your time catching up on your homework, planning ahead, and thinking seriously about your future. Some Librans may decide to begin a new course of study or to apply for some additional job training. You are definitely thinking in the right direction. Your lucky number is 4.

Saturday, August 2 (Moon Gemini to Cancer 1:04 a.m.) The weekend mood comes upon you, and you are inspired to get out and go places in the company of people who are more stimulating than your usual milieu. Some Librans will be meeting someone whose prominent standing in the community can really help in terms of future advancement. For anyone, a Gemini or a Virgo could be a real boon companion today.

Sunday, August 3 (Moon in Cancer) You may have to pull in your horns a bit more today and pay more attention to people around you—especially a parent or other family member who really wants your company.

For some, a sentimental gift or other token of affection will be a real morale booster. You should think about doing the same for someone else. You would do well to slow down your pace and muster up as much patience and diplomacy as you can.

Monday, August 4 (Moon Cancer to Leo 12:26 p.m.) Look around you today and make mental notes of all the "players" in your job situation. It is important to adopt a waiting game now where career moves are concerned. In any situation, you are better off learning the story behind the story before you plunge ahead. In many cases, a true friend will come through, and help you see the situation as it really is. It could be a Pisces. Your lucky number is 7.

Tuesday, August 5 (Moon in Leo) Full steam ahead; you can really make things happen if you want to. In many cases, Librans will be profiting from past efforts that now make them look extremely good—particularly with an authority figure. It is an excellent time to make that important move—in love or in business.

Wednesday, August 6 (Moon Leo to Virgo 9:44 p.m.) You are going to have to make a decision about whether or not you want to go on seeing someone who drains you but gives little in return. Any Libran will feel strongly now that a wider scope is needed for his/her native talents; some may find the avenue through a new group or organization. You are recognizing your true potential, and that is a positive sign. Your lucky number is 9.

Thursday, August 7 (Moon in Virgo) For many Librans, a love relationship is blossoming behind the scenes, but it may be difficult to keep it hush-hush. The glow in your eye and the look on your face could be a real giveaway. If this is not your current scenario, rest assured that soon you will attract someone rather romantic—and very daring. Keep on hoping!

Friday, August 8 (Moon Virgo to Libra 5:05 a.m.) You may be tempted to force an issue today, but do not do it. Continue to remain in the background in spite of a very strong desire to be in the spotlight. You could be extra sensitive today to imagined slights; realize that only your own fears and self-doubts are holding you back.

Saturday, August 9 (Moon in Libra) Now the dark clouds disappear and you find yourself quite popular, and very much sought after. With your lunar cycle so high, you can call your own shots. Your social life should be excellent now. A Sagittarian or a Gemini could be an excellent companion.

Sunday, August 10 (Moon in Libra) Try to avoid extremes today, and concentrate on self-improvement instead. If you want, you will have the discipline needed to begin a diet or an exercise program. You can also prove yourself to someone who wants to believe in you very much. The lucky number today is 4.

Monday, August 11 (Moon Libra to Scorpio 10:36 a.m.) Events today may take an unexpected turn, and you should be ready for it. The written or spoken word will play a very important role. In some cases, what you begin for your own satisfaction could turn into a moneymaking proposition. No matter what happens, be prepared for a lot of questions to which you must give very fast answers. Your lucky number is 5.

Tuesday, August 12 (Moon in Scorpio) Money again takes the spotlight. Anything you spend on home or family will pay much greater dividends than you think in terms of greater happiness and harmony. You should really investigate that home improvement or renovation program that's been somewhere in the back of your mind. Consult with a Taurus or another Libran who really knows the ropes.

Wednesday, August 13 (Moon Scorpio to Sagittarius 2:17 p.m.) If you allow your self-esteem to be based on what others think or say, you are going in the wrong direction. Your own value system may need rethinking. If you can, take time out to be by yourself and to do some soul-searching. You may find a very special message within yourself. The lucky number is 7.

Thursday, August 14 (Moon in Sagittarius) This is definitely not a halfway day. Some will find themselves making promises that can involve long-term commitments. The subject may be romance and marriage. In other cases, you will find yourself in an important discussion of career objectives, and you should listen to every word. A Cancer or a Capricorn could play a significant role.

Friday, August 15 (Moon Sagittarius to Capricorn 4:22 p.m.) You may feel as if you can't get away from people today. However, you should try to rise above petty differences and decide to end a situation that is limiting you and continually makes you feel as if you are in the wrong. At all costs, do not allow others to belittle you. Seek the people who have different standards. And better ones.

Saturday, August 16 (Moon in Capricorn) The emphasis today is on new projects and on building a firmer foundation for the future. If a change is indicated—possibly to a better location—prove that you can be daring and innovative. Many Librans will be drawing romantic attention to themselves because of their high degree of personal magnetism. Make the most of it! The lucky number is 1.

Sunday, August 17 (Moon Capricorn to Aquarius 5:44 p.m.) Many of you will be finding happiness right in your own backyard—or some place equally close. Family feeling, good food, warmth, and affection—all are on the menu today. Savor them as much as you can. A Cancer or a Capricorn may be right there beside you.

Monday, August 18 (Moon in Aquarius) This is an excellent day to be on the move—socializing, investigating, and giving free rein to your creative imagination. You may find yourself in a face-off with a very bright person; you may take the opposite viewpoint just to stir things up. Be sure you don't take on more than you handle.

Tuesday, August 19 (Moon Aquarius to Pisces 7:52 p.m.) You are going to need a lot of patience and self-discipline today. Particularly if you are involved in some kind of creative venture. The full moon may make you feel as if you are being pulled in several different directions at one time. The answer is to stick with your obligations and not attempt to dump them on someone else. Your lucky number today is 4.

Wednesday, August 20 (Moon in Pisces) You may have already realized that better communication will pay off in your workplace. There are ways you can understand others, and they can understand you. Some Librans must be willing to change their schedules on a very short notice in order to accommodate other people. If you play your cards right, a romantic situation could easily develop—a Gemini or a Virgo could be your opposite number.

Thursday, August 21 (Moon in Pisces) Others are likely to hand you more than your share of duties and responsibilities today—or at least more than you would like to handle. Do your part, but don't do anything that someone else should really be doing. It is not necessary. When it comes to meal times, avoid rich foods and anything else that could upset your digestive system. Or add weight. Your lucky number is 6.

Friday, August 22 (Moon Pisces to Aries 12:27 a.m.) If you try to escape from a situation in which you must take the needs of someone else into consideration, it will only lead to problems. Face up to it. And realize that you may not be seeing the situation in a realistic light. If you listen with a truly sympathetic ear and maintain a compassionate attitude, you will be a lot better off. Withhold judgment for now.

Saturday, August 23 (Moon in Aries) Don't groan if someone older and wiser wants to give you some advice; you can really benefit from it. Also, don't try to go it alone. Realize that other people are in your court willing to provide emotional and financial support. If you play a relationship by the rules, it could become much more what you want it to be.

Sunday, August 24 (Moon Aries to Taurus 8:36 a.m.) You can really expand your vistas today as well as share love and inspiration with someone who is very important to you. You are likely to start out the day on a very up note; do not let it descend into petty wrangling over money and expenses. Realize that a truly altruistic attitude is necessary now. Your lucky number is 9.

Monday, August 25 (Moon in Taurus) This is a day to make love or money—with style and flair. You can take the lead in a relationship or in a business enterprise; you have what it takes. Your innovative ideas and magnetic personality can serve you—and make others happy as well. A Leo could be very prominent.

Tuesday, August 26 (Moon Taurus to Gemini 8:00 p.m.) A hunch could easily pay off, particularly with relation to your finances. However, the emphasis is likely to be on saving rather than spending. Keep your security needs and the approval of other people uppermost in your mind. When it comes to budgetary matters, be willing to share decision. Perhaps with a Cancer.

Wednesday, August 27 (Moon in Gemini) Travel, education, and planning for the future are high on the list of the day's priorities. Take care not to spread yourself too thin or to take on more than you can handle. It's nice to be popular, but realize that you could simply be spinning your wheels. A Gemini is exciting, but could string you out by the end of the day. Your lucky number is 3.

Thursday, August 28 (Moon in Gemini) If you must travel today—no matter how short a distance—plan your route carefully in advance. It is important to avoid extremes of any kind, and to recognize the limitations of both time and money. You may have to put business in front of pleasure today, because there is a practical, work-oriented tone to this period. An Aquarian may be in the picture, and may help you see the larger scheme of things.

Friday, August 29 (Moon Gemini to Cancer 8:40 a.m.) Be careful that you don't let your reputation suffer from careless words you utter in public today. Someone important may be listening when you least expect it. Focus your energies instead on making contacts that will add to your prestige. You could easily sell or promote something effectively today, especially yourself.

Saturday, August 30 (Moon in Cancer) If you have any artistic or decorating skills at all—and you should—you can utilize them very well today. And get a lot of applause for your efforts. Someone who shows up at a gathering could be very important to your future career; do not ignore him/her because you are too busy. Another Libran may be very prominent in the picture.

Sunday, August 31 (Moon Cancer to Leo 8:08 p.m.) Someone you admire and respect will give you a special uplift today—and possibly some spiritual inspiration. Don't toss it off as unimportant. For many Librans, this is a good day to get close to nature—it is a better way to spend your time than in trying to impress others. Get away from it all for a little while, and try to get it back together again. Your lucky number is 7.

SEPTEMBER 1986

Monday, September 1 (Moon in Leo) A romantic message could easily make your day. However, it could come in disguise. You may be on the brink of translating your dreams into concrete reality, and you should consult friends who seem to know better than you where you should go from here. Take care what you say today; it will be long remembered. A Gemini or a Virgo could be very much on the scene, and play a very imporant role.

Tuesday, September 2 (Moon in Leo) The accent is on family affairs and community involvement. You may have to be a master diplomat and utilize all your powers to bring together some diverse factions. Some Librans will entertain and should do so with a lavish hand. Your home can be a great source of pleasure to you now. For others, an artistic friend could be a great source of inspiration. The lucky number is 6.

Wednesday, September 3 (Moon Leo to Virgo 5:06 a.m.) This may be a more subdued day than you would like it to be. Spend some time helping someone else by listening to his/her secrets, and by indicating that you do understand and care. There is an air of mystery about this day, and some intrigue may be going on behind the scenes. Pisces may be involved.

Thursday, September 4 (Moon in Virgo) Get set for some new responsibilities. Many of you are working on something very important, but it is essential to keep the whole thing under wraps until someone higher up gives the green light. You won't lose anything by waiting now. Your lucky number is 8.

Friday, September 5 (Moon Virgo to Libra 11:33 a.m.) Now's the time to finish something off and to get ready to take advantage of some new opportunities that are on the way. Some things that have been under wraps may be out of the bag by the middle of the day.

Then you can begin to make long-range plans with confidence and self-assurance. You did your part!

Saturday, September 6 (Moon in Libra) This is a high-cycle, high-powered day. If you want to, you can press your advantage and set out on a bold new course. Cinch the deal by wearing something bold and distinctive that draws attention to your better points. It's time you were noticed! In many cases, Librans will find themselves showered with attention. The person who showers could be a Leo.

Sunday, September 7 (Moon Libra to Scorpio 4:12 p.m.) There is a subtle shift in the emphasis today, and it ends up on money and security. You may be waiting for someone else to show you what you're worth; but only you can set your own value. You are better off not pushing today, but surveying the scene and getting a feel for the situation. It could be a very positive one for you. The lucky number is 2.

Monday, September 8 (Moon in Scorpio) You may feel inclined to "grab the check" or otherwise spend money to be popular today. It is not necessary. You will be able to win a lot of friends and influence people simply through your optimistic manner and your witty talk. A shopping trip could be delightful, and very beneficial—if you don't buy everything you see! Watch a Sagittarian!

Tuesday, September 9 (Moon Scorpio to Sagittarius 7:40 p.m.) Settle down to routine and detail now. That means, pay the bills, and balance your checkbook. If you know what you really owe, you will know what is really yours to spend. Some Librans may be inclined to escape from necessary duties now; realize that is no way to start building for success. Your lucky number is 4.

Wednesday, September 10 (Moon in Sagittarius) Love and romance could be very close to you—in fact, right under your nose. The key is to open up the lines of communication with someone who shares your emotional life. Ask yourself, "Have I said 'I love you' lately?" Prepare yourself for some surprises when you open up and state how you feel. A Gemini could very well be in the picture.

Thursday, September 11 (Moon Sagittarius to Capricorn 10:28 p.m.) For many Librans, a change of residence may be up for discussion. Don't make a move until you have checked out everything—including property values and what is available. Understand that your eye for the beautiful will be a great asset in evaluating the situation. Your lucky number is 6.

Friday, September 12 (Moon in Capricorn) Don't allow a misunderstanding to escalate into full-scale war—particularly in a matter concerning home and family. Realize that you have your head in the clouds now, and may not realize that other people think you are ignoring them. Try to explain, if you can. A Pisces individual may be very helpful in clarifying the situation.

Saturday, September 13 (Moon in Capricorn) Take that first big step in a matter that has been on your mind for some time. A parent or someone else in a supportive position is squarely behind you, lending influence and possibly even cash backing. For some Librans, a deep commitment could be made now that could involve love and marriage. Show how stable you can really be. Your lucky number is 8.

Sunday, September 14 (Moon Capricorn to Aquarius 1:07 a.m.) Your ability to put someone else's interest before your own can work wonders now. Particularly where romance is concerned. If you decide that minor differences really don't matter at all, you can start planning big things together. In other Libra cases, entertainment and social life will take on a lot of glamour and glitter now. Enjoy!

Monday, September 15 (Moon in Aquarius) Matters of the heart continue to be on the top of the charts for Librans. In some cases, "love" could take the form of creativity; show that you are willing to take an unpopular path in order to express what you are really feeling. There are lots of new opportunities around you now, and you should not hesitate to grab them. Your lucky number is 1.

Tuesday, September 16 (Moon Aquarius to Pisces 4:27 a.m.) You might be feeling a bit on the emotional side today. Mood swings and extremes of feeling are likely to be the order of the day. Don't expect other people to understand why you're feeling so touchy; they have their own problems. Watch your health, and at all costs don't eat while you're under pressure—or in too much of a hurry. Talk over your problems with a Cancer.

Wednesday, September 17 (Moon in Pisces) Okay, now's the time to dress for success and step right out in front of everyone else. Your eye for color, design, and style are particularly acute today. You may receive a very important invitation on top of it. Realize that your appearance is a real asset and can help you move ahead. Your lucky number is 3.

Thursday, September 18 (Moon Pisces to Aries 9:33 a.m.) There is full-moon tension in the air, and it may be difficult for you to keep your mind on your work. However, devotion to duty is called for today, and there is no way you can escape it. Stick to the routine, and keep your eye on every detail. Above all, don't indulge in office gossip or idle chatter. Let others take their lives in their hands!

Friday, September 19 (Moon in Aries) Realize that someone may be playing games with your mind or your heart. Insist on communication that is constructive; however, you must be prepared for anything. If someone suddenly switches gear, be right there with an answer.

This is a roller-coaster day, and your heart could definitely be feeling the effects.

Saturday, September 20 (Moon Aries to Taurus 5:25 p.m.) Quiet diplomacy is the way to win today. If you have to take a back seat to someone else, do so—you have nothing to lose and everything to gain. For many Librans, home is where the heart is, and domestic talents are featured. Luxuriate in your love of beauty now for true pleasure. You can remove a disturbing influence if you try. Your lucky number is 6.

Sunday, September 21 (Moon in Taurus) Reject a proposition that seems to offer something for nothing. Get to the root of the matter and decide what is actually being offered. You may decide you are better off not coming to any important decisions today—particularly in money matters. You are right! A Pisces or a Virgo may try to influence you.

Monday, September 22 (Moon in Taurus) Step right up and into a business deal today, confident that you can get the support and backing you desire. This is a day when you can really expect the breaks, and they can affect a serious relationship or get you into an inner circle of prestigious people. Take advantage of every opportunity that comes along. Your lucky number is 8.

Tuesday, September 23 (Moon Taurus to Gemini 4:13 a.m.) Don't expect to find answers right under your nose. You are going to have to do a little digging. One thing that could help a lot is discussing things with people who have a more long-range view on the situation than you do. Your other best bet is to let go of people and situations that are holding you back. You do not need them. Let an Aries show you the way.

Wednesday, September 24 (Moon in Gemini) For many Librans, the proverbial "fascinating foreigner" could drop onto the scene, possibly drawn by your personal magnetism and charisma. For all of you, a taste for romance and adventure may take you on a journey or expedition that seemed much too daring in the past. You are right to pull out all the stops now. Your lucky number is 1.

Thursday, September 25 (Moon Gemini to Cancer 4:44 p.m.) A strong hunch or impression may come upon you today; be sure to pay attention to it. If necessary, retreat from center stage and observe the scene without participating in it. Though this may seem like a rather quiet day, you could be traveling a million miles in your imagination. And gaining a lot by it. An older woman could easily be in the picture.

Friday, September 26 (Moon in Cancer) Something you dreamed up yesterday can be brought to the attention of important people today; it could also be the key to your future success. Don't feel shy or hang back. In personal matters, you'll be sociable, popular, and lighthearted. However, make sure not to promise more than you can deliver. Your lucky number is 3.

Saturday, September 27 (Moon in Cancer) The emphasis is squarely on basic issues and routine matters today. Realize that someone is watching you closely and taking careful note of whether or not you follow the rules. You may not like being observed this way, but don't delegate details to someone else anyway. Realize that solid rewards are coming to you for a job well done.

Sunday, September 28 (Moon Cancer to Leo 5:39 a.m.) Now you feel as if a great burden is lifted and restrictions are off. Enjoy your freer feelings and freer time by associating with some rather witty types who either teach, write, or entertain. In some cases, a new love could develop so quickly that your head will spin. Let a Gemini or a Virgo help you figure out how to handle it.

Monday, September 29 (Moon in Leo) Try to be diplomatic with a friend who comes up with some ideas and schemes that are quite different from yours. Warmth and affection are much more needed than criticism. Realize that restoring harmony to this situation is more important than the issue itself. For many Librans, a social function will allow you to express your very special talents. The lucky number today is 6.

Tuesday, September 30 (Moon Leo to Virgo 1:57 p.m.) Today you may feel rather out of it; look into yourself for answers. You may discover that you really need a little time out for meditation and reflection. The best medicine may be to think about those who are less fortunate than you are and who need your sympathy and compassion. Isn't there someone who is waiting to hear from you? Do something about it right away. Your lucky number is 7.

OCTOBER 1986

Wednesday, October 1 (Moon in Virgo) There are some confidential matters that desperately need discretion now; it is wise to keep them "all in the family." It's possible you have been trying to hide something, but it is much better brought out into the open and handled—diplomatically of course. Those who love you certainly will understand. And you will have greater peace of mind. Your lucky number is 6.

Thursday, October 2 (Moon Virgo to Libra 8:03 p.m.) It's wise to work behind the scenes today; you have some latent talent that can be developed if you give it some time and attention. Some may be feeling rather confined, but soon that feeling will vanish. Be glad of the fact that you have time to be alone and think things through. A Pisces or a Virgo could be very helpful.

Friday, October 3 (Moon in Libra) This is the best moon in Libra time of the year for you. In fact, it could bring important and significant events into your life during the coming months. Today your ambitions and business goals are accented, but there is still time for concentrating on a relationship. Something could be getting a lot more serious and intense. Are you ready for this?

Saturday, October 4 (Moon Libra to Scorpio 11:35 p.m.) You may get a lot more accomplished today than you thought you would. For one thing, your sense of timing is excellent, and you should be able to polish off certain things quite handily. Join up with some forward-looking people who are a lot more aggressive than you, and are quite able to steer you in the right direction. It's someplace you want to go. Your lucky number today is 9.

Sunday, October 5 (Moon in Scorpio) You are definitely ready for something new, especially in your appearance. Some Librans are getting a bit bolder now and stepping out in real style. If you haven't reached that point, today's the day to make a start. Your sense of style and taste are quite individualistic now. Let a Leo show you how.

Monday, October 6 (Moon in Scorpio) You have an instinctive feeling about both spending and saving now; you are right to follow your hunches. Because your sense of security is accented now, you will want to put something away for the proverbial rainy day. Listen to someone who has a good suggestion, even if it is a family member. At least talk it over. Your lucky number is 2.

Tuesday, October 7 (Moon Scorpio to Sagittarius 1:48 a.m.) You may have a strong urge to communicate today—but make sure you aren't just talking for the sake of talking. Concentrate on the content of your ideas and not just your style. It would be easy for you to go to extremes today and run around a bit too much. Don't take on more than you can handle. The lucky number today is 3.

Wednesday, October 8 (Moon in Sagittarius) Slow and steady wins the race today. You've got to pay attention to details in order to get anything done, even if you do not feel like doing so. If you don't expect anything terribly exciting today, you will not be disappointed. But you could easily feel a glow of satisfaction at what you have accomplished by the end of the day.

Thursday, October 9 (Moon Sagittarius to Capricorn 3:52 a.m.) A family situation has been bugging you, and now is the time to get to the bottom of it. However, both you and someone else are going to have to lay your cards on the table. Set aside some time for the two of you to talk it over quietly. For many Librans, exciting developments are also on the agenda—including a definite change of scenery.

Friday, October 10 (Moon in Capricorn) You may feel an urge to splurge today, and it would not be a bad idea to do something to lift your morale. And that of people around you. It could be as simple as buying a bouquet of flowers—or as expensive as a real luxury item for the home. No matter what you do or decide to buy, you will be feeling especially sentimental and gracious today. It's an excellent evening to entertain at home.

Saturday, October 11 (Moon Capricorn to Aquarius 7:45 a.m.) If nothing exciting happens today, you are going to have to create your own form of entertainment. The desire for "escape" is strong as is the taste for mystery and intrigue. Don't get so carried away that you upset the applecart in your romantic life. If you keep someone guessing too long, he/she could easily decide it isn't worth the wait. Share your tender emotions.

Sunday, October 12 (Moon in Aquarius) Now you're going to have to be absolutely blunt and tell someone how much you really care. Or don't care. Definite commitments are going to be expected from you, and you must be ready to give them. Many Librans will be in the mood to solidify a relationship, so your tendency will be to say, "yes I do." In other areas, this can be an excellent day—if you follow the rules.

Monday, October 13 (Moon Aquarius to Pisces 11:03 a.m.) It may be very difficult for you to get down to work this morning; you aren't ready to accept the fact that a great weekend is over. If you look at the big picture rather than all those little things, you can make great strides. This is no time for tunnel vision. It is important to plan ahead. Your lucky number is 9.

Tuesday, October 14 (Moon in Pisces) Once again, it is important to give in to those creative feelings and let them guide you no matter what task is before you today. It's also a day you could get by on your charm, because your personal magnetism is quite strong. If there's a job or a promotion that looks good to you, today's the day to go for it. A Leo could easily be involved.

Wednesday, October 15 (Moon Pisces to Aries 5:13 p.m.) A lot of people may be depending on you today, even if you wish they wouldn't. Don't let your own possibly heavy mood create an unpleasant atmosphere. If you are feeling ultrasensitive, use that feeling to empathize with other people's problems. A Cancerian could be extremely helpful today. Your lucky number is 2.

Thursday, October 16 (Moon in Aries) Today you positively radiate enthusiasm. However, your curiosity about the world could run away with you. If you scatter your forces or spread yourself too thin, you won't accomplish very much. Don't try to be everyone's friend. Your lucky number today is 3.

Friday, October 17 (Moon in Aries) Don't give in to the temptation to cut corners today. There is no way you can skirt the rules and get away with it. Devotion to duty is a must today. The full moon will create a lot of touchiness all around you, so you should make an especially strong attempt to keep yourself on an even keel. In order to do so, you may have to give in to others.

Saturday, October 18 (Moon Aries to Taurus 1:35 a.m.) You may get a rather surprising insight into the deepest feelings of someone else today; it could take place during what should be a romantic encounter. It will make you realize this is no time for a light flirtation or simply playing games. Be thankful that you can reach each other on a very emotional level now. For other Librans, there may be a prophetic glimpse into the future.

Sunday, October 19 (Moon in Taurus) You can smooth the waters where they have been troubled by money matters recently. But you may have to pay for it—possibly in the form of a special gift or a great dinner out. No matter what, it's time to get budget conscious and to talk over the subject—no matter how much you or a partner may want to avoid it. It's important not to play the heavy; just be understanding. Your lucky number is 6.

Monday, October 20 (Moon Taurus to Gemini 12:15 p.m.) Get some niggling financial affairs out of the way early in the day; later on you won't be in the mood for handling details. As a matter of fact, most Librans will be feeling rather dreamy and escapist today. It could make you think about traveling—or even doing something tangible about it. If you can't literally get away from it all, concentrate on your loftier values and ideals. It will give you a real lift.

Tuesday, October 21 (Moon in Gemini) You sense that you can do better than you are actually doing now; you are right to consider furthering your education in order to put yourself ahead of the game. If you are serious about committing yourself to something, the money and help you need will be forthcoming. Talk it over with someone who has the know-how as well as the wherewithal. Your lucky number is 8.

Wednesday, October 22 (Moon in Gemini) You should feel proud of yourself for being able to make a definite break with the past. In some cases, the break will be between you and someone who has been bringing you down. This is no time for small thinking; be ready to transcend your usual boundaries. One way is by associating with people who are looking ahead instead of backwards. An Aries could be one of them.

Thursday, October 23 (Moon Gemini to Cancer 12:37 a.m.) If there's something that's got to be decided, don't deal with people on a lower echelon; go right to the top. Realize that someone in an influential position has had his/her eye on you, and knows about your creative ideas. If necessary, blow your own horn, and show your true individuality. Now is the time your career can take off. It all depends on you.

Friday, October 24 (Moon in Cancer) Now's the time to go back to a low-key image. Let someone else take the glory today, while you act as a backup. Some Librans will be looking for warm affection and a secure environment today; someone will definitely be "there for you" to provide it. It could actually be one of your parents or a parent substitute. Your lucky number is 2.

Saturday, October 25 (Moon Cancer to Leo 1:02 p.m.) Early in the day, your mind may still be on your work life; however, later on you will be more than willing to break loose and look for some excitement. Some will have the good fortune to meet a rather clever type who has similar ideas about life. Others will find themselves the center of a special celebration. If you're looking for adventure, you will find it.

Sunday, October 26 (Moon in Leo) Now you should be able to sit back and enjoy the rewards of some hard work you put in recently. Some Librans will also be making long-range plans that focus on a goal that's near and dear to your heart. It's an excellent day for laying foundations and attending to basics; if you take a "no frills" approach, you will put yourself ahead of the game. Your lucky number is 4.

Monday, October 27 (Moon Leo to Virgo 11:20 p.m.) After a temporary downturn, the pace picks up; a change of plans is a high possibility. Don't let it throw you. Some of you will find yourselves smack in the middle of a group with stimulating ideas you can exchange for your own. One will be a standout—and could turn into a romantic interest. A Gemini will play a key role today.

Tuesday, October 28 (Moon in Virgo) It's definitely time to pay some attention to yourself—especially with regard to your appearance. It's possible you have been doing more giving than getting recently. Pamper yourself in some way today. Some Librans should prepare themselves for a secret meeting which includes some very special self-indulgence. Enjoy!

Wednesday, October 29 (Moon in Virgo) Now you've got to get realistic—particularly about an affair of the heart. Is it possible you are expecting more than someone can give? If necessary, take some time out to be alone and get more in touch with what is going on inside of you. This is no day to force an issue; diplomacy will get you much more. Your lucky number is 7.

Thursday, October 30 (Moon Virgo to Libra 6:04 a.m.) Whatever soul-searching you did yesterday will pay off today. Now you are ready for dynamic action, and you should not hold yourself back in any way. You should be on the move—in love or career. For some, greater prestige is on the way, and part of it could arrive today. A Capricorn will figure very prominently.

Friday, October 31 (Moon in Libra) Don't be tempted to drop the ball; it is imperative to finish what you began yesterday. Then, you will be able to reevaluate your game plan and possibly revise it on a higher level. Someone around you will be rather competitive, but remember that the odds are still in your favor. It is important to rise above petty jealousy. The lucky number today is 9.

NOVEMBER 1986

Saturday, November 1 (Moon Libra to Scorpio 9:19 a.m.) It's okay to be a little mysterious today; however, you should draw the line at outright deception. Many of you will be exuding an aura of glamour now, and should have fun with that image. Prepare yourself for the fact that others will be looking to you for leadership and inspiration. Are you ready to give it? Your lucky number today is 7.

Sunday, November 2 (Moon in Scorpio) Many will come to the firm conclusion today that a new start financially is necessary. It is an excellent day to "make your garden grow." Your business sense is sharp and your ambitions are high. Concentrate on long-range plans in that area. Some Librans would do well to seek advice from someone who has a proven track record. Others will have to curb an urge to be greedy.

Monday, November 3 (Moon Scorpio to Sagittarius 10:19 a.m.) A generous mood could come upon you today and you could be willing to share what you have with someone less fortunate. Good for you! However, some should be careful not to make someone more dependent than they already are. Be discriminating and tread carefully. Don't let someone drag you into an argument over petty issues, and keep your eye on the big picture.

Tuesday, November 4 (Moon in Sagittarius) It may be difficult for you to keep your mind on your work today; you probably would much rather be "somewhere over the rainbow." If you can manage it, take some time out to get in touch with someone you haven't seen in a while; the contact will satisfy at least some of your desire for mental stimulation. Better yet—drop in at a travel bureau and pick up some tempting folders. You can dream, can't you?

Wednesday, November 5 (Moon Sagittarius to Capricorn 10:49 a.m.) No matter what the weather is today, you should be feeling warm and cozy. It's an excellent day to share things with someone you love—from a table for two to pleasant memories. All should be in a sentimental mood, and for some it will be a close relative who provides the sense of security you are yearning for. Don't hesitate to ask for what you want. In general, a slow pace is the best one today.

Thursday, November 6 (Moon in Capricorn) Don't blame other people for distracting you today; it's your own restlessness that's causing your mind to wander from your work. You are impelled to keep things stirred up and to divert your interest in multiple directions. Though you should make an effort to concentrate, you probably are best off going with the flow. A Sagittarian could help keep you hopping.

Friday, November 7 (Moon Capricorn to Aquarius 12:29 p.m.) Okay, now it's easier to get down to work. Dig into that pile of stuff that's waiting to be done, because only you can cut through it. Most Librans should have the necessary self-discipline to plunge into some home repairs and family obligations that have seemed rather weighty in recent days. Today your lucky number is 4.

Saturday, November 8 (Moon in Aquarius) You should have a lot of physical and mental energy today. Some should try to burn it off with active sports; others in the company of people who give you a run for your money, intellectually speaking. You should feel especially expressive today, and should find a profitable area to express yourself. Change and variety are very much part of the scenario.

Sunday, November 9 (Moon Aquarius to Pisces 4:30 p.m.) Some Librans will have a sharp face-off with another person today. However, if you prepare yourself for a difference of opinion, you will be able to keep things on an even keel. At a family party or other kind of gathering, on the other hand, you may find yourself acting the referee! Some Librans can expect a sentimental gift from the heart.

Monday, November 10 (Moon in Pisces) You will find it difficult to settle down to routine tasks today. However, you will achieve great satisfaction from working with and for people who need sympathy and compassion. No matter what the day brings, keep your secrets to yourself. There are those who would like to ferret them out—and spread them around. Your lucky number is 7.

Tuesday, November 11 (Moon Pisces to Aries 11:14 p.m.) It should be easy for you to take the lead today—especially at your place of employment. You possess some excellent organizational skills, and they should serve you well now and impress those who count. Make the most of this significant day, and take every opportunity that comes along for getting ahead. Your lucky number is 8.

Wednesday, November 12 (Moon in Aries) You may be intimidated by a rather dynamic person who has ideas that seem to be ahead of the time. Let him/her take the lead today, and go along with it. You will inspired to use talents you had almost forgotten about and to develop greater potential for the immediate future. If you are able to put jealousy aside and stay above personality issues, you can really learn a lot now.

Thursday, November 13 (Moon in Aries) A mellow mood should be upon you today, and you should be able to attract love and affection from a warm, caring partner more easily than usual. The reason may be that you are willing to temporarily suppress your individualistic tendencies. In some cases, the balancing act is a rather tricky one, but most Librans are up to the task. Your lucky number today is 1.

Friday, November 14 (Moon Aries to Taurus 8:24 a.m.) Money problems may be weighing heavily on you now, but you don't have to carry them alone. Discuss it openly with another person who is both understanding and involved. If you have a meeting of the minds, this is an excellent day to begin a long-range savings program. It is possible to avoid problems like this in the future.

Saturday, November 15 (Moon in Taurus) Let your curiosity take you where it will today; it is an excellent time to look into something complicated that intrigues you. Though your purpose is serious, your mood should be lighthearted. Don't put any limits on your thinking now, because you will only sell yourself short. If education and travel are real goals, keep them in mind—and do something about them.

Sunday, November 16 (Moon Taurus to Gemini 7:26 p.m.) This could be a rather unsettling day, with the full moon partially to blame. Your wisest course is to stick to routine matters and associate with stable, solid people. Financial matters may be causing you some jitters; don't just throw up your hands over the situation; if you take time to carefully analyze things, you will realize there is a lot that can be done.

Monday, November 17 (Moon in Gemini) Now you are ready to break out of the mold and throw over the status quo. As a sense of restriction lifts, you should not be afraid to change plans—even in midstream. Any kind of adventure—of the body or the mind—will be a source of inspiration to you. You'll be back in the routine soon enough. Your lucky number is 5.

Tuesday, November 18 (Moon in Gemini) Your desire to please is very strong today. It should make you work hard—either at your usual job, or at something special to make a loved one smile. Some Librans may be preparing for a rather large get-together. Others may receive a surprise call or letter from someone at a distance. All in all, it is or should be a lovely day.

Wednesday, November 19 (Moon Gemini to Cancer 7:46 a.m.) In contrast to yesterday's mood, today you could be feeling a bit sorry for yourself. Try to translate that into compassion for others. Some Librans may find it necessary to step aside and let someone else have the glory. Congratulate yourself for this willingness to concede. Confusion in plans is highly likely, so check and double-check all arrangements. Your lucky number is 7.

Thursday, November 20 (Moon in Cancer) You will be able to throw yourself into your work today and take on a lot of responsibility. However, don't think your efforts will go unnoticed. Something that happens today plants the seed of future accomplishment. If you want to reap the rewards eventually, stick to your commitments now. For some, the commitment may be an emotional one.

Friday, November 21 (Moon Cancer to Leo 8:25 p.m.) Some Librans will find themselves in the middle of a competitive situation. Whether it's honor, recognition, or some other award, don't worry about whether you win or lose. This time it's truly a case of playing the game well. And fairly. If you look beyond your personal advantages, you will gain important insight. Be a good loser!

Saturday, November 22 (Moon in Leo) Now the accent is on originality and new things and new people. Some Librans are destined to be the center of attention at some kind of gathering today. In some cases, there could be several people competing for your attention and affection. The winner will be a fiery, warmhearted person who really hits up your affections. The lucky number is 1.

Sunday, November 23 (Moon in Leo) You don't have to prove anything to anybody today; just quietly enjoy what is. The key word in your vocabulary today will be security—more the emotional than the financial kind. Your best bet for social life is family and close friends. Within your circle, a Capricorn or a Cancer will stand out.

Monday, November 24 (Moon Leo to Virgo 7:46 a.m.) You may be in the mood for fun and games, but you will quickly realize that certain other people are not. You may have to make your own amusement, and direct your active mind into solitary pursuits. Underneath your bright spirits, however, you may have some fears or some doubts. Don't let them dampen this good day. Your lucky number is 3.

Tuesday, November 25 (Moon in Virgo) Your wisest course is to learn the rules before you break them. Whatever studying you do now will pay off in the future. Many Librans will feel inclined to wrestle with details today and be happy just to settle down to routine. Some kind of research could be your best form of relaxation.

Wednesday, November 26 (Moon Virgo to Libra 3:59 p.m.) You should start out the day with some very bright ideas, good enough to put down on paper. Later in the day, when the moon moves into your sign, you will have a real chance for self-expression. Your wits will be very sharp—and they may even attract a rather sharp person. It could be the beginning of a romance. Your lucky number is 5.

Thursday, November 27 (Moon in Libra) Today is one of those days you may take a look in the mirror and decide something's got to be done. In this high of your moon cycle, it's an excellent time to take yourself in hand and create a brand-new style. Most Librans have rather good taste, and it will be even better under these influences. It's okay to be a bit self-indulgent today—but you might share the fun with someone lively, like an Aries.

Friday, November 28 (Moon Libra to Scorpio 8:13 p.m.) You may be more comfortable out of this world today than in it. Not that things will be so bad, but because your imagination is taking you on such pleasant adventures. However, someone may demand that you come back from outer space and tend to the things at hand. Your artistic talents are at a high point today.

Saturday, November 29 (Moon in Scorpio) You are on a much more practical wave-length today, and money and material things may be very much on your mind. Some of you will spot a real thing—and should grab it. Others will see a business opportunity that has been a closed door up until now. In some ways, it is a serious day. And you will be asked to take a serious attitude—toward both money and love. Your lucky number is 8.

Sunday, November 30 (Moon Scorpio to Sagittarius 9:08 p.m.) Your thoughts are on a much higher level, and you may be feeling rather altruistic. You are right to give in to those generous impulses and help other people today. However, make sure that the help that you give is constructive; ultimately, others will have to help themselves. Did anyone ever tell you you really are a good person?

DECEMBER 1986

Monday, December 1 (Moon in Sagittarius) No matter what "neighborhood" you find yourself in today, you will prove yourself a good neighbor. Your prestige is on the rise in the community of people that surrounds you—past efforts will pay off in the form of a lot of admiration. For some, money will also be forthcoming. The future should look rather bright today.

Tuesday, December 2 (Moon Sagittarius to Capricorn 8:26 p.m.) Communication is the name of the game today. If there's a message you've been hesitating to deliver, today's the day to lay it on the table—and to expect positive results. Some of you will get a real boost when an efficient person shows you some faster ways of getting things done. They put you in the right spot for a much bigger project.

Wednesday, December 3 (Moon in Capricorn) Someone is going to impress you very much today by his/her "together" way of doing things. Cultivate this person because he/she could figure prominently in your life in the immediate future. Romantic opportunities are increased right now, so you should make the most of them. The lucky number is 1.

Thursday, December 4 (Moon Capricorn to Aquarius 8:23 p.m.) No matter what you must do today, home will be very much on your mind. Some will be entertaining there; others may come to the realization that some renovations are in order. Keep your eye out for an older person—possibly a woman—who really has some excellent advice. The lucky number is 2.

Friday, December 5 (Moon in Aquarius) This is your day—and evening—to shine. Most should have several opportunities for partying—or at least meeting new people. Don't expect to get a lot accomplished in the way of work today, but do expect some early holiday cheer and good humor. Travel might even be involved. Enjoy it!

Saturday, December 6 (Moon Aquarius to Pisces 10:48 p.m.) You may have to work hard at having fun today. Some will get stuck with the details of a party or other recreational event. Don't complain, because you will be giving much pleasure to others. As well as to yourself. An Aquarian could easily be in the picture. Try to be as practical as possible, no matter what you do.

Sunday, December 7 (Moon in Pisces) Your nerves could be a bit of a problem today unless you give both your mind and your body a workout. Some form of physical exercise could be very beneficial—possibly even just a brisk walk. Expect to have a lot of companionship, because there should be a number of congenial people around you today. The lucky number is 5.

Monday, December 8 (Moon in Pisces) Someone approaches you with a rather serious personal problem today, and you should be willing to listen. For some, it will be necessary to be as tactful as possible. Others should go out of their way if necessary to purchase a special gift that will delight someone whose feelings are a bit ruffled. A Scorpio or a Taurus could play a key role today.

Tuesday, December 9 (Moon Pisces to Aries 4:49 a.m.) Confusion threatens to unsettle a relationship today. No matter what you say, express yourself clearly. Better yet, play a waiting game and try to see the situation as it really is—not as you would like it to be. Are you expecting more from someone than he/she is able to give? Try to be more realistic.

Wednesday, December 10 (Moon in Aries) This is an excellent day to sign, seal, and deliver an agreement with someone you love. Also to make important decisions about the future, and promises you will keep. However, in most cases, it is better to let the other person make the first move; you have time on your side. It's a great day to ask for a favor and have it granted to you.

Thursday, December 11 (Moon Aries to Taurus 2:10 p.m.) Try to stay away from arguments by avoiding petty issues. Relax and look at the big picture, no matter what other people do. Later in the day, things look up—and you may even get the money or backing you've been looking for. A positive approach will win the day. And your way over an Aries or a Libra.

Friday, December 12 (Moon in Taurus) Generosity and extravagance could go hand in hand today; many will be tempted to make a grand gesture. Make sure it is not grander than your pocketbook can afford. Try to be innovative and original, and save yourself some money. No matter what your scenario, you should be rather creative today. The lucky number is 1.

Saturday, December 13 (Moon in Taurus) You may be feeling rather sensitive today, and sentimental as well. It's an excellent time to take a stroll down memory lane with someone who shares your past. Others should catch up on some rest and relaxation in order to bring back vitality. You will need it for some fast times that are coming.

Sunday, December 14 (Moon Taurus to Gemini 1:41 a.m.) The mood is lighter and brighter today, and you should be feeling a lot more energetic. You may be tempted to go all out with a burst of enthusiasm and energy; just make sure you save some of it for yourself. Some of you will be traveling a fair distance to get together with friends. Minor snags may make it necessary for you to keep your sense of humor in hand.

Monday, December 15 (Moon in Gemini) Something or someone could test your patience today. You may find you are not as well prepared as you should be to meet a challenge. However, you're going to have to see the thing through and should not give up when you meet the first obstacle. Remember that you are building a foundation for future success. The lucky number today is 4.

Tuesday, December 16 (Moon Gemini to Cancer 2:09 p.m.) Your head may be spinning with ideas and opportunities today; the full moon could be a factor in making you feel confused. Rub your eyes and realize that your reputation depends on choosing what is best, and rejecting the rest. In some cases, a chat with someone at the top will help you make an important decision. The lucky number is 5.

Wednesday, December 17 (Moon in Cancer) It's okay to go ahead and use your connections now. In fact, it could be the key to success. Others should be very grateful for the love and support of people near and dear. Perhaps you should show your gratitude in some tangible way. A family gathering is highly likely. And another Libra could figure prominently.

Thursday, December 18 (Moon in Cancer) This is one of those times when you could discover that it really is lonely at the top. Success isn't always what it's cracked up to be. Your best course is to focus on those who are less fortunate than you and figure out how they can share in your good fortune. Search your heart for your real values and what you consider the "best things in life." Your lucky number is 7.

Friday, December 19 (Moon Cancer to Leo 2:44 a.m.) Many Librans will find themselves in a rap session today where they exchange ideas about ambitions and long-range dreams. Realize that someone important is hearing what you have to say, and can help make some of those dreams come true. In love and romance, it's an all-or-nothing day, so be on your guard. If you make a promise, you will be expected to keep it.

Saturday, December 20 (Moon in Leo) Both the season and your personal cycle could make you feel rather humanitarian today and in a mood to be charitable. This is one of those times you really believe it is better to give than to receive. Good for you! Some

Librans will have to use their social skills today, and will play an important role in an important event. Another Aries or another Libra could be involved.

Sunday, December 21 (Moon Leo to Virgo 2:30 p.m.) You should start out the day on an upbeat, dynamic note. However, you could lose heart if things don't continue to go your way later on. Don't let self-doubts get in the way of your enjoyment—or your progress. The best things most Librans can do today is boost the esteem of someone else. That way you will forget about your own little fears. The lucky number is 1.

Monday, December 22 (Moon in Virgo) Someone may drop a hint to you today—or possibly confide a secret. Be sensitive to what someone else is going through, and try to help as much as possible. Take a parental role, no matter what age the person is who needs you. Togetherness should be your watchword today, and sharing is the most productive activity. The lucky number is 2.

Tuesday, December 23 (Moon in Virgo) This is a day for true intimacy. Someone who both admires and shares your way of thinking may engage you in a rather deep discussion. It is wise to keep this relationship on a light good-humored basis before plunging in too deeply. For some Librans, a Sagittarian or Gemini may be the key to the day's events.

Wednesday, December 24 (Moon Virgo to Libra 12:05 a.m.) There is a great deal to be done today, and the burden of it may fall upon you. However, with the moon in your sign, you should be more than up to it. Your personality and sense of style are very much accented now, but don't let too many invitations tempt you to overindulge. You are very much the center of attention, and that should be enough to satisfy your appetite. Your lucky number is 4.

Thursday, December 25 (Moon in Libra) This should be one of the best holidays you've had in years.

Your mood should be upbeat, and you should be able to bring everyone up with you. No matter where you are, you will be spreading joy and charm all around. Expect a day full of good talk and a quick-changing schedule. Changes of plan should not upset your excellent frame of mind.

Friday, December 26 (Moon Libra to Scorpio 7:06 a.m.) If the post-holiday blues threaten to descend, count your real blessings. No matter how much you owe, you have a great deal of real value right around you. Love and affection of people close to you should be especially precious now. Many Librans will be feeling rather sentimental, and their generosity of spirit should keep the good time flowing. Your lucky number is 6.

Saturday, December 27 (Moon in Scorpio) You could be very vulnerable today—particularly to a sales talk of any kind. If something sounds too good to be true, it probably is. Though your head is in the clouds, you should attempt to keep your feet firmly on the ground. And count your change in every respect.

Sunday, December 28 (Moon Scorpio to Sagittarius 8:20 a.m.) You've made a big impression on a rather impressive person. He/she indicates a willingness to help, and you should be prepared to make a decision. Are there any strings attached? Keep in mind that nothing will occur halfway on this day. That means that if you want to throw your own weight around, you are in an excellent position to do so. The lucky number is 8.

Monday, December 29 (Moon in Sagittarius) Stand up for your rights and your point of view today. In some cases, Librans will find themselves fighting for an underdog. You are right to let go of limiting conditions now; one of your most important New Year's resolutions should be to broaden your horizons. You are especially able to do so now.

Tuesday, December 30 (Moon Sagittarius to Capricorn 7:54 a.m.) Many Librans will get a rather heartwarming message today. Tuck it in the back of your mind to keep you warm on some possible future "chilly" day. You should be particularly able to take a bold stand now and not waiver from a point of view. That is an excellent thing in a Libra. Many of you will be testing the waters for exciting changes to come in the New Year.

Wednesday, December 31 (Moon in Capricorn) This is an excellent New Year's Eve to stay at home by the fire with someone you love—and possibly a circle of close friends. Your sense of home and family will be particularly strong, and you will feel that "all you need is love." It's a nice and secure feeling. Your lucky number is 2. Happy New Year!

About the Author

Born on August 5, 1926, in Philadelphia, Omarr was the only astrologer ever given full-time duty in the U.S. Army as an astrologer. He also is regarded as the most erudite astrologer of our time and the best-known, through his syndicated column (300 newspapers), and his radio and television programs (he is Merv Griffin's "resident astrologer"). Omarr has been called the most "knowledgeable astrologer since Evangeline Adams." His forecasts of Nixon's downfall, the end of World War II in mid-August of 1945, the assassination of John F. Kennedy, Roosevelt's election to a fourth term and his death in office ... these and many others ... are on record and quoted enough to be considered "legendary."

About This Series

This is one of a series of
Twelve Day-by-Day Astrological Guides
for the signs in 1986
by Sydney Omarr

COUPON

PROF. LALLEMEND
Dept SO-8 • POB 252
BROOKLYN, N.Y. 11204

516 Fifth Ave., NY., NY. 10036

Dear Reader,

You do not have to 'merely believe' Professor Lallemend, the renowned astrologer, because he will **PROVE** to you how he can help you make your life better!

Just fill out this form and mail it. Professor Lallemend will prepare **YOUR HOROSCOPE** and predict—without charge **TWO ESSENTIAL EVENTS IN YOUR LIFE.** You will be thoroughly convinced by the precision of the forecast and will also learn how you can gain success and inner contentment, as well as avoiding everything which can be an obstacle in the path of your happiness. You will receive his advice absolutely free of charge. All you have to do is, answer the questions below, and mail the coupon TODAY.

Please send me free of charge and without any obligation on my part my horoscope and two predictions in an unmarked envelope.

My Birthdate ....

Time .... Place ....

Please let me know as well, my lucky numbers. I enclose here a number between 0 and 9 which suddenly comes to my mind:

_____

NAME......................

ADD.......................

....

CITY......................

STATE .... ZIP ....

How well do you know yourself?

This horoscope gives you answers to these questions based on your exact time and place of birth...

How do others see you?
What is your greatest strength?
What are your life purposes?
What drives motivate you?
How do you think?
Are you a loving person?
How competitive are you?
What are your ideals?
How religious are you?
Can you take responsibility?
How creative are you?
How do you handle money?
How do you express yourself?
What career is best for you?
How will you be remembered?
Who are your real friends?
What are you hiding?

Many people are out of touch with their real selves. Some can't get ahead professionally because they are doing the wrong kind of work. Others lack self-confidence because they're trying to be someone they're not. Others are unsuccessful in love because they use the wrong approach with the wrong people. Astrology has helped hundreds of people with problems like these by showing them their real selves.

You are a unique individual. Since the world began, there has never been anyone exactly like you. Sun-sign astrology, the kind you see in newspapers and magazines, is all right as far as it goes. But it treats you as if you were just the same as millions of others who have the same Sun sign because their birthdays are close to yours. A true astrological reading of your character and personality has to be one of a kind, unlike any other. It has to be based on exact date, time, longitude and latitude of your birth. Only a big IBM computer like the one that Para Research uses can handle the trillions of possibilities.

A Unique Document Your Astral Portrait includes your complete chart with planetary positions and house cusps calculated to the nearest minute of arc, all planetary aspects with orbs and intensities, plus text explaining the meaning of:

★ Your particular combination of Sun and Moon signs.
★ Your Ascendant sign and the house position of its ruling planet. (Many computer horoscopes omit this because it requires exact birth data.)
★ The planets influencing all twelve houses in your chart.
★ Your planetary aspects.

Others Tell Us "I found the Astral Portrait to be the best horoscope I've ever read." —E.D., Los Angeles, CA
"I could not put it down until I'd read every word. It is like you've been looking over my shoulder since I arrived in this world!" —B.N.L., Redding, CA
"I recommend the Astral Portrait. It even surpasses many of the readings done by professional astrologers." —J.B., Bristol, CT

Low Price There is no substitute for a personal conference with an astrologer, but a good astrologer charges $50 and up for a complete chart reading. Some who have rich clients get $200 and more. Your Astral Portrait is an analysis of your character written by some of the world's foremost astrologers, and you can have it not for $200 or $50 but for only $22. This is possible because the text of your Astral Portrait is already written. You pay only for the cost of putting your birth information into the computer, compiling one copy, checking it and sending it to you within two weeks.

Permanence Ordinarily, you leave as astrologer's office with only a memory. Your Astral Portrait is a thirty-five-page, fifteen-thousand-word, permanently bound book that you can read again and again for years.

Money-Back Guarantee Our guarantee is unconditional. That means you can return your Astral Portrait at any time for any reason and get a full refund of the purchase price. That means we take all the risk, not you!

You Hold the Key The secrets of your inner character and personality, your real self, are locked in the memory of the computer. You alone hold the key: your time and place of birth. Fill in the coupon below and send it to the address shown with $22. Don't put it off. Do it now while you're thinking of it. Your Astral Portrait is waiting for you.

© 1977 Para Research, Inc

Para Research, Dept. BT, P.O. Box 61, Gloucester, Massachusetts 01930 I want to read about my real self. Please send me my Astral Portrait. I understand that if I am not completely satisfied, I can return it for a full refund. ☐ I enclose $22 plus 1.50 for shipping and handling. ☐ Charge $23.50 to my Master Card account. ☐ Charge $23.50 to my VISA account.

Card number		Good through Mo.	Day	Yr.
Mr/Ms		Birthdate Mo.	Day	Yr.
Address		Birthtime (within an hour)		AM/PM
City		Birthplace City		
State	Zip	State	County	

Know in advance the changes in your life

Wouldn't it be useful to know when important events in your life are going to happen? How would you respond? What will you experience emotionally, intellectually and psychologically? And how will these experiences affect your life.

Your transits can provide valuable clues to various trends or stages of personal growth. This is especially true for the slower moving outer planets—Jupiter through Pluto. The transits for these planets are long lasting and profound in their psychological consequences. Many occur only once in a lifetime. The Astral Forecast is all about the outer planets.

This horoscope provides a reliable tool for astrological forecasting. The Astral Forecast will show you how the outer transits affect your sense of timing, that is, the times that are appropriate for you to take certain kinds of actions and inappropriate for others. This horoscope includes every significant transit to your outer planets that occurs in a twelve-month period. You can use your Astral Forecast to better understand how the outer planets affect such important life issues as career, child rearing, love, marriage and more.

For example, when Jupiter is in the first house, this transit represents a major growth cycle in your life. This is the best time for you to explore who you really are as an individual. Under this transit, you will feel more secure about yourself and the impression you make on others. Therefore, understanding yourself and your influence on others can make this transit an especially powerful and

important time in your life. This is also a time for learning and gaining new experience. All this is part of your present need for personal growth, which affects not only yourself, but also the way you deal with the world as a whole. This is one time when persons and resources are likely to be drawn to you, and you should take constructive advantage of them.

You can find out in advance what your transits are going to be. But if you do it on your own, you will have to consult several astronomical tables to find the positions of each of the transiting planets every day and then compare them mathematically to the positions of the planets at the time of your birth.

There's an easier way to learn of your transits. Our IBM System/36 computer will handle all the calculations and provide you with information on all your outer transits based on your exact time and place of birth. With the Astral Forecast you not only receive the most accurate calculation of your personal transits for the next twelve months, you will also receive an extensive printout interpreting the character and significance of your individual transits.

Your Astral Forecast is the most accurate and authoritative guide to the outer transits that you can receive. It is based on the work of Robert Hand, one of America's most famous astrologers, and the author of several astrology books.

Like all Para Research horoscopes, the Astral Forecast is inexpensive. For just $16.00 you can have the same kind of advice that would otherwise cost you hundreds of dollars. This low price is possible because the astrological data is stored in our computer, and can be easily formatted and printed. Also, the mathematical calculations can be done in a matter of minutes. Your only cost is the cost of putting your personal information into the computer, producing one copy and then mailing it.

When you order your Astral Forecast, you receive an unconditional money-back guarantee. This means you can return your Astral Forecast at any time and get a full refund of the purchase price. We take all the risk.

Order your Astral Forecast today. Discover how the transits can bring energy to each part of your personality, fulfill your potential and help you gain more control over your own life.
© 1983 Para Research, Inc.

Para Research, Dept. BT, P.O. Box 61, Gloucester, Massachusetts 01930 Please send me my Astral Forecast. I understand that if I am not completely satisfied, I can return it for a full refund. ☐ I enclose $16 plus $1.50 for shipping and handling. ☐ Charge $17.50 to my MasterCard account. ☐ Charge $17.50 to my VISA account.

Card number		Good through Mo.	Day	Yr.
Mr/Ms		Birthdate Mo.	Day	Yr.
Address		Birthtime (within an hour)		AM/PM
City		Birthplace City	State	
State	Zip	Start calendar with Mo.	Yr.	

Don't Let A TERRIBLE THING HAPPEN TO YOU!

SECRET KNOWLEDGE REVEALED THAT HAS BEEN HANDED DOWN THROUGH HISTORY- TO HELP GIVE YOU A RICHER, LOVE FILLED, HAPPIER LIFE.

Will The POWER Of The OCCULT DOLL Work For YOU?

● **OCCULT SUPPLIES**—For centruies It was and still is a tradition that in Secret Ancient Rituals and Magic of Haiti, Africa, and Latin America, dolls were used to carry out every purpose desired. Used for Love, Luck, Riches to gain power. These ancient rituals were rare a constant source of comfort and hope to those who pratice.

We have been making these OCCULT DOLLS and RITUALS for certain customers with Special Problems to see if they were able to help. We are happy to tell you that we feel they have been a great success. Each Doll is made of a certain color with Amulets, Charms, and Herbs sewn in. Believed to attract WHAT YOU WANT. Each Doll is handmade with Great Care by one who knows and believes. Comes with full Instructions.

● **LOVE DOLL**
We feel the Most Powerful Love Occult Ritual is done with Red, and special items sewn in. Used to bring a love back to you or get your relationship back to the love and excitement you once had we believe. Comes with special Red tipped pin, powerful instructions
D300 . . . . 5.98

● **MONEY DRAWING DOLL**
Green Doll handmade with coins and herbs sewn in. We believe that Green has the power of attracting money to one in need. Strong money directions included.
D500 . . . . 5.98

● **OCCULT RITUAL HANDBOOK**
Everything you always wanted to know about Occult Rituals and Magic—songs, chants, spells for every purpose. Use of Roots, Herbs, Oils plus ceremonial rites and more. The secrets are here.
Bk120 . . . . 4.98

Triple Win BINGO BAG

Did you ever wonder why some people always win at BINGO? Do they have a secret? Now you can have your own secret! Your own BINGO BAG to carry with you.

NOW YOU CAN WIN TOO! When your numbers are called, you be the one to shout BINGO! You get Bingo Oil, Gemstone, Charm, Seal plus Green Bag and full Instructions.
KK795 All 7 items 7.95

LOVE RUB

Rub on your hands or body — or on the body of the one you love. Get what you want and use it wisely.

K371-Red-Passionate Love
K372-Pink-Win love and conquer Evil
K373-Green-Money Drawing
K374-Light Blue-Power to Find a Job

3.98 Any 3 for 11.50

FOLLOW ME COLOGNE

Comes with "LUCKY FORTUNE" A Few Drops Does the Trick. To attract your love, wear this whenever you go out. Sprinkle in your draws also.

K297 Large 4 oz. size
4.98

SPIRITUAL OILS

Used by many thousands of satisfied people because the fragrance charms the senses. Try them today!

2.25 Save 77¢ Order any 3 Only 5.98

K-4 — Attraction	K-14 — Lady Luck
K-100 — Commanding	K-11 — Lodestone
K-2 — Compelling	K-112 — Lovers
K-101 — Concentration	K-113 — Lucky Money
K-102 — Crossing	K-114 — Lucky Hand
K-103 — Dragon Blood	K-8 — Money Drawing
K-16 — Fast Luck	K-7 — Power
K-104 — Finance	K-117 — Protection
K-105 — French Love	K-121 — Spirit
K-106 — Good Luck	K-8 — Success
K-107 — High Conquering	K-122 — Uncrossing
K-109 — Holy Spiritual	K-123 — Van Van
K-110 — Jinx Removing	
K-111 — King Solomon	

SPECIAL INCENSE

2.25 Save 77¢ Order any 3 Only 5.98

Burn incense to attract, to dispel wicked odors. Best incense available, attracting fragrances, satisfying results.

NUMBER IN EVERY BOX
People are used to buying incense with a number. And considering it lucky. We don't claim these numbers as such.

K-77 — Commanding	K-48 — Success
K-42 — Compelling	K-34 — Jinx Removing
K-78 — Concentration	K-84 — Lady Luck
K-97 — Crossing	K-86 — Lovers
K-80 — Dragon Blood	K-87 — Lucky Hand
K-41 — Fast Luck	K-88 — Lucky Money
K-33 — Finance	K-91 — Masters
K-81 — French Love	K-47 — Money Drawing
K-82 — Good Luck	K-39 — Power
K-83 — High Conquering	K-43 — Van Van
	K-35 — Uncrossing

Write to: **ANN HOWARD DEPT.SY1 200 West Sunrise Highway, Freeport, N.Y. 11520**

$5 Dollar Deposit on all C.O.D. Orders! Prepaid Orders Please Add $1.95 for Postage. FREE- Latest Catalog-Candles, Oils, Incense, Spells, More. Just Write. No claims are made. These alleged powers are gathered from writings, books, folklore & occult sources. Sold as curios.

"Next to my mother, you have been the greatest inspiration of my life."

You'll be amazed!
When you read what Marguerite Carter has to say about your life in the year ahead you'll be amazed. She delves into the most important areas of your life: romance, money, goals, and significant changes. You'll find out all the wonderful ways you can live a better life when you have your Unitology Forecast prepared for you by Marguerite Carter.

She'll help you.
Marguerite Carter has counseled thousands of enthusiastic followers around the world for decades. She has been the guiding light and helping hand for people from all walks of life: business leaders, hollywood stars and just everyday folks. There is a good reason why they seek her services year after year. They get the help they need in the most important areas of their lives!

'. . . it was amazing.'
People write all the time telling about how Marguerite Carter has helped them.

". . . it was amazing. I just can't believe it." W.C., Canada

". . . could not put it down until I read it cover to cover." M.L., Illinois.

"Without a doubt, next to my mother, you have been the greatest inspiration of my life. Many others could probably say the same thing." M.A., PA

MARGUERITE CARTER

In letter after letter people comment on the realistic guidance they've received for getting what they want from life. They've found the help they need in times of decision or resolving personal problems. These are judgments by a caring counselor, not some impersonal computer.

Hidden Opportunities
The things you want most may not be out of reach. Marguerite Carter says, "Many people are completely unaware that the opportunities for money, love or advancement are passing them by almost daily . . ." Without knowledge of when the conditions are favorable or unfavorable, the chances for success and happiness are greatly diminished.

Get your Unitology Forecast with special notations by Marguerite Carter. It will be prepared to your specific birthdate information. Remember that you will receive a full year of guidance, regardless of when your request is received, and you'll know that your forecast has come from one of the world's most highly respected astrologer-counselors.

O-6

Marguerite Carter • P.O. Box 807 • Indianapolis, Indiana 46206

☐ Yes Miss Carter, Please send me my Unitology Forecast for the year ahead. Enclosed is my remittance of $9.95 plus $1.00 for postage and handling. (First Class $1.30) Make all checks payable in U.S. funds. Allow 4 weeks for delivery.

Name _____

Address _____

City _____ State _____ Zip Code _____

Birthplace _____

Month _____ Day _____ Year _____

Place _____ Hour _____

Astrology Questionnaire

Help us bring you even better astrology guides by filling out this survey and mailing it today.

A. Book Title (Sign): _____

B. Using the scale below how would you rate this astrological guide? (Place one rating from 0–10 in the space provided.)

Poor	Not So Good	O.K.	Good	Excellent
0 1	2 3	4 5 6	7 8	9 10

Rating

Overall Opinion of book

Essay On:
1. Defining Terms _____
2. Your House of The Sun _____
3. The Geometry of Relationships _____
4. Twelve Places at the Table _____
5. Moods of the Moon _____
6. Venus and Mars _____
7. Venus Sign Position Chart _____
8. Mars Sign Position Chart _____
9. The Planets as "Stars" _____
10. Astrotrivia _____
11. Sun Sign Changes _____
12. Your Sign: The Big Picture _____
13. Your Sign: Objectives and Obstacles _____
14. Pairing Off With Your Sign _____
15. Your Sign's Sex Role Dilemma _____
16. Your Sign: Female _____
17. Your Sign: Male _____
18. Your Sign: Help Wanted _____
19. How "Pure" a _____ are you? _____
20. Find Your Rising Sign _____
21. Your Sign: Astro-Outlook for '86 _____
22. 15 Months of Day-By-Day Predictions _____

C. In total about how many astrology guides have you purchased for yourself in the past 12 months?
   # of books _____

D. What topics would you be interested in having Sydney Omarr write about in the 1987 Astrology Guide?
   _____
   _____

E. What is your education?

   1( ) High School   3( ) 4 yrs college
   2( ) 2 yrs college 4( ) Postgraduate

F. What is your occupation? _____

G. What is your marital status?

   1( ) Single   3( ) Divorced   5( ) Widowed
   2( ) Married   4( ) Separated

H. Age: _____   I. Sex: 1( ) Male
                         2( ) Female

Please Print Name:_____

Address_____

City_____State_____Zip_____

Phone # ( )_____

Thank you. Please send to New American Library, Research Dept., 1633 Broadway, New York, NY 10019